THE MODERN USE OF THE BIBLE

THE MODERN USE
OF THE BIBLE

BY

HARRY EMERSON FOSDICK, D.D.

MORRIS K. JESUP PROFESSOR OF PRACTICAL THEOLOGY
UNION THEOLOGICAL SEMINARY, NEW YORK

New York

THE MACMILLAN COMPANY

1925

59. 2101

PRINTED IN THE UNITED STATES OF AMERICA BY
THE BERWICK & SMITH CO.

To Two Members of the Younger Generation
ELINOR WHITNEY FOSDICK
DOROTHY FOSDICK

THE LYMAN BEECHER LECTURESHIP
FOUNDATION

The Lyman Beecher Fund in the School of Religion, Yale University, was established May 2, 1872, by a gift of ten thousand dollars from Henry W. Sage, Esq., then of Brooklyn, New York, in memory of Lyman Beecher, of the Class of 1797, Yale College, who died January 10, 1863. In accordance with the wishes of the donor, this gift was devoted by the Yale Corporation to the establishment of a Foundation "to be designated as 'The Lyman Beecher Lectureship on Preaching,' to be filled from time to time, upon the appointment of the Corporation, by a minister of the Gospel, of any evangelical denomination, who has been markedly successful in the special work of the Christian ministry." With the authorization of the donor, the Corporation, in May, 1882, voted "that henceforth the Lyman Beecher Lecturer shall be invited to lecture on a branch of pastoral theology or any other topic appropriate to the work of the Christian ministry." In December, 1893, the donor authorized the Corporation "if at any time they should deem it desirable to do so, to appoint a layman instead of a minister to deliver the course of lectures on the Lyman Beecher Foundation."

PREFACE

These lectures have just been delivered on the Lyman Beecher Foundation at Yale University and are now given to the publishers in the hope that, although left in the style of spoken address, they may prove useful beyond the original circle of auditors. Nothing new or startling can be promised to the reader who is well informed in the realm of modern Biblical scholarship. Nevertheless, after ten years of dealing with this subject in the classroom with special reference to the practical problems of Christian preachers and teachers, I hope that some service may be rendered by the systematic statement which I have endeavored to make.

Upon the basis of the approach to the Bible here set forth I have done my preaching from the beginning of my ministry, and for the last decade I have been trying to set forth this approach in orderly fashion in lectures at the Union Theological Seminary. To the many students who have worked with me in the classroom on this course of thought and whose encouraging letters from the pastoral and missionary fields have testified to its practical feasibility and have furnished incentive for this publication, I am profoundly grateful.

A word may be needed about the bibliographies, printed one at the close of each lecture. These lists of books are intended merely to be suggestive of read-

PREFACE

ing likely to aid the interested student in carrying further the line of thought begun in the lectures. Obviously, they are not exhaustive and could not well have been made so.

It is useless to try adequately to express my sense of indebtedness for help received in the preparation of these lectures. My secretary, Miss Margaret Renton, has given tireless and efficient service. President Arthur Cushman McGiffert and Professor Julius A. Bewer, of the Union Theological Seminary Faculty, have each read portions of the manuscript greatly to my profit. Especially, I owe an unpayable debt to my friend and colleague, Professor James Everett Frame, who has read the entire manuscript and has given me many valuable suggestions.

The position represented in this book will of course be distasteful to those bound by a theory of literal inerrancy in their approach to the Bible. I am hoping, however, that many not so bound but anxious, it may be, over the possible effects of modern scholarship, may be led to see how consonant with a reverent estimate of the Book and an inspiring use of it the new views are.

HARRY EMERSON FOSDICK

New York, May 3, 1924

CONTENTS

THE MODERN USE OF THE BIBLE

LECTURE I

THE NEW APPROACH TO THE BIBLE

I

Some of the most lively and perplexing problems that trouble Christian thought to-day center in the subject which we have chosen. Quite apart from the lecturer's amazement and delight at finding a topic with which but one of his forty-odd predecessors on this Foundation has dealt at all,[1] he may claim interest in his theme because around it gather many of our most serious questions and controversies.

To more ministers than one likes to think the use of the Bible is a difficult enigma. Some reveal this by avoiding wide areas of the Scripture altogether. All the king's horses and all the king's men could hardly drag them into dealing with certain passages that used to be the glory of our fathers' preaching. Others make their embarrassment clear by their use of texts—no longer treasuries of truth from which they draw the substance of their message, but convenient pegs on which they hang a collection of their own thoughts. Others reveal their discomfort and confusion when they try to discuss Biblical problems, such as miracles. They are ill at ease in handling

[1] George Adam Smith: Modern Criticism and the Preaching of the Old Testament.

I

these Scriptural categories, reminding one of a comment which Longfellow once made on a preacher: "I could not tell what he was driving at, except that he seemed desirous not to offend the congregation." And still other preachers cut the Gordian knot by practically surrendering the Bible as the inspiration of their thought and teaching, save as by courtesy they use it in some oblique and cursory fashion to point a moral, or adorn a tale.

Of course, such a summary does not include all ministers, but one fears that it applies to a growing percentage. Years ago, here at Yale, Dr. William Newton Clarke made this comment on the preacher's problem with the Book:

> "I tell no secret—though perhaps many a man has wished he could keep it a secret—when I say that to the average minister to-day the Bible that lies on his pulpit is more or less an unsolved problem. He is loyal to it, and not for his right hand would he degrade it or do it wrong. He longs to speak with authority on the basis of its teaching, and feels that he ought to be able so to do. He knows that the people need its message in full power and clearness, and cannot bear to think that it is losing influence with them. Yet he is not entirely free to use it. Criticism has altered the book for his use, but just how far he does not know." [1]

Surely, it is worth while to attempt, from the preacher's point of view, a constructive contribution

[1] The Use of the Scriptures in Theology, 161.

in this field. It would be worth while if only a few ministers, laboring under the handicap of the prevalent confusion, were helped to handle the Bible with new zest, freedom, honesty, and power.

Quite apart from the special needs of the preacher, an intelligent understanding of the Bible is indispensable to anybody in the Western world who wishes to think wisely about religion. By no possibility can any one of us be independent of the Bible's influence. Our intellectual heritage is full of its words and phrases, ideas and formulas. Ignorance of it constitutes a hopeless handicap in the endeavor to understand any great Western literature, and as for our English classics, take from them the contribution of the Scriptures and the remainder would resemble a town in Flanders after the big guns were through with it.

No man in the Western world, therefore, can think about religion as though the Bible did not exist. He might as well try to think legally without reference to the Common Law—a psychological impossibility. Even though he never read a law-book, all the presuppositions with which he starts, the problems with which he deals, the mental grooves in which his thought inevitably runs, are set in advance by the inherited tradition. If a man wishes to think independently of the Common Law he must first thoroughly know the Law and then deliberately break away from it.

Similarly, in our religious thinking we may agree with the Bible or disagree with it, use its structural ideas sympathetically or hostilely, or even be unaware that we are using them at all, but in any case we are under duress. One way or another we are thinking with reference to the Biblical tradition. That is inbred in our consciousness and we cannot get rid of it. It will never do, therefore, for us to play ostrich with reference to the problems which the modern use of the Bible presents. We must see them straight or we will see nothing else straight. In the last analysis all the controversies that vex our modern churches come back to this central matter: how are we using the Bible? There is no hope of unsnarling our sadly perplexed religious thinking until we achieve and make popularly effective an intelligent employment of the Scriptures.

When to this basic need which affects everybody's religious thinking in the Western world are added the special problems of the preacher, the necessity of a well-instructed and fruitful use of the Bible becomes overwhelming. For one thing, in most congregations there are folk drilled in the older methods of employing Scripture. They are often the salt of the earth— folk of consistent and effective Christian lives and of reliable devotion to the kingdom. The man who ministers to them must know the Bible. If he disagrees with their way of handling it he must not give the impression of doing so ignorantly or flippantly, without long reflection, sound reason, and conscientious decision. They must feel that he is a thorough, thoughtful, reverent student of the Book. If they are sure of that they will give him large liberty. But if they see that he is using texts for convention's sake and not because he is concerned with the message of the Bible or has any well-ordered and intelligent view of it as a whole, they will rightly distrust his intellectual integrity. He seems to be trifling, and he is.

Upon the other hand, multitudes of people, so far from being well-stabilized traditionalists, are all at sea in their religious thinking. If ever they were drilled in older uses of the Bible they have rebelled against them. Get back to the nub of their difficulty and you find it in Biblical categories which they no longer believe—miracles, demons, fiat creation, apocalyptic hopes, eternal hell, or ethical conceptions of Jehovah in the Old Testament that shock the modern conscience. Their inherited way of thinking about the Bible has been to them indissoluble from their religion. An artificial adhesion, none the less strong because it is irrational, has been set up between their deepest and most beautiful spiritual experiences on the one side and their accustomed use of Scripture on the other. When the one goes the other threatens to collapse. In many cases it has collapsed.

The man who ministers to them must have an intelligible way of handling the Bible. He must have gone through the searching criticism to which the last few generations have subjected the Scriptures and be able to understand and enter into the negations that have resulted. Not blinking any of the facts, he must have come out with a positive, reasonable, fruitful attitude toward the Book. Only so can he be of service in resolving the doubts of multitudes of folk to-day. If they can see that the Bible is not lost but is the more usable the better it is understood, that the new knowledge has not despoiled it but has set its spirit free for its largest usefulness, that its basic experiences are separable from its temporary forms of thought, and that in its fundamental principles of life lie the best hopes of the world to-day, they are set at liberty from a great fear that their faith is vain. In the end, like many of us, they may see more in the Scriptures now than ever they saw under the old régime.

At any rate, whether we consider the preacher's private thinking or public ministry, few things are so important as that he should achieve an intelligent and spiritually effective use of the Bible.

II

The results of the modern study of Scripture can be grouped under two heads, and to one of these we now turn our attention.   For the first time in the history of the church, we of this generation are able to arrange the writings of the Bible in approximately chronological order.   That statement, like other summaries of human knowledge such as that the earth is round, can be swiftly and simply made, but its involved meanings reach far and deep.   The total consequence of all the work of the Higher Criticism is that at last we are able to see the Bible a good deal as a geologist sees the strata of the earth; we can tell when and in what order the deposits were laid down whose accumulated results constitute our Scriptures.   Was there ever such an unfortunate label put upon an entirely legitimate procedure as the name "Higher Criticism"?   Were one to search the dictionary for two words suggestive of superciliousness, condescension, and destructiveness, one could hardly find any to surpass these. Yet the Higher Criticism simply asks about the books of the Bible: who wrote them, when and why they were written, and to whom. Every efficient Sunday School teacher, according to his own ability, has always been a Higher Critic. This process, however, armed with our modern instruments of literary, historical, and archeological research, pushed with unremitting zeal and tireless labor, after following many false trails and landing in many cul-de-sacs, has gotten a result, at least in its outlines, well assured. We can arrange the documents of the Bible in their approximately chronological order. Endless minor uncertainties, difficulties, and unanswered questions remain but, for all that, it is possible now for Dr. Harlan Creelman to give us his volume in which the strata of the Old Testament are chronologically distinguished, and for Dr. Julius Bewer to give us his continued story of Hebrew literature from its first emergence to its canonization.[1]

From the purely scientific point of view this is an absorbingly interesting matter, but even more from the standpoint of practical results its importance is difficult to exaggerate. It means that we can trace the great ideas of Scripture in their development from their simple and elementary forms, when they first appear in the earliest writings, until they come to their full maturity in the latest books. Indeed, the

[1] Harlan Creelman: An Introduction to the Old Testament Chronologically Arranged; Julius A. Bewer: The Literature of the Old Testament in its Historical Development.

general soundness of the critical results is tested by this fact that as one moves up from the earlier writings toward the later he can observe the development of any idea he chooses to select, such as God, man, duty, sin, worship. Plainly we are dealing with ideas that enlarge their scope, deepen their meaning, are played upon by changing circumstance and maturing thought, so that from its lowliest beginning in the earliest writings of the Hebrews any religious or ethical idea of the Bible can now be traced, traveling an often uneven but ascending roadway to its climax in the teaching of Jesus.

That this involves a new approach to the Bible is plain. To be sure, our fathers were not blind to the fact that the New Testament overtops, fulfils, and in part supersedes the Old. They had the Sermon on the Mount and the opening verses of the Epistle to the Hebrews to assure them of that. But our fathers never possessed such concrete and detailed illustration of that idea as we have now. We shall have occasion later to applaud the school of interpretation made notable by Theodore of Mopsuestia and to appreciate great exegetes like Calvin, but even such interpreters never dreamed of arranging the documents of the Bible in chronological order and then tracing through them the development of those faiths and ethical ideals that come to their flower in the New Testament. Rather, they lacked both the historical apparatus that could have made this possible and the idea of development which interprets everything in terms of its early origin and gradual growth. In consequence, the older interpreters of the Bible consistently tended to read

the meanings of the New Testament back into the
Old, to level up the Old Testament toward the New,
until there was nothing in the New Testament which
could not by direct statement, by type, symbol, or
allegory, be found in the Old.

To us it would seem obvious that the Christian
doctrine of the Trinity arose after the church had begun to meditate on the significance of Jesus. But our
fathers found the doctrine of the Trinity all through
the Old Testament. Luther found it in the opening
chapter of Genesis: "Let us make"; [1] he found it in
Psalm 67:

> "God, even our own God, will bless us.
> God will bless us." [2]

Calvin, a superb exegete, had to rebuke those ancient
fathers who, as he thought, had carried this process
much too far. They had based argument for the
Trinity upon the story that at the sacred oak of
Mamre Abraham had bowed once when greeting three
heavenly visitors and so had recognized one God in
three persons.[3]

This leveling up of the Old Testament by reading
into it the message of the New is most familiar to us
through the deeply ingrained habit of finding definite
references to Jesus throughout the older record.

[1] Commentary on Genesis, Ch. I, verse 26a, in translation by J. N.
Lenker, Vol. I, 109.

[2] Dictata super Psalterium 1513–1516 Glossa: Psalmus LXVI
(LXVII) lines 20–23, 40–41, in Werke, Kritische Gesammtausgabe,
Weimar, Vol. 3, 383.

[3] John Calvin: Commentary on Genesis, Ch. XVIII, Sec. 2, last ¶,
in translation by John King, Vol. I, 470.

Luther said that Genesis contained more figures of Christ and his kingdom than any other book in the Bible.[1] The book of Proverbs would hardly suggest itself to us as likely to yield rich doctrinal material, but probably few passages in Scripture have been more consistently used as proof of the divine nature of Jesus than the eighth chapter of Proverbs. In a word, the Bible has not been conceived as a record of developing ideas and ideals, but as a repository of truth in which from beginning to end could be found everything that New Testament Christians believed. From Genesis to Revelation it has been supposed to speak with unanimous voice the theology of the early church. In this respect Athanasius is typical of the general method of ancient interpretation. "Athanasius saw no development of truth through the ages of biblical history," says Gilbert, "and no differences of doctrinal type. All parts of the Bible were equally good, in his judgment, as sources of proof-texts." [2]

If one supposes that the Reformation changed this general view and use of Scripture, he can readily disabuse himself by reading the commentaries and books of apologetics. Indeed, one wishes that one were not dealing with such typical material when he quotes from Pfeiffer, a Lutheran superintendent of the sixteenth century. According to him Genesis "must be received strictly"; "it contains all knowledge

[1] In Genesin Declamationes, closing ¶, in Weimar edition quoted above, Vol. 24, 710.

[2] George Holley Gilbert: Interpretation of the Bible; A Short History, 121.

human and divine"; "twenty-eight articles of the Augsburg Confession are to be found in it"; it is "an arsenal of arguments against all sects and sorts of atheists, pagans, Jews, Turks, Tartars, papists, Calvinists, Socinians and Baptists"; it is "the source of all sciences and arts, including law, medicine, philosophy and rhetoric"; it is "the source and essence of all histories and of all professions, trades and works"; it is "an exhibition of virtues and vices" and "the origin of all consolation." [1]

Fortunately for us, spiritual efficiency in the use of the Bible is not entirely dependent upon correctness of exegesis. These older interpreters who used the Book in ways now impossible for us did not on that account fail to find there the sustenance and inspiration which we may miss if we trust too much to our keener instruments and too little to spiritual insight. Just as men raised life-sustaining crops from the earth's soil long before they analyzed the earth's strata, so they got from Scripture the bread of life even if the chronological arrangement of the documents was yet undreamed. Nevertheless, it is of obvious importance that a new approach to the Bible has been forced upon us. No longer can we think of the Book as on a level, no longer read its maturer messages back into its earlier sources. We know now that every idea in the Bible started from primitive and childlike origins and, with however many setbacks and delays, grew in scope and height toward the culmination in Christ's Gospel. We know now that

[1] Andrew D. White: A History of the Warfare of Science with Theology in Christendom, Vol. II, 312.

the Bible is the record of an amazing spiritual devel-·
opment.[1]

III

The first book of which I know that endeavored to
take this general idea and fill in its outline with definite
content by actually tracing through the Scripture the
development of significant ideas was written by Professor Toy of Harvard, and was published thirty-
four years ago.[2]   Since then the material has grown
richer year by year.   Probably the emergence of the
hope of resurrection among the Hebrews and its consummation in the New Testament has been more
fully traced than any other subject.   But whether it
be the hope of life eternal or the idea of God, righteousness, sin, sacrifice, worship, the story of the
development of Scriptural concepts is at least partially
available.   No preacher ought to go into his work
without the equipment and stimulus which this new
approach to the Bible gives.

Obviously this is no place for tracing in detail the
various roadways through Scripture which the great
faiths and ideals of the Gospel traveled from their
primitive origin to their consummation in the New
Testament.   But we may well give clarity and content

[1] The reader, of course, must never take the actual order of documents in our Bible as indicative of the chronological order in which
they originally were produced.   The first chapter of Genesis, for
example, is very late.   For information see Bibliography at the close
of this lecture.

[2] Crawford Howell Toy: Judaism and Christianity; A Sketch of
the Progress of Thought from Old Testament to New Testament.

to what we are saying by brief illustrations of this fresh and rewarding approach to the Book. In the field of ethics, for example, the development of moral ideals within the Bible presents a fascinating story. When one turns to the first conceptions as to the nature of duty and its range, one is impressed with certain clearly marked characteristics of early Hebrew thought. For one thing, the range of duty was strictly limited to special social groups. A man's obligations to his family, his clan, his tribe, his nation—to the social groups, that is, in which his membership was recognized—were set forth often on a high plane. But obligation outside these boundaries was very dim, if it was there at all.

This, of course, was associated with the geographical limitation of Jehovah himself. As the early writings of the Old Testament clearly reveal, Jehovah, at first one among many gods, dwelt with his own special people and exercised no jurisdiction beyond their boundaries. So long, then, as religious imagination conceived of God as limited in his interest and power by the territory of his people, the sense of moral obligation could have no wider range. Men who cannot think of their God as caring for other peoples will not themselves care for them. So long as Jehovah and Chemosh were both real characters with settled hostility a natural estate between them, the Hebrew people of Jehovah could not be expected to recognize ethical responsibilities to the Moabitish people of Chemosh.

Here we have the explanation of those deeds in the Old Testament which from our youth have shocked us by their barbarity. The ruthless extermination of the Amalekites—"both man and woman, infant and suckling" [1]—was due not to inhumanity as a theory of moral action, but to the limitation of the field within which humane action was a duty. Samuel's oft-quoted words, "to obey is better than sacrifice," [2] were a high-minded man's indignant rebuke because Saul had not killed Agag. Samuel was doubtless humane within the social group where such an attitude was virtuous, but it never had occurred to him that the realm of moral obligation took in Agag and his people.

Here, too, is the explanation of the ethics of the book of Deuteronomy. Its humane quality is extraordinary. Few more beautiful passages can be found than its injunctions to philanthropy. Its legal applications of the spirit of mercy make it one of the most remarkable of ancient books. All this goodwill, however, was expended upon Israel and her proselytes; the horizons never lifted to take in moral obligations to alien people.

Start now with this tribal morality and the roadway leading up to the New Testament, where all boundaries are down and God is calling all humanity into his kingdom, is alike one of the most significant that man ever traveled and one of the most rewarding that man can study now. To see in the Bible new world-contacts breaking down the old walls of isolation, to watch prophets enlarging their thought of God and thereby widening their sense of moral obligation, to feel the significance of great hours of vision,

[1] I Samuel 15:3.   [2] I Samuel 15:22.

as when Isaiah hears God say, "Blessed be Egypt my
people, and Assyria the work of my hands, and Israel
mine inheritance," [1] to rejoice in the widening internationalism of books of propaganda, like Jonah, until
at last, under the influence of Jesus, religion is uni-
versalized, human personality regardless of national
or racial lines is made the supreme treasure, men of
every tribe, tongue, people, and nation are welcomed
into one brotherhood, and a kingdom of God on earth
is promised to which men shall come from east, west,
north, and south—so to see the Bible is to enter
creatively into what God was really doing in that
amazing spiritual development whose record the
Bible is. Moreover, it gives the preacher a new grip
on the significance and necessity of his message. All
too clearly he sees how far back in the Old Testament
the world still is living, how much our morality belongs to the days of Saul and Samuel, how little we
have lifted it to the level of the Christian Gospel.

Consider another illustration of this approach to the
Bible. Prayer as intimate personal fellowship with
the unseen Friend is to us, however lamely we may
exercise our privilege, the very center of our inward
relationship with God. But the Bible at its beginning
had no such idea of man's relationship with God, and
the reasons are clear. For one thing, the idea of God
in the earliest writings of the Bible was such that few
would desire to have intimate fellowship with him.
Read Exodus 4:24–26, for example, and see that a
God who, out of pure caprice, at a wayside inn started
to kill a man on sight and was only estopped by the

[1] Isaiah 19:25.

quick action of the man's wife in circumcizing her son, was not a God with whom close communion would be desirable. Or when on Sinai "thunders and light-nings, and a thick cloud upon the mount"[1] were the evidences of the divine Presence, one would not be allured by such a thought of God to intimate fellow-ship. Rather, the people stood afar off and said to Moses, "Speak thou with us, and we will hear; but let not God speak with us, lest we die."[2] For a long time in the development of Old Testament religion, the conception of God was lacking in those qualities which would have led anybody to enter into his inner chamber, and having shut his door, to pray to his Father who is in secret.[3]

Moreover, even though one had wished so to pray, it would have been impossible. God was not thought of as a spiritual Presence everywhere available to the devout and seeking soul. He was localized. He dwelt on Sinai, or later in the Ark, or later in the Canaanitish high places reconsecrated into shrines of Jehovah. In those days in Israel, if a man wanted to perform an act of worship he did not think of entering into his inner chamber; he went up into his village's high place and made an offering. "In every place where I record my name," says Jehovah in Exodus, "I will come unto thee."[4]

Deeper yet in making impossible the New Testa-ment idea of secret prayer was the limitation of Jehovah's interest. He was not at the beginning thought of as caring for individuals one by one. He

[1] Exodus 19:16.   [2] Exodus 20:19.
[3] Cf. Matthew 6:6.   [4] Exodus 20:24.

was the God of the nation and he regarded individuals only as they were incidentally affected by the national fortunes. Not yet had the personality of the individual been shaken loose from its submergence in the mass. Not yet was religion the relationship of the soul with God; it was the relationship of the social group with its heavenly chieftain.

Even in earthly justice the individual was treated only as part of the group. When Achan secreted booty from Jericho his whole family was put to death; [1] because Saul slaughtered the Gibeonites his two sons and five grandsons were handed over to be killed and hung up in the mountain of Gibeah; [2] because Ahab had allowed Naboth to be killed, Jehu killed Ahab's son Joram.[3] Everywhere in early Hebrew history, as with all primitive peoples, the individual had no standing save as an item in the corporate mass. When Jehovah visits "the iniquity of the fathers upon the children, upon the third and upon the fourth generation of them that hate" him,[4] we are dealing not with a premonition of modern ideas of heredity, but with a very ancient idea of corporate responsibility in which the separate rights of the individual had no place. Of course, so prevalent a conception affected religion; of course religion was not a personal, intimate fellowship of the soul with God.

Start now with this beginning in the Old Testament—a God from whom one would wish to stand far off in awe and fear, a God localized so that his spiritual Presence is not available in secret prayer, a

---

[1] Joshua, Ch. 7.   [2] II Samuel 21:1–9.
[3] II Kings 9:24–26.   [4] Exodus 20:5.

God who does not even care for individuals save as
they are temporarily members of the social group—
how lowly a beginning it was and how magnificent is
the development which leads us up and out into the
New Testament!

One who knows the Book can trace the major steps
of this amazing growth.   He can feel the effect of the
Exile as it shattered the social group and threw individuals back on God.   He can watch prophets like
Ezekiel in his eighteenth chapter stalwartly attacking
the old theology which submerged the individual in
the mass, or like Jeremiah breaking quite over old
restraints into deep personal piety and trust: "O
Jehovah, my strength, and my stronghold, and my
refuge in the day of affliction." [1]   He can see the hope
of resurrection emerging into confident faith, with all
the heightening of personal worth which it involved,
for death, as another said, is not a factory gate through
which men go in crowds, but a turnstile through which
they go one by one.   At last, in some of the later
Psalms, one finds a view of God full of New Testament anticipations:

> "Whither shall I go from thy Spirit?
> Or whither shall I flee from thy presence?
> If I ascend up into heaven, thou art there:
> If I make my bed in Sheol, behold, thou art there.
> If I take the wings of the morning,
> And dwell in the uttermost parts of the sea;
> Even there shall thy hand lead me,
> And thy right hand shall hold me." [2]

As for the New Testament itself, the old limitations

[1] Jeremiah 16:19.   [2] Psalm 139:7-1c.

with which the process started are there quite done away. God is severe in punishment upon impenitent iniquity, but to those who seek him he is infinitely good and gracious—who would not wish him for an unseen Friend? He is universally available for every willing soul, "a Spirit: and they that worship him must worship in spirit and truth." [1] He cares for men individually, loving us every one as though there were but one of us to love. And prayer is not now sending a delegate up Sinai to brave his thunders, but going into the inner chamber, shutting the door, and speaking to the Father who seeth in secret.

Did a dubious morning twilight ever break into a more glorious noon?

IV

There are four ways in which to know the Bible. The first is to be acquainted with its beauty spots, and this, of course, is the way in which the great majority of people know the Book. Some of the choicest narratives in the Old Testament, notably the matchless stories of Joseph, a few of the greatest Psalms, preeminently the 23d, select samples of the resonant eloquence of Isaiah, a few of the parables of Jesus and the Sermon on the Mount, some of Paul's supreme passages, especially the 13th chapter of First Corinthians—such is the Bible which most people know. Read Cromwell's letters and you get a fair idea of the way our fathers knew the Scripture. They knew it all. Its minor characters were as familiar as

[1] John 4:24.

its stars, and to Cromwell's correspondents reference to Phinehas was evidently as understandable as reference to Paul. But it is not so with us. As Dr. Charles Sylvester Horne once put it: "To-day this great territory of Scripture is like a modern continent; extreme and unhealthy congestion at certain well-known centers, and vast tracts of country uncultivated and unknown." [1]

The second way to know the Bible is to know its individual books. Many a man has vainly struggled to find interest and sense in some sections of the Scripture, like a collection of prophetic sermons in the Old Testament or an epistle in the New, and then, discovering what the book really was about, what kind of man wrote it, when he wrote it, why he wrote it, to whom he wrote it, has seen the light break until what was dull and opaque became luminous and clear. I never think of Paul's letter to Philemon without seeing Tychicus and Onesimus when first they carried it across the Empire from Rome to Colossæ. Onesimus must have clung to it as his only hope of escaping the dire penalties of a runaway slave. One who has traveled and trembled with that returning man and seen him thrust Paul's letter fearfully into his master's hand will not thereafter read it without a thrill. But to read the books of the Bible without thus knowing their vivid settings is like listening to one half of a telephone conversation.

A third way to know the Bible is to know its characters. For the Bible is biography and he who would understand its meaning must familiarly acquaint

[1] The Romance of Preaching, 216–217.

himself with the men and women who throng its pages and illustrate its truth. As a lad I started to read the Scripture through according to the familiar schedule, three chapters each week-day and five on Sunday, by which we were assured that in a single year we could complete the reading of the Book. I got safely through Numbers and Leviticus, even Proverbs did not altogether quench my ardor, but I stuck in the middle of Jeremiah and never got out. I do not blame myself, for how can a boy read Jeremiah in its present form and understand it?   To-day, however, there is no character in the Old Testament who in my estimation towers so high as Jeremiah. His was the richest experience of personal religion, I think, known on earth before our Lord. Get Driver's translation of his book, Skinner's monograph on him, " Prophecy and Religion," George Adam Smith's new exposition, and, for homiletical suggestions, Cheyne's "Jeremiah, His Life and Times" and Gillies' "Jeremiah, the Man and His Message," and acquaint yourself with this great prophet. A braver, gentler, more exquisite, or more courageous soul has not often walked the earth, and his spiritual pioneering in the realm of personal religion made him a forerunner of Jesus and one of the eminent benefactors of the race.

If one is to know the Bible well he must so know its characters. Its men and women must be real people in his imagination and his affection. He must come up to what the Bible says by way of the lives through whom the Bible says it, until Amos the shepherd of Tekoa, or Hosea of the ruined home and broken heart, Peter the vacillating changed to rock, or Paul of the indwelling Christ and the unconquerable passion for the Cross, are his familiar friends.

But indispensable as are these three ways of knowing the Book—its beauty spots, its individual writings, its revealing characters—all of them together are not enough. Only as a man is able to trace up through the whole Scripture the development of its structural ideas does he really know the Bible.

To start with God conceived like a man who walks in a garden in the cool of the day, or as one who comes down from the sky to confuse men's speech lest they should build their tower so high as to reach his home; to know the road that leads out from that beginning until in the New Testament God revealed in Christ is the spiritual Presence in whom we live, and move, and have our being, whose name is love, and whose temples are human hearts; and to be able in any book or passage to locate oneself with reference to this progressive revelation of the meaning of God—that is to know the Bible.

To start with man whose only soul is his physical breath and who, lacking alike separate rights here and immortality hereafter, is identified with his body and lost in his social group; to see the individual shaken loose from the mass and lifted up into royal worthfulness, and within the individual the spiritual distinguished from the physical until in the New Testament man is spirit, inwardly renewed though the outward man perish; to know the details of the journey which men made from that starting point to that conclusion, with all its rough acclivities, its devious wanderings, its glorious vistas, its doubts and its victory—that is to know the Bible.

To start with the demands of God on man interpreted in terms of tribal custom, with ethics and rubric jumbled together so that God equally hates David's sin with Bathsheba and David's taking of a census, or requires alike freedom from murder and the refusal to seethe a kid in its mother's milk; to see the prophetic task so magnificently performed by which righteousness was made central in the character of God and in his requirements of mankind, until in the Gospel God's will, freed from clinging ceremonialism, is completely moralized and men to please him must be inwardly right in thought and outwardly merciful in life; and at any point in this development to know the men whose insight brought new light, and the books and passages which represent the crucial hours of choice—that is to know the Bible.

To start with man's suffering as a curse from God, with all trouble regarded as divine punishment, so that wherever there was misery at all there was the double misery of interpreting it as a sign of God's disfavor; to see wiser, truer ideas of God surely but hardly dislodging more ancient thoughts as the book of Job argued against the old theology, or Isaiah's 53d chapter sounded a new note in the interpretation of suffering; to see suffering gradually redeemed from its old interpretation until, while some of it is still punishment, more of it is welcomed as spiritual discipline, and a part of it is lifted up into the glory of vicarious sacrifice; to see the process crowned in the Cross of Christ, where suffering becomes voluntary sacrifice as the means by which alone God can save the world; and at any point in this whole development to know the road by which the truth had traveled hitherto and where it is going next—that is to know the Bible.

From our youth up many of us have been familiar with the phrase "progressive revelation." It is a good phrase. But now the means are in our hands to fill it with rich, substantial content. Not only can we believe that the Bible does represent a progressive revelation, but we can clearly and in detail watch it progress. We can know where the Scripture's major ideas started; we can trace the routes they took; we can watch them in periods of rapid traveling and in days when the going was difficult and slow. We can enter into their defeats, their hair-breadth escapes, and costly victories; and we can see the way the Gospel of Jesus carried them up to a great height "not to destroy, but to fulfil."

That is the new approach to the Bible.

V

Certain results follow from this approach which ought to give relief to the thought, and power to the work, of every preacher who uses it.

For one thing, we are saved by it from the old and impossible attempt to harmonize the Bible with itself, to make it speak with unanimous voice, to resolve its conflicts and contradictions into a strained and artificial unity. How could one suppose that such internal harmony ever could be achieved between writings so

vital and real, springing hot out of the life of the
generations that gave them being, and extending in
their composition over at least twelve hundred years?
Listen to Ecclesiastes:

> "A living dog is better than a dead lion.   For
> the living know that they shall die: but the dead
> know not anything, neither have they any more
> a reward; for the memory of them is forgotten.
> As well their love, as their hatred and their envy,
> is perished long ago; neither have they any more
> a portion for ever in anything that is done under
> the sun"; "For that which befalleth the sons of
> men befalleth beasts; even one thing befalleth
> them: as the one dieth, so dieth the other; yea,
> they have all one breath; and man hath no pre-
> eminence above the beasts: for all is vanity." [1]

And here is a passage from First Corinthians:

> "For this corruptible must put on incorrup-
> tion, and this mortal must put on immortality.
> But when this corruptible shall have put on in-
> corruption, and this mortal shall have put on
> immortality, then shall come to pass the saying
> that is written, Death is swallowed up in victory.
> O death, where is thy victory?   O death, where
> is thy sting?" [2]

No ingenuity of exegesis ever can make those two
agree. The fact is that at the beginning Hebrew religion had no hope of immortality. Its future state in

---

[1] Ecclesiastes 9:4–6 and 3:19.   [2] I Corinthians 15:53–55.

Sheol was shadowy semi-existence concerning which
the dreariest words in the Hebrew vocabulary were
used. It was the land of "forgetfulness," [1] of "silence," [2] of "destruction;" [3] and when one psalmist
thought of it he said,

> "Oh spare me, that I may recover strength,
> Before I go hence, and be no more." [4]

Then the hope of resurrection began to grow in Israel.
The story of its emergence, its struggle, its victory, is
one of the most thrilling in the Book. But there were
some who fought against this new faith with all their
might and scorn. The book of Ecclesiastes is their
voice. It is the Rubáiyát of Omar Kháyyám in the
Old Testament. Not for the world would I have the
book of Ecclesiastes taken out of the Bible; it supplies
an indispensable element in the record of a marvelous
development; but the endeavor to harmonize it with
the hope of immortality which glows in the 73d Psalm
and is brought to light in the whole of the New Testament is now a process as unnecessary as it is impossible.

Again, read the ninth chapter of Esther, where the
writer rejoices in a vengeful massacre, or the closing
words of the 137th Psalm, which even Gounod's glorious music cannot redeem from brutality:

> "Happy shall he be, that rewardeth thee
> As thou hast served us.
> Happy shall he be, that taketh and dasheth thy little ones
> Against the rock."

[1] Psalm 88:12.
[2] Psalm 94:17.
[3] Job 26:6.
[4] Psalm 39:13.

The task of harmonizing such ethical conceptions with the Sermon on the Mount surely is too much for human wit or patience. The Old Testament exhibits many attitudes indulged in by men and ascribed to God which represent early stages in a great development, and it is alike intellectually ruinous and morally debilitating to endeavor to harmonize those early ideals with the revelations of the great prophets and the Gospels. Rather, the method of Jesus is obviously applicable: "It was said to them of old time . . . but I say unto you."

Moreover, the new approach to the Bible saves us from the necessity of apologizing for immature stages in the development of the Biblical revelation. From the beginning of the church many things in the early documents have been a stumbling-block to the faithful. Indeed, before the church began, Philo of Alexandria with great candor faced difficulties that have troubled modern minds. He was a passionate believer in Judaism and gave his life to the task of commending it to the acceptance of the Greek world. But he says that it would be a sign of great simplicity to think that the world was created in six days; [1] that the literal statement that woman was made out of a man's rib is fabulous; [2] that to suppose Cain actually built a city is "not only extraordinary, but contrary to all reason;" [3] that to picture God literally planting

[1] Philo Judæus: Treatise on the Allegories of the Sacred Laws, Book I, Sec. II, in translation by C. D. Yonge, Vol. I, 52.

[2] Ibid., Book II, Sec. VII, 85.

[3] Treatise on the Posterity of Cain, Sec. XIV, same volume as above, 297.

a garden in Eden is "impiety" and "fabulous non-
sense." [1]   In general Philo would regard it as utterly
missing the Old Testament's real meaning to take any
of the anthropomorphic representations of God in the
Old Testament as representing literal fact.

Now, the older Hebrew and Christian interpreters,
lacking the modern historic point of view and scientific apparatus, had one resource in their difficulties.
They allegorized away the things they did not like.
They read out the literal sense and read in the sense
they wished to find.   They ascribed to ancient writers
a mystical knowledge of all later learning and made
the early stories of a childlike age the parables and
symbols of the Greek philosophy or of Christian
theology.   Such a resource is no longer possible to us.
We know that the early writings of the Bible meant
what they said.   But we do not need to apologize for
their crudities.   They are early stages in a great development.   Their lack is the lack of immaturity, not of
perversion.   They are as acorns to the oak, fountains
to the river, and as such they require no defending as
though they were impertinences in the revelation of
God.   They are the infancy of a progressive unfolding
of the divine character and purpose, and they are to
be judged, as all things are to be judged, by what they
came to in the end.   And what they came to in the
end was Christ and his Gospel.

VI

This leads us to our final statement about the consequences of the new approach to the Bible.   It re-

[1] Treatise on the Allegories of the Sacred Laws, Book I, Sec. XIV, 63.

stores to us the whole Book. It gives to us a comprehensive, inclusive view of the Scriptures and enables us to see them, not piecemeal, but as a whole. Those of us who accept the modern knowledge of the Bible as assured and endeavor to put it to good use are continually being accused of tearing the Book to pieces, of cutting out this or that, and of leaving a mere tattered patchwork of what was once a glorious unity. The fact is precisely the opposite. The new approach to the Bible once more integrates the Scriptures, saves us from our piecemeal treatment of them, and restores to us the whole book seen as a unified development from early and simple beginnings to a great conclusion.

One who has mastered the new approach is at home in any part of the Bible and can use all of it. He opens its pages at any point and knows where he is. He knows the road by which the thought that he finds there has traveled. He knows the contribution that there is being made to the enlarging revelation. He knows where next the road will turn and climb, and he knows where it all comes out in the Gospel. Once more, in a new way, he has regained what once our fathers had and what recently the church has lost: ability to see the Bible in its entirety and to use it as a whole.

For no part of it is without its usefulness. People to-day are living in all the stages of development which its records represent. Its earliest, crudest sins and shames, views of God, and ideals of man are all among us. As one travels through the Book there is no place on the road where one does not meet some problems which modern folk are facing, some points of view which they ought to get or ought to outgrow, some faiths which they ought to achieve or ought to improve upon. So long as a man knows the whole road and judges every step of it by the spirit of Christ, who is its climax, he can use it all.

This is the finest consequence of the new approach to the Bible: it gives us the whole Book back again.

If some one protests that it spoils the idea of inspiration, I ask why. We used to think that God created the world by fiat on the instant, and then, learning that the world evolves, many were tempted to cry out that God did not create it at all. We now know that changing one's idea of a process does not in itself alter one's philosophy of origins. So we used to think of inspiration as a procedure which produced a book guaranteed in all its parts against error, and containing from beginning to end a unanimous system of truth. No well-instructed mind, I think, can hold that now. Our idea of the nature of the process has changed. What has actually happened is the production of a Book which from lowly beginnings to great. conclusions records the development of truth about God and his will, beyond all comparison the richest in spiritual issue that the world has known. Personally, I think that the Spirit of God was behind that process and in it. I do not believe that man ever found God when God was not seeking to be found. The under side of the process is man's discovery; the upper side is God's revelation. Our ideas of the method of inspiration have changed; verbal dictation, inerrant manuscripts, uniformity of doctrine between

1000 B. C. and 70 A. D.—all such ideas have become
incredible in the face of the facts.   But one who
earnestly believes in the divine Spirit will be led by
the new approach to the Bible to repeat with freshened
meaning and deepened content the opening words of
the Epistle to the Hebrews:

> "God, having of old time spoken unto the
> fathers in the prophets by divers portions and in
> divers manners, hath at the end of these days
> spoken unto us in his Son."

BIBLIOGRAPHY

Religion of Israel, E. Kautsch, in the Extra Volume of A Dic-
tionary of the Bible, edited by James Hastings. Scribner's.
Development of Doctrine in the Apocryphal Period, W. Fair-
weather, in the same volume.
The Religion of the Hebrews, John Punnett Peters. Ginn & Co.
The Moral Life of the Hebrews, J. M. Powis Smith.   Univer-
sity of Chicago Press.
The Religious Ideas of the Old Testament, H. Wheeler Robin-
son. Scribner's.
God in the Old Testament, Robert Alexander Aytoun.   Doran.
The Problem of Suffering in the Old Testament, Arthur S.Peake.
Robert Bryant.
The Literature of the Old Testament in its Historical Develop-
ment, Julius A. Bewer. Columbia University Press.
An Introduction to the Old Testament Chronologically Ar-
ranged, Harlan Creelman. Macmillan.
The Origin and Permanent Value of the Old Testament, Charles
Foster Kent. Scribner's.
The New Testament in the Christian Church, Edward Caldwell
Moore. Macmillan.
The New Testament in the Twentieth Century, Maurice Jones.
Macmillan.

The Approach to the New Testament, James Moffatt. Doran.
The Story of the New Testament, Edgar Johnson Goodspeed.
University of Chicago Press.
The Historical Bible, Charles Foster Kent. Scribner's.
The Bible; its Origin, its Significance, and its Abiding Worth,
Arthur S. Peake. Hodder & Stoughton.
How the Bible Grew, Frank Grant Lewis. University of Chicago
Press.
The Christian Doctrine of Man, H. Wheeler Robinson. T. and
T. Clark.
The Use of the Scriptures in Theology, William Newton Clarke.
Scribner's.

LECTURE II

THE OLD BOOK IN A NEW WORLD

I

The results of the modern study of the Bible, as we have said, can be grouped under two heads, and the second of these, by far the more difficult to handle and the more troublesome to modern minds, now claims our thought. If we begin, not with the critical processes which have produced the result, but with the practical consequence itself as it affects the minds of multitudes of people, the matter can be simply put: the Bible appears an ancient book difficult to read, understand, believe, and follow in the modern world.

One wonders how many folk have felt misgivings over the situation described by Dr. Robinson:

> "A business man, harassed by the industrial problems of modern democracy, drifts in to the service of an English cathedral. The majesty of his surroundings carries him back to the religion and art of the thirteenth century. The Creeds take him on a longer journey to the early centuries of the Catholic Church. But the First Lesson demands the longest pilgrimage of all, for he must listen, perhaps, to the story of Jezebel, of whose body was found no more than the skull, and the feet, and the palms of the hands. It is

worth while to try and realise the strangeness of
the history which has incorporated such flotsam
and jetsam of Semitic story into the ritual of an
English cathedral in the twentieth century after
Christ.   But many at the present day are concerned less with the wonder than with the in-
congruity of it." [1]

If this difficulty of naturalizing the Bible in the
modern world concerned only stories like those about
Jezebel, it might be comfortably arranged.   The real
problem lies deeper.   When one moves back to the
Scripture with a mind accustomed to work in modern
ways, he finds himself in a strange world.   The people
who walk through its pages often do not speak his
language, nor use his intellectual viewpoints, nor explain occurrences by his categories.   Knowing modern
astronomy he turns to the Bible to find the sun and
moon standing still or the shadow retreating on Ahaz'
dial.[2]   Knowing modern biology he hears that when
Elisha had been so long dead that only his bones were
left, another dead body, thrown into the cave where
he was buried, touched his skeleton and sprang to life
again, or that after our Lord's resurrection many of
the saints long deceased arose and appeared in Jerusalem.[3]   Knowing modern physics he turns to the
Bible and reads that light was created three days
before the sun and that an axe-head floated when

<hr>

[1] H. Wheeler Robinson: The Religious Ideas of the Old Testament, 212–213.

[2] Joshua 10:12–13; II Kings 20:11.

[3] II Kings 13:21; Matthew 27:52–53.

Elisha threw a stick into the water.[1] Knowing modern medicine he finds in the Scripture many familiar ailments, epilepsy, deafness, dumbness, blindness, insanity, ascribed to the visitation of demons.[2] Knowing that the sky is blue because of the infinite number of dust-particles that catch and break up the light, he finds himself in the Bible living under a solid "firmament" "strong as a molton mirror," or a "paved work of sapphire stone" from which a fiery chariot can come down to snatch a living man by literal levitation from the flat earth to his heavenly reward.[3]

Here is the perplexity which more than any other afflicts the minds of educated men. They honor the Bible. They know that in it are the springs of the noblest elements in our civilization. They stand uncovered before Jesus Christ. But they are honestly bothered by many things in Scripture. They do not know what to make of them. They find it hard to use one set of mental presuppositions and categories in every other realm of life and another set in religion. They have to shift their mental gear too suddenly when they turn from their ordinary intellectual processes to the strange ways of thinking that the Bible contains.

II

If this practical difficulty in using the old Book in the new world so confuses many minds to-day it is

[1] Genesis 1:3–5, 16–19; II Kings 6:5–6.

[2] Matthew 17:15,18; Mark 9:25; Matthew 9:32; 12:22; Luke 8:27, 35.

[3] Genesis 1:6; Job 37:18; Exodus 24:10; Psalm 136:6; Isaiah 11:12; II Kings 2:11.

important to understand the process that has caused the problem. What has happened can be briefly put: historical knowledge has given us a vivid understanding of the old world from which the Scriptures came until we see the Bible's original, native meanings in terms of the time when it was written; and, on the other side, the new world in which we live has become very new, with ways of thinking that never were on earth before; and these two worlds stand over against each other alien at a multitude of points. What once was said of Jehovah can in a different sense be said of the Book—its thoughts are not our thoughts, neither are its ways our ways. This is the second result of our modern study of the Bible. It has made the Scriptures appear in the light of an old Book in a new world.

The ultimate cause of this problem is to be found in the ambition of all Biblical scholarship to get at the original meaning of Scripture, to discover in terms of its historic significance just what any passage meant to the folk who first wrote it and first read it. Surely, this is not only an innocent ambition; it is an indispensable goal for any interpreter of ancient literature to seek. Nor is it new in the church's attitude toward the Bible. Go back to the Syrian school of interpretation with Theodore of Mopsuestia for its scholar and John Chrysostom for its preacher, a school that is alike the glory and despair of the early church because it rose so splendidly and then was so soon quenched by ignorance, and you find an honest, earnest, and energetic endeavor to get at the original historic sense of Scripture. Those first great exegetes, in spite of the prevalent allegorizing of their time, sought to know what the Bible meant to say in terms of the time when it was written. This, too, is the strength of Calvin's work, which causes one modern admirer to call him "the first scientific interpreter in the history of the Christian Church."[1] How could the Golden Rule of exegesis be better put than in Calvin's dedicatory letter to his Commentary on Romans: "This is in a manner his [the interpreter's] whole charge: namely, to show forth the mind of the writer whom he hath taken upon himself to expound."

If, then, those older interpreters, with an eager desire to get at the historic sense of the Bible, did not fully achieve their end, it was not for lack of will but for lack of means. Though they hungered and thirsted for the original connotation of the Book, they did not yet have the apparatus, historical, documentary, linguistic, archeological, which could put them in possession of the setting out of which the Bible came, the ways men used to think, their social customs, intellectual categories, and prevalent beliefs. What is new in our situation is the achievement of new instruments. As never was true before in the church's history, the scientific desire to get at the historic sense of Scripture has scientific machinery with which to work. Now we are able, as our fathers were not, vitally to enter into the understanding of older civilizations, their mental habits and social institutions, and in particular by many new avenues to get at the world out of which the Bible came. We can understand the original meaning of its words and

[1] Kemper Fullerton: Prophecy and Authority, 133.

ways of thinking until, for those who know, that old world lives again with picturesque vividness.

Consider the various disciplines that enter into Biblical scholarship to-day and see how they all contribute to one aim: to make luminous and clear the historic meaning of the texts. First of all, *knowledge of the ancient languages* has supplied an indispensable instrument for the understanding of what the Bible originally meant to say. In 1800 not a word of the inscriptions of Egypt had been deciphered. In 1802 the Rosetta Stone began to surrender its secret. By 1832 decipherment of Egyptian inscriptions had been put upon a secure basis. Since that time, as Driver says, "the history, the art, the antiquities, the manners and customs, the domestic life of an entire civilization extending over some 4,000 years, have been disinterred and made intelligible to the present generation." [1] In 1849 not a word of all the Assyrian inscriptions had been translated except the names of Nebuchadnezzar and his father. In 1851 Major Rawlinson published, with grammatical notes, a translation of a tri-lingual inscription of Darius. Since that time we have seen the rediscovery and reconstruction of a great civilization of almost incalculable antiquity which was once immensely influential on Hebrew religion and which now is indispensable to its full understanding. Even the linguistic relationship of Hebrew, Aramaic, Arabic, Ethiopic, and Amharic, as dialects of one original language, was not securely established before 1800, and since then students of the Book have had put into their hands not

[1] S. R. Driver: Modern Research as Illustrating the Bible, 4.

only an organized knowledge of Hebrew, but of all the allied Semitic tongues and the different languages of Egypt, to say nothing of a greatly improved knowledge of the Hellenistic Greek in which the New Testament was written.[1]

For another thing, the *discovery and translation of contemporary literatures* have thrown a luminous light upon the historic meanings of the Scripture. To be sure, the church has always known Josephus and Philo, and certain apocalyptic books, notably Enoch, have been used from the days of Origen and Jerome. Yet, in a way no longer true, the Bible once stood out sharply from antiquity, and the thought and life of man that had lain around it remained in the shadow, largely unregarded. Now the light spreads as current books which sprang out of the same situations come within our ken and, with others long known, are subjected to careful scrutiny, and what in our knowledge of Biblical times was incomplete is, by the new information, often rounded out and fulfilled. So the Jewish apocalypses have been brought to light in these last few years, their importance has been vividly realized, and the study of them has illumined the development of apocalyptic hopes in Judaism. So the work of Cumont, Reitzenstein, and others is making clearer the meaning of those Hellenistic mystery religions which surrounded and rivaled Christianity and which affected some of the thought and phraseology of the New Testament.

All this added knowledge of language and literature has made *textual criticism* a powerful help in correct-

[1] Ibid, 13–14.

ing obscure and perverted renderings and in getting back as nearly as we can to the original autograph copies of the Scriptures. How many people do not know that the most ancient extant manuscript of the Old Testament dates from the ninth century A. D. and the most ancient extant Greek manuscript of the New Testament from the fourth century; that the versions are variant at so many points that one could say of them what Jerome said of the Latin translations of his day, that there are almost as many forms of texts as there are copies? [1] The clearing up of the texts, therefore, the selection of the more ancient or more sensible renderings, the correction of obviously mistaken copying, have in all cases been useful and in some cases, as with Jeremiah, have rescued a book from obscurity.

To this same end of lighting up the original meaning of the Bible, *history* makes an important contribution. Nobly and rightly distinguished are those fathers of history whose writings are still unexhausted quarries of information, Herodotus, Thucydides, Livy, and Tacitus, yet Professor Shotwell is justified when he exclaims, ' By what miracle has the long lost past been at last recovered, in our own day, so that we are checking up Herodotus by his own antiquity, correcting the narrative of Livy or Tacitus by the very refuse deposited beneath the streets upon which they walked?'' [2] No longer the story of dynasties alone,

[1] St. Jerome: Preface to the Four Gospels (in Vulgate Version of the New Testament), in The Nicene and Post-Nicene Fathers, Second Series., Vol. VI, 488.

[2] James T. Shotwell: An Introduction to the History of History, 2.

but of peoples, their customs, laws, domestic habits, mental categories, religious faiths, their folk-lore and folk-ways, history, with its many modern auxiliaries, has done for old civilizations whose influence lay around and permeated the Bible what the spade has done for Pompeii. Once more we can walk the ancient streets, and, while life is gone, the memorials of its presence are so clear that in imagination we can reconstruct the humanity that once toiled, dreamed, thought, and suffered there.

Add to the list *archeology* and no long comment is needed to make clear the incalculable service which has been rendered by modern research to the understanding of the Bible. At innumerable points the Scriptures have been corroborated, illumined, supplemented by the manifold results that have come from the "romance of the spade." It was only in 1872 that George Smith, working over some clay tablets from the library of Asshurbanipal, found the first parallels of the deluge story. The Daily Telegraph of London offered him a thousand guineas to go to Nineveh and describe his discoveries. He found more of the deluge tablets and all the creation tablets. Nor is the end yet. Every new discovery binds the Book more closely to the life out of which it sprang and reveals more clearly what its narratives, laws, rituals, doctrines, and customs meant in terms of the generations when they arose.

Last but not least, *comparative religion* has made an immense contribution to our understanding of the original meanings of the Bible. Once the Hebrew religion and its Christian fulfilment stood alone and

the religious life of the world outside was either
shrouded in obscurity or else was lumped in one
general condemnation as heathenism. Gone was the
noble catholicity of the early church's greater minds,
when on the basis of the doctrine of the Logos "which
lighteth every man," cosmopolitan Christians recognized all the world's wisdom and goodness as part
of the divine revelation. Gone was the breadth of
vision which had stirred Paul on Mars Hill and which
had made Clement of Alexandria say that philosophy
was given by God to the Greeks as "a schoolmaster
to bring the Hellenic mind . . . to Christ." [1] The
older cosmopolitanism of the Græco-Roman world was
finally lost when the Empire fell, when the Turks shut
off the Orient from the Occident, and the shadows of
the medieval age closed in.

But the new world of broken boundaries and open
avenues has brought back to us interest in other
religions than our own, and with that interest, made
effective by the diligent study of the legends, cosmologies, rituals, doctrines of other people, new light has
come upon our sacred books. Supreme they may be,
but they are not, in their typical ways of conceiving
the world and describing events, isolated and alone.
Primitive cosmology, animal sacrifice, offering of
first fruits, circumcision, clean and unclean foods,
shrines on high places, priestly garments of linen,
sacred trees like the oak of Shechem, sacred chests
like the holy Ark, instruments for obtaining divine
oracles like the Urim or Thummim, ordeals to deter-

---

[1] See, e. g., The Stromata, Book I, Ch. V, first ¶, in The Ante-
Nicene Fathers, Vol. II, 305.

THE OLD BOOK IN A NEW WORLD   43

mine guilt or innocence,[1] angelic or demonic visitations, and all manner of miracles, are familiar elements of man's religious life wherever its records
reveal the past or its present practises and beliefs
preserve unchanged an older heritage.   Often, lec-
turing on some ancient idea or custom indicated in
our Bible, I hear from a missionary student a perfect
parallel out of the religious life of the people among
whom he works.

This, then, is the result which follows from all these
disciplines of modern scholarship converging on one
point: the world in which the Bible first was written
lives again in our thought. We can enter into its mind,
understand its problems, catch the native connotation of its words. Historic imagination has well-
accredited data on which to work and can picture
how men lived, thought, talked, and hoped in Scriptural times. Perhaps what has been gained is as
nothing in comparison with the light that yet shall
come but, for all that, it is true that when we read the
Book to-day we read it with increasing clearness in
terms of its contemporary meanings. In a way never
true in Christian history before we stand face to face
with the historic sense of the Scriptures.

In the meantime, while this old world of the Bible
has been growing more vivid in our apprehension, the
new world in which we actually live has been growing
very new. Science has remade from top to bottom
our outlook on the physical universe; philosophy has
restated its problems, reformed its methods and,
when discussing old questions or new ones, uses pre-

[1] See, e. g., Numbers 5:11-31.

suppositions and structural ideas of which the ancient world never heard; the inductive method of scientific investigation has revolutionized man's ways of discovering and using truth; the idea of evolution in biology has blossomed out into the idea of progress in human life, a conception as far as possible removed from the static view which controlled the ancient world; ethical problems have so changed that polygamy, chattel slavery, imperialistic government and war are rightly recognized as sins to be hated and overcome, although all of them are taken for granted in large areas of the Bible without reproof, and in some of the older documents are inculcated and encouraged; democracy has arrived and has introduced ideas to which older theories of the state were utter strangers; the machine has remade our industry, and our whole economic life, alike in its extent, its methods, and its problems, is far removed from the economic background of the Bible. We live in a new world, we picture with increasing clearness the contemporary meanings of an old world, and we feel the incompatibility between them—that is the difficulty which multitudes of modern folk are having with the Bible.

On the one side is the Semitic world-view with its flat earth surrounded by the sea, and the solid firmament a little way above; on the other our modern universe of immeasurable distances. On the one side is a world where God's providence is specially revealed in miracle; on the other our world of law where God is seen, not in the irregular, but in the regular. On the one side we find a world thronged with demons who cause sickness, drive men mad, inspire sin, and enter into a universal conspiracy to overthrow God; on the other a world where the fear of demons is a superstition. On the one side are apocalyptic hopes where expectations of God's triumph center in a supernatural invasion of the world; on the other are our social hopes that foresee a prolonged fight ahead, with many a catastrophe, and many a long, hard pull. In the Bible immortality is associated with the resurrection of the body; among us immortality is conceived as escape from the body. There the person of our Lord is interpreted in terms of the Jewish Messiahship or of Alexandrian Platonism; here are philosophical methods and structural ideas that have no kinship with apocalypses or with Philo. There is an ethic developed in a theocracy under autocratic governments; here an ethic inevitably shaped by the new democracy and the new economic order.

That is the problem which the modern man faces with his Bible, and to say that it is serious is to speak mildly.

III

We may make this problem more vivid by illustrating it in the realm where the church met it first and where we have had the longest time to adjust our thought—the changed views of the physical universe. If we could divest ourselves of the scientific information into the possession of which we were born and reared, and with quite unsophisticated minds could look out on the physical world, we should see it a good deal as men used to see it in the childhood of the race. The world looks flat; travel far enough in any

direction and you come to water, which evidently
surrounds the earth; dig deep enough and you come
to water, which evidently underlies the earth. Look
up and you see a blue canopy or vault, which encloses
and covers the earth; across this vault's inner side
move lights to illumine the earth by day and night;
water falls from the sky in rain, so that on the other
side of the vault there must be a sea, and there must
be apertures in the firmament through which the rain
comes down. That is the world-view which is presented by things as they look. That world-view inevitably constituted the early cosmology of man.
One finds it as the background of all Semitic thought
about the universe, and it is indicated in every passage
of the Bible that indicates anything at all about the
physical world.

In the Scriptures the flat earth is founded on an
underlying sea; [1] it is stationary; [2] the heavens are like
an upturned bowl or canopy above it; [3] the circum-
ference of this vault rests on pillars; [4] the sun, moon,
and stars move within this firmament of special purpose to illumine man; [5] there is a sea above the sky,
"the waters which were above the heavens," [6] and
through the "windows of heaven" the rain comes
down; [7] within the earth is Sheol, where dwell the
shadowy dead; [8] this whole cosmic system is suspended over vacancy; [9] and it all was made in six

[1] Psalm 136:6, 24:1–2, Genesis 7:11.   [2] Psalm 93:1, 104:5.
[3] Job 37:18, Genesis 1:6–8, Isaiah 40:22, Psalm 104:2.
[4] Job 26:11, Psalm 104:3.   [5] Genesis 1:14–18.
[6] Genesis 1:7, Psalm 148:4.   [7] Psalm 78:23, Genesis 7:11.
[8] Isaiah 14:9–11.   [9] Job 26:7.

days, each with a morning and an evening,[1] a short and measurable time before.   This is the world-view of the Bible.

Moreover, it remained the world-view of the Christian church for a long time.   Augustine, with uncompromising strictness, stated the authority of Scripture in matters such as this: "Scripture, which proves the truth of its historical statements by the accomplishment of its prophecies, gives no false information." [2]   Those early fathers have been severely handled because they thus clung to a world-view which might have been outgrown long before it was, had not their literalism barred the way.   In this insistence upon an old cosmology, however, they were but children of their age.   To be sure, Lactantius, a Christian writer of the fourth century, ridiculed the idea of people on the other side of the earth.   He writes:

> "Is there any one so senseless as to believe that there are men whose footsteps are higher than their heads? or that the things which with us are in a recumbent position, with them hang in an inverted direction? that the crops and trees grow downwards? that the rains, and snow, and hail fall upwards to the earth?   And does any one wonder that hanging gardens are mentioned among the seven wonders of the world, when philosophers make hanging fields, and seas, and cities, and mountains? . . .   I am at a loss what to say re-

[1] Genesis, Ch. I.

[2] The City of God, Book XVI, Ch. 9, first ¶, in The Nicene and Post-Nicene Fathers, First Series, Vol. II, 315.

specting those who, when they have once erred,
consistently persevere in their folly, and defend
one vain thing by another." [1]

It will not do, however, to charge this against Christianity, for Plutarch, the brill'ant pagan, held precisely the same scornful attitude about the antipodes. [2]

It is true also that many of the church fathers
treated all scientific investigation with high disdain.
Basil of Cæsarea thought it a matter of no interest to us whether the earth is "spherical or cylin-
drical, if it resemble a disc and is equally rounded in
all parts, or if it has the form of a winnowing basket
and is hollow in the middle." [3]   Said St. Ambrose:
"To discuss the nature and position of the earth does
not help us in our hope of the life to come." [4]   Said
Eusebius: "We have justly kept aloof from the un-
profitable and erroneous and vain labor of them all,
and do not busy ourselves at all about the said subjects, for we do not see the utility of them, nor any
tendency to benefit and gain good for mankind." [5]

While, however, an extreme other-worldliness was

[1] The Divine Institutes, Book III, Ch. XXIV, first and third ¶¶,
in The Ante-Nicene Fathers, Vol. VII, 94, 95.

[2] Lynn Thorndike: A History of Magic and Experimental Science,
during the First Thirteen Centuries of our Era, Vol. I, 219.

[3] The Hexæmeron, Homily IX, 1, in The Nicene and Post-Nicene
Fathers, Second Series, Vol. VIII, 101.

[4] St. Ambrose: Hexæmeron, Liber I, Cap. VI, ¶ 22, in Patrologiæ
Latinæ, ed. by J. P. Migne, Vol. XIV, Column 132.

[5] Preparation for the Gospel, Book XV, Ch. LXI, in translation by
E. H. Gifford, Part II, 852c.

in part responsible for this contempt of scientific inquiry, there was another motive which introduces a new element into our judgment of the case. All investigation of cosmology in the early centuries was inextricably tied up with astrology. The whole ancient world into which Christianity went believed that the stars controlled and forecast human events. This astrological fatalism permeated the life of the people through and through. Nor was it a mere popular superstition; the foremost scientific minds that the early centuries produced believed it. Pliny expounded the predictive power of comets; [1] Seneca believed that the planets forecast the future and that unusual celestial phenomena were to be looked upon as prodigies and portents; [2] Ptolemy vigorously defended astrology and sheltered it from defeat for many centuries by the authority of his great name; even Galen, the pioneer of scientific healing, devoted two entire books to the presentation of astrological medicine.[3] This tremendously powerful influence affected many minds in the church and one wonders whether in our New Testament the beautiful story of the star of Bethlehem is not associated with the desire to connect so great an event as the birth of Jesus with some unusual portent in the heavens. At any rate, more than one Christian teacher, notably John Chrysostom, worked hard to dissociate the story from

[1] Natural History, Book II, Ch. XXIII.

[2] See, e. g., Physical Science (Quaestiones Naturales), Book VII, Ch. XXVIII, in translation by John Clarke, 302–303.

[3] Lynn Thorndike: A History of Magic and Experimental Science during the First Thirteen Centuries of our Era, Vol. I, 110.

astrology, lest the Scripture itself should be made the friend of superstition.[1]

The Christians hated astrological fatalism, rightly looking upon it as a deadly enemy of the Gospel, and because astrology and astronomy had not yet been differentiated, the early church was often hostile to or negligent of scientific inquiry.

Whatever motives entered into the situation, however, and whatever mitigations of judgment may be proposed, the story of the church's attitude toward the enlargement of scientific knowledge is pathetic. Gradually and painlessly, to be sure, the Ptolemaic cosmology took the place of the flat earth. This new astronomy rounded out the earth into a sphere but still left it stationary. Different, therefore, as the Ptolemaic system was from Biblical science, it could without too great violence be accommodated to the texts. But when the Copernican system was proposed the storm broke. It was a war of texts against facts. Even Luther called Copernicus a fool for suggesting that the earth moved, and roundly capped his argument by calling to witness the Scripture which says that Joshua made the sun stand still and not the earth.[2]

What has happened since is now common property. We hold a world-view whose structural bases were not laid down by Moses in the thirteenth century B. C., but by Copernicus and Galileo in the sixteenth century

[1] The Gospel of St. Matthew, Homily Six, Secs. I–IV, in The Nicene and Post-Nicene Fathers, First Series, Vol. X, 36–39.

[2] Tischreden, Vol. I (in Kritische Gesammtausgabe, Weimar), Nr. 855, 3d ¶, 419.

THE OLD BOOK IN A NEW WORLD

A. D.   Upon these structural bases an entirely new
conception of the physical universe has been built up.
It may be that temporarily Newton's theory of
gravitation did "tend to infidelity" [1] as John Wesley
said, but, for all that, it has been accepted and with
its corollaries has revolutionized man's thought.   It
may be that the evolutionary hypothesis is dangerous
to the religious faith of many folk who welcome it
to-day, as some conservatives think, but, for all that,
the more facts we know the better founded does the
hypothesis appear.   We live in a new world.   We have
not kept the forms of thought and categories of explanation in astronomy, geology, biology, which the
Bible contains.   We have definitely and irrevocably
gotten new ones diverse from and irreconcilable with
the outlooks on the universe which earlier ages in
general and the Bible in particular had.   Whatever
we may think of it, this is a fait accompli.

Recently I received from a man in Massachusetts a
letter attributing most human ills to the Copernican
astronomy.   Everything had gone wrong, he said,
since men began believing in a round and moving
earth.   As for him, he was sure that alike Copernicus
and Newton were wrong.   The Scripture is against
them, he wrote, and the facts sustain the Scripture's
claim.   He is the only thoroughgoing literalist with
whom I ever dealt.   He really believes the Bible from
cover to cover.   He has not deceived himself with any
of those devious schemes by which less ingenuous
minds read into the first chapter of Genesis conceptions of the universe that never were thought of before

[1] Edwin Tenney Brewster: The Understanding of Religion, 26.

the modern age. But there are not many of him left. He seems like one born out of due time and alive after his day.

Do not suppose that one, granting all this, picks up the first chapter of Genesis with condescension. For myself, I think it holy ground. If you wish to know how great a thing was done there of which we are the illimitable debtors, come up to the creation story in Genesis from the so-called parallels that are found in the creation tablets of Babylonia. Folk call them parallels, but I do not see how they do it if they have read them. They are full of the quarrels of gods, the fear of primeval dragons, the war of Tiamat and the hosts of chaos against Marduk and the gods of light. They do, indeed, give us the same cosmology, but Marduk builds it up by slitting Tiamat like a flat fish and making the firmament of her upper half and the earth of her lower. When one turns from this welter of mythology to the first chapter of Genesis, with its stately and glorious exordium, "In the beginning God created the heavens and the earth," one feels as though he had left miasmic marshes for a high mountain with clean air to breathe and great horizons to look upon. Here a victory was gained for pure religion for which we never can be too thankful. In place of polytheism, ethical monotheism; in place of mythology with ugly dragons and disgraceful fights, one God transcendent, who says "Let be," and it is; in place of political desire to exalt Marduk, god of Babylon, a religious devotion which makes the chapter read more like a psalm than a cosmology; in place of man created that the gods may have some one to offer sacrifices to them, man

meant to be and fitted to be the friend and son of God
—such are a few of the contrasts between the so-called
parallels of Babylonia and the magnificent first chapter
of the Book.   The only way in which to feel the force
of this is to read the documents.   See if you do not
come from the old Semitic heritage to the Biblical
account as Stade came from the so-called Eden story
of Babylonia to the Eden story of the Scripture, saying that it was like passing from the slough of a village
cesspool to a clean mountain spring.[1]

This is the fair and rational approach to a true
estimate of the account of creation in Genesis: we
must come up to it from contemporary thinking, not
go back to it from modern science.

Nevertheless, the problem still remains.   The
science of the Bible is not our science.   That fact
troubles multitudes of minds.   They are bothered by
it and spiritually disturbed.   And when one goes to
church and hears some sermons one cannot blame
them.   Let a Christian layman put into his own urgent
words the difficulty which many feel when they try
to read the old Book in this new age:

"Six days in the week we live in an ordered
world.   On the seventh, we open the church door
on a land of topsy-turvy, where axes float, dry
sticks change to serpents, cities are let down out
of the sky, angels stir the water of wells, bedeviled
swine run violently into the sea.   We say prayers
for rain an hour after we have consulted a government bulletin to see whether we shall need an

[1] A. R. Gordon: The Early Traditions of Genesis, 56.

umbrella before we get home. We solemnly
repeat, '. . . Maker of heaven and earth . . .
descended into Hell . . . sitteth on the right
hand of God . . .' Yet all the while we know
perfectly well that heaven is not ' up ' nor hell
' down,' that this universe was never 'made' by
anybody in any such sense as the 'apostles' supposed, nor has it any such topographical relations
as they assumed. Whoso has sat with his eye at
one end of a brass tube and a fragment of the
everlasting mystery at the other, knows that no
living being, from pond scum to mammal, ever
gets into this unintelligible world by virtue of any
process that in the least resembles anything that
the days of ignorance meant by '*conceptus*'; while
as for '*carnis resurrectionem*,' which, as a piece of
psychophysics, we inherit from the followers of
Zarathustra by way of the Pharisees and St.
Paul, most of us actually do hold the diametri-
cally opposite opinion—the Platonic doctrine of
the immortality of the soul." [1]

What shall we preachers say to an educated layman who talks to us like that?

IV

The basis of the answer, to whose completion the
following lectures will be devoted, is, after all, not
difficult to state. The most abiding elements in
human history are the fundamental experiences of
man's spirit. Everything else in man's life changes;

[1] Edwin Tenney Brewster: The Understanding of Religion, 27–28.

outwardly his environments and inwardly his mental categories alter; but at the heart of him is something that changes but little if at all. This is not a matter of pious desire; it is a matter of historic fact. "It is more than doubtful," says Dr. Crump in his Logic of History, "whether any varieties of human character have disappeared during the ages of which we have knowledge, or whether any new types of character have come into existence. The motives that act on men have altered but little." [1]

One must always distinguish, therefore, between man's abiding experiences and their temporary expressions. We no longer put on sackcloth and ashes, but that does not mean that any important change has taken place in the griefs and miseries which sackcloth and ashes once expressed. We do not live in tents under patriarchal rule; we live in modern apartment houses with all the complicated appliances of our scientific age; but if we are fortunate we understand a story like that of Isaac and Rebekah as well as though it were written yesterday— "And Isaac brought her into his mother Sarah's tent, and took Rebekah, and she became his wife; and he loved her." [2]

This contrast between the fundamental experiences of man and their temporary expressions holds just as good in the intellectual as it does in the practical realm. Man's way of looking at the world, rationalizing his life, and explaining what happens to him, is always changing. Man is forever getting a new mental framework in which to arrange his experiences. But the experiences themselves go on. This very much

[1] C. G. Crump: The Logic of History, 49.   [2] Genesis 24:67.

needs to be said. Fairly intoxicated with the newness of this modern world, we are tempted to forget that all the while there is a world of experience here, not new at all but as old as the race: sin and its consequence, hunger and thirst after righteousness, love, hate and jealousy, heartbreak, grief and tragedy, joy, hope, and the need of God. You will find them in Homer and in Shakspere, in Job and in Goethe. Pick up an old scientific book, like Pliny's Natural History, and compare it with The Outline of Science, by Thomson, and what a difference! But when you turn to biography and read the story of men's lives, their hopes and fears, temptations, motives, and desires, loves, hates, griefs, struggles, defeats and victories, it is all alike a thousand years before Christ or two thousand years after. For there you have stepped out of the shifting world into the deeps of the human spirit where dwell the abiding experiences of men.

Since a preacher who is about his business is dealing all the while with this inner world of man's spiritual experience, he may be entirely aware of the contrasts between the Biblical categories and his own and yet may go on year after year untroubled by it. Perhaps he ought not to go untroubled, but it can be done. On Sunday morning, as Ruskin said, he has "thirty minutes to raise the dead in." He has lived through another week of intimate dealing with the elemental needs of human souls. When he mounts the pulpit he is thinking of them and not of Copernicus versus Genesis. With these ancient yet ever new needs of man's spirit on his mind, he is not first of all impressed by the changes of mental category which have taken

place between Biblical times and his own.   What
most impresses him is the amazing timelessness of the
Bible when it deals with the spiritual life of men.
As Dr. Moffatt says, "The alterations of civilization
leave the heart of vital religion untouched as nothing
else." [1]

"Blessed are the pure in heart: for they shall see
God"—what have time and change to do with that?
"Enter into thine inner chamber, and having shut thy
door, pray to thy Father who is in secret"; "God is
love; and he that abideth in love abideth in God, and
God abideth in him"—what have time and change to
do with that?   "Let all bitterness, and wrath, and
anger, and clamor, and railing, be put away from you,
with all malice: and be ye kind one to another, tender-
hearted, forgiving each other, even as God also in
Christ forgave you"—what have time and change to
do with that?   And supremely when one thinks of
Jesus, the quality of his spirit and the central emphases
of his teaching, I should suppose that no man would
care to be a Christian minister if he could not say
what George Matheson said, "Son of Man, whenever
I doubt of life, I think of Thee . . . Thou never
growest old to me.   Last century is old, last year is
old, last season is an obsolete fashion; but Thou art
not obsolete.   Thou art abreast of all the centuries,
nay, Thou goest before them like the star.   I have
never come up with Thee, modern as I am." [2]

No mere outgrowing of old world-views, therefore,
will ever make the Bible old to a man who is concerned

[1] James Moffatt: The Approach to the New Testament, 174.
[2] Searchings in the Silence, 20–21.

with the cure of souls. The only thing that ever
would make the Bible old to him would be to have
mankind's spiritual experiences and needs so change
that they were no longer mirrored in the Book and
met in the Gospel. And that day is a long sea-mile
away.

No one at this point need fear for a moment that
we shall fail in these lectures to wrestle as manfully
as we know how with the intellectual differences between the Scripture and ourselves. They are important. They do present a serious problem. But,
surely, this more basic truth needs first to be emphasized. Underneath this new world of shifting
circumstance and changing category is a very old
world. On every hand we hear folk talking about the
newness of this modern world and the way that old
things have gone. We hear about new geology, new
biology, new astronomy, new theology, new world-
contacts, new economic problems, and the general
impression sinks in that the whole world is new and
that old things have disappeared. But one who thinks
more deeply, hearing such talk over much, becomes
rebellious and wishes to cry so that the whole generation can hear him: What is new, really new? To be
sure, countless external arrangements of human life
are new and, as well, almost all the mental frameworks
by which we apprehend and interpret experience; but
underneath, in the world where most of all we live,
what is new? Selfishness, lust, greed, and cruelty;
love, friendship, and self-sacrifice—are these new?
Are sin, remorse, pardon, and reconciliation new?
Are the desires of men new for peace, for brotherhood,

for a kingdom of righteousness upon the earth, for "a house not made with hands, eternal, in the heavens"? The strength of the Bible has always been its appeal to this deep and abiding realm of man's basic experiences, for out of that realm the Bible came.

V

A man, therefore, can go on preaching the Bible year after year and can pay little attention to changing thought-forms and outgrown categories. He can do it by choosing his lessons from those wide areas of Scripture where no outmoded ways of thinking trouble him, or, in other areas, he can neglect those which he knows are there. But this method of treating the Bible, if exclusively used, is becoming increasingly unsatisfactory and perilous. One of the most intelligent and conscientious ministers I ever knew looked at me once in wistful surprise when I told him of a large class which I taught every Sunday in the church. "I rejoice in preaching," he said, "but I should not dare to teach a class; they might ask me questions." That is the trouble with the attitude which we just have been describing if it is exclusive of all others. The one who uses it is not facing, often he does not know how to face, sometimes he is afraid to face, the questions by which the more thoughtful minds in his congregation are really troubled. He is not taking into account some of the intellectual stumbling-blocks over which many young people are falling when they read the Bible. He is not answering questions which. however secondary in importance to the profound needs of the moral and religious life, are nevertheless real barriers against the free and glad acceptance of the spiritual help which the Bible ought to bring.

Moreover, not only is this too easy content with the abiding spiritual messages of the Book increasingly unsatisfactory for the preacher; it is increasingly dangerous for the church. Is not this in part the explanation of the appalling renaissance of obscurantism which afflicts us to-day? Once there was a well standardized way of using Scripture. Practically everybody recognized it. It was drilled into children alike in home and school, and in the church it furnished the unquestioned method of the preacher. This method did not use merely the Bible's abiding experiences; it used the Bible's scientific concepts and ways of thinking from Genesis to Revelation.

Then came the new age with its disturbing influences. The old use of the Bible became impossible to many preachers who, as much as ever was true of their fathers, believed in Jesus Christ as the world's Savior and wanted to proclaim his Gospel as the power of God unto salvation. These preachers, therefore, having lost an old method of using the Bible and not having gotten a new one, let go Biblical conceptions that seemed outgrown and quietly fell back on the unquestioned messages of the Book—its central spiritual hopes and timeless inspirations. This often produced great preaching; certainly its tendency has been to produce more vitally helpful preaching than much that the older dogmatism issued in. But it has perilous lacks. It has not been teaching the people

how to think in the realm of religion.   It has been
practical, human, encouraging, vital, but it has been
intellectually loose-jointed and rickety.   It has evaded
real questions.   It has surrendered old intellectual
frameworks without getting new ones.   It has let the
church drift before the breezes of inspirational preaching upon the rocks of intellectual confusion.

We are paying for it now.   On the one side we are
paying for it in multitudes of churches waiting to be
swamped by theological obscurantism, fanatical pre-
millennialists, anti-evolutionary propaganda, or any
other kind of reactionary movement in religious thinking against which no intellectual dikes ever have been
raised by thoroughgoing, consistent teaching as to
what our new knowledge really means to religion.   On
the other side we are paying for it in the loss of our
more intelligent young people.   Sure as most of them
are that the foundations of religion are secure, many
are alienated from the churches.   When they read
the Bible or go to worship they feel their inherited
religious thinking, set forth in the Book and taken for
granted in the pulpit, so out of place in the modern
world that like the Jews in Babylon they cry, "How
shall we sing the Lord's song in a strange land"?

Deeply as we rejoice, therefore, in the timelessness
of the Bible's central messages, and true as it is that
our preaching must mainly deal with the realm of
unchanging experience, where the deeps of the Book
call to the deeps of the human heart, it will not do to
leave the matter there.   The old Book has moved out
into a new world.   There are sharp contrasts between
some ways of thinking in the Bible and our own.

There is no use obscuring the fact. We would better set it out in the clear light and deal with it. For if we who are the disciples of the Lord do not do it in the interests of his people and his cause, it will be ruinously done for us by those who are his enemies.

Nor is there good reason why we should approach this task with fearfulness or reluctance. We may well approach it triumphantly. See what the church already has done so wisely and so well in wide areas of her life. When the new music came, when Palestrina, Bach, Beethoven, Handel began using new instruments and new methods, did the church say, "None of that! Sackbuts and psalteries—they are the holy instruments"? Upon the contrary, she captured the new music, she claimed it for Christ, so that the noblest harmony of the centuries has been set to the high task of praising God.

When the new art came in, when out of old stiffness and unreality painting began to move into lifelikeness with expanding use of line and color, did the church turn away and say, "None of that! We will go back to the old outlines that Christians first drew upon the walls of the catacombs"? Upon the contrary, the church captured the new painting. She said to Cimabue, Giotto, Raphael, Michelangelo: "All that you know and the best that you can do for the glory of Christ!" And the rememberable consequence of that attitude is with us still in pictures before which generations of Christians have stood in awe.

When the new architecture came, when men began dreaming their aspirations in Gothic stone, did the church turn her back on that and say, "No, we will return to worship as the apostles did, in an upper room"? Upon the contrary, she captured Gothic architecture, building with it cathedrals that, in Ruskin's words, are "vast illuminated missals bound with alabaster instead of parchment."

See what the church has done so wisely and so well in wide areas of her life where she has taken things new and true and made them ministrant to religion. Why cannot we do that same thing gladly, triumphantly in every realm of this new world? If there are fresh things to learn concerning the physical universe, let us have them, that we may find a deeper meaning when we say, "The heavens declare the glory of God." If there are new ways of approaching men's minds, new methods of argument and apologetic, let us have them and not fight like fools with bows and arrows at Verdun, when the One we are fighting for is so worthy of the best that we can do. If there are new powers disclosed by science, let us have them and put them at the disposal of the Lord of life to make our service more efficient! All that we know at the service of the Highest that we know—that is the ideal!

Surely, in a universe with a living God, the burden of proof is not upon us who would urge that attitude. The burden of proof is upon those who would endeavor to withhold us from it.

BIBLIOGRAPHY

The Understanding of Religion, Edwin Tenney Brewster. Houghton Mifflin.

A History of the Warfare of Science with Theology in Christendom; Ch. III, Astronomy, Andrew D. White. Appletons.

The Old Testament in the Light of To-Day, William Frederic Badè. Houghton Mifflin.

Hebrew and Babylonian Traditions, Morris Jastrow, Jr. Scribner's.

The Early Traditions of Genesis, A. R. Gordon. T. and T. Clark.

Archæology and the Bible, George A. Barton. American Sunday-School Union.

Modern Research as Illustrating the Bible, S. R. Driver. Oxford University Press for British Academy.

Sixty Years with the Bible, William Newton Clarke. Scribner's.

The Rise of Modern Religious Ideas, Arthur Cushman McGiffert. Macmillan.

LECTURE III

THE ANCIENT SOLUTION

I

Before we consider further the problem presented by the old Book in a new world, we may well put historic horizon around our thought by understanding as clearly as we can the ancient solution of this same problem. For the necessity of accommodating venerable scriptures to new conditions has been faced again and again by every religion that has had sacred scriptures at all. Ours is not the first modern age. Ours is not the first generation that has found itself surrounded by new circumstances and using new modes of thought. Therefore, ours is not the first occasion in history when folk who venerated and believed in a sacred book have been distressed and puzzled because so many things in it seemed unfitted to their modern world.

In this recurrent situation there has been one supreme resource: allegory. No other method of interpretation, whether in our Hebrew-Christian tradition or in the use of sacred scriptures by other peoples, has been so wide-spread, so deep-seated, so indefatigable. That the roots of allegory are deep in the problem which we are considering is clear. Homer's poems, for example, became the sacred scriptures of the Greeks. They were the source of religious instruction; their myths were embodied in venerable customs of worship; they were glorified in art and were the fountainhead of creative literature; and on any question in heaven above or on the earth beneath argument could be clinched by a text from Homer.

Then came a modern age. The crude anthropomorphism of Homer's theology shocked the developed thought of a new generation. The scandalous amours and quarrels of Homer's gods became intolerable to maturer consciences. Moreover, new problems arose on which men wanted light and of which Homer never had thought or sung, yet on which sacred scripture had to give light if it was to fulfil the functions of sacred scripture at all. Under these circumstances the dilemma was distressing. On the one side the Greeks might have broken with the old poems altogether, might have disowned them and torn the Homeric heritage from their literature, art, worship, and apologetic. Of course they did no such thing. They chose the other horn of the dilemma. They allegorized Homer. They said that he never meant literally what he literally said; that all his stories had a hidden sense; that one must find beneath their superficial meaning the mystic significance which the poet had in mind. The necessity which moved their modern age thus to get rid of the historical sense of their ancient scriptures and to put new sense in its place was plainly stated by Heraclitus. He said of Homer: "He was altogether impious if he was not allegorizing." [1]

[1] Homeric Problems, i, lines 5–6.

The Stoics systematized and carried to perfection this method of using their literary heritage. They found their whole modern system of thought in the Iliad and Odyssey. The gods were not gods but allegorical figures for the elements out of which the cosmos was made. Zeus was ether, fire, law, reason, fate, or providence, as any one might wish; Athena, too, was ether; Hades was the heavy air that is in the earth, and Hera was the air above. Rhea and Demeter were earth itself, and Poseidon, water.[1] So the old stories of the gods, that had sprung from their fore-fathers' primitive life, became parables of the fully developed philosophy of a modern age, until Cicero could taunt Chrysippus, the Stoic, with endeavoring "to accommodate the fables of Orpheus, Musæus, Hesiod, and Homer . . . in order that the most ancient poets, who never dreamed of these things, might seem to have been Stoics." [2]

This method of accommodating an old bible to a new age has been so prevalent wherever sacred scrip-tures have existed, and in particular it has so con-trolled the preaching of the Christian church through-out the greater part of her history, that a clear under-standing of it is indispensable as a background for our present discussion.

II

The conditions out of which in the past allegorical interpretation has invariably issued are not difficult

[1] George Foot Moore: History of Religions, Vol. I, 520.
[2] On the Nature of the Gods, Book I, Sec. XV.

to state. First, there must be a sacred literature which by its antiquity has become venerable and by long usage has been woven into the thoughts, affections, customs of the people. If added to this practical authority a high doctrine of inspiration has developed, like the Platonic conception of ancient poets possessed by the divine afflatus and writing in a trance, then the scriptures become so exalted that nothing in them can be trivial, and so holy that to doubt them becomes blasphemy. If the people possessing such a body of sacred writings could always remain in the same culture and circumstance as were theirs when the scriptures were produced, the perfect harmony between their book and their life would not be disturbed. But no people ever do remain so static. Circumstances alter, new philosophies come in, new ethical problems and ideals emerge, new religious conceptions arise, and new cosmologies are proposed. Sooner or later the people with their book find themselves in a modern age with elements in it with which the book does not agree. Then they allegorize. They go behind the natural historic sense of the passages which they object to or do not understand and read into them the sense they wish to find there.

This is being done all over the world to-day in every religion with a sacred literature. You find it in India. Out of the ancient Hindu faith have come reform movements whose devotees have been affected by modern ideas and customs. They are proposing something new but they still are passionately desirous to be true to Hinduism and they so regard themselves.

Such loyalty to the ancient faith, however, involves loyalty to the ancient books. How shall they harmonize their sacred writings with their own modernity? Allegory is the panacea. Even stories like Krishna's amours with the cow-girls, which in fact are primitive tales like Homer's from an age when gods were freely credited with the passions of mankind, are allegorically interpreted to mean the yearning of the soul for union with God. This same process is going on in Muhammadanism. The Koran has all the sacredness with which long usage, passionate fidelity, and a high doctrine of inspiration can endow a book. No one could be a true Muhammadan who did not venerate it. But the deeps of the human soul are too powerful in their upheavals to postpone action just because a book, however sacred, once was written and still is ardently believed. New types of religious life not contemplated in the Koran and far removed from the experience and teachings of Muhammad do appear in Muhammadanism. The Sufis, for example, are mystics. They have passed to another religious realm altogether from that occupied by Allah and his message. No longer even believing in a personal Creator, they are pantheists; no longer defining duty as submission to divine law in hope of future reward, they define it as surrender to divine love in a mystical experience which is its own reward. But still they believe in the Koran. They insist with ardent faith that they alone understand it and are true to it. They are doing with the Koran what the Greeks did with Homer. They hold that it does not mean what it literally says, that it has an inner, allegorical sense, and many of them maintain that they alone are truly interpreting what that sense is.

So clear are the conditions under which allegorical interpretation arises and so repeated and unfailing is its emergence wherever these conditions are fulfilled, that the law of the procedure can be confidently stated. It has been well put by Dr. J. Massie:

> "When any literature has so deeply inwrought itself into the hearts and lives of a people as to have become a sacred and inseparable constituent of their nature, and when time has nevertheless so far changed the current of thought as to make that literature apparently inconsistent with the new idea, or inadequate to express it,—then the choice for the people lies between a ruinous breach with what is, by this time, part and parcel of themselves, and, on the other hand, forcing the old language to be a vehicle for the new thought." [1]

III

When now we turn to the Hebrew-Christian tradition, we find no exception to this rule. The Jewish rabbis allegorized their own Scriptures. How could they avoid it? Some of the ritual and customary laws incorporated in the code had sprung up out of early conditions and could no longer be literally fulfilled. Yet those laws stood in Scripture, where surely the divine Spirit would allow nothing to be written which was either inapplicable or unimportant. Even

---

[1] J. Massie: article on Allegory, iii, in A Dictionary of the Bible, ed. by James Hastings.

Rabbi Ishmael, who tried his best to avoid allegory, struck some passages where he was sure that an allegorical interpretation must be given.[1] Moreover, the rabbis faced the necessity of defending their developed oral tradition from the sacred Scriptures. Some of them said frankly that many of their new developments of thought and ritual were not obviously in the Scripture and "hung only by a hair." This slender support, necessary to sustain the rabbinical tradition, was often found in the allegorical interpretation of some ancient text.

Indeed, one whole book is in our canon of Scripture to-day because allegory was employed to give it sacredness. Rabbi Akiba, although he feared the allegorizing of the law, was the first teacher thus to allegorize an entire book—the Song of Songs. This dramatic poem is obviously a beautiful lyric of pure love, and, save as human love at its best is itself religious, there is no religion in the book at all. For many years the Song was kept out of the Hebrew canon. Toward the close of the first century A. D. the opposition against it still was strong. But allegory won the day. The Song was interpreted out of its original sense into mystic meanings as a lyric on the love of Israel and Jehovah, and Christians reallegorized it as a love-song of Christ and his church. So it stands in our Bible now and the headings of the King James Version still bear witness to the allegorical accommodation of an old book to a new age.

[1] On this subject see Louis Ginzberg: article on Allegorical Interpretation, in The Jewish Encyclopedia, ed. by Isidore Singer; and George Holley Gilbert: Interpretation of the Bible; A Short History, 25.

When Judaism moved still further away from its ancient setting into the Hellenistic world and in cities like Alexandria grew to both intellectual and political importance, the need of accommodation was even greater. The Hellenized Jews, thoroughly impregnated with Neoplatonic ideas were not on that account less devoted to their sacred books. The conditions for allegory, therefore, were perfectly fulfilled and a florescent exhibition of it resulted. The whole Hellenistic philosophy was found in the Old Testament. Nor has Judaism, moving from land to land and from generation to generation, ever lacked those pursuers of the mystic sense who in the old words have discovered a new meaning. Here is an example of successful allegory finding medieval mysticism in an ancient Hebrew law. In Exodus 21:7-11 there is a provision guarding the interests of daughters who have been sold by their fathers into slavery. The law provides that a daughter so sold, if she does not please her master as a concubine, can be redeemed by her father; she certainly shall not be resold to a foreign people; and if she is not decently treated her free return to her father shall be allowed. Obviously, the social and ethical background which required such a law is primitive. To the medieval Jew it was shameful that such a commandment should stand in his Torah. Allegory, however, solved the problem: the father who sells the daughter into slavery is God; the daughter is the human soul; her going into slavery is the soul's birth into this material world; the object of this bondage is that the soul at last shall be redeemed to its father; and this must be done lest the soul be sold to a foreign people, that is, the evil angels. The outline of medieval mysticism is thus discovered in a primitive law.[1]

From these repeated exhibitions of allegory, always arising when an old book is introduced into a new world, one turns to the New Testament and is amazed that there is so little allegorizing there. The conditions were perfect. The ancient Hebrew Scriptures were received by the first Christians as their Bible; the new revelation in Christ was regarded by them as divine; in consequence they faced the apologetic necessity of finding the new Gospel in the old Book. The setting for allegory could not be better. And allegory is there. Paul declared that the law prohibiting the muzzling of oxen when they trod out the corn meant that Christian ministers should receive financial support;[2] he allegorized the rabbinical legend of the rock that followed the Israelites through the wilderness as meaning Christ;[3] he definitely called the story of the two sons of Abraham an allegory of the old dispensation and the new:[4] and in such interpretations he was doing for Christian purposes what he doubtless had heard rabbis like Gamaliel do in accommodating the old Bible to the understanding and need of a later generation. What is surprising is not these few mild examples of allegory in the New Testament but the extraordinary fact that in a situa-

[1] Louis Ginzberg: article on Allegorical Interpretation, ¶ on General Allegorization of the Law, in The Jewish Encyclopedia, ed. by Isidore Singer.

[2] Deuteronomy 25:4; I Corinthians 9:9-14.

[3] I Corinthians 10:4.   [4] Galatians 4:21-31.

tion which might have called out a tropical luxuriance of allegorizing there is so little of it.

When, however, one turns from the New Testament's restraint to the church at large, the barriers are down. Allegorizing appears everywhere. The original motive for its use is lucidly displayed in Origen. No modern ever recognized more clearly or handled more frankly than he did the fact that the Old Testament contains ideas, laws, customs, and ideals which cannot stand the test of developed thought and morals. The first chapters of Genesis, taken literally, seem to him absurd:

> "For who that has understanding will suppose that the first, and second, and third day, and the evening and the morning, existed without a sun, and moon, and stars? and that the first day was, as it were, also without a sky? And who is so foolish as to suppose that God, after the manner of a husbandman, planted a paradise in Eden, towards the east, and placed in it a tree of life, visible and palpable, so that one tasting of the fruit by the bodily teeth obtained life?" [1]

The anthropomorphisms of the Old Testament shocked him. With reference to the literal interpretation of Moses' seeing God's "hinder parts" on Sinai, he exclaims against "those old wives' fables . . . invented by ignorant persons respecting the anterior and posterior parts of God." [2] Such ideas as God's having

[1] De Principiis, Book IV, Ch. I, 16, in The Ante-Nicene Fathers, Vol. IV, 365.

[2] Ibid., Book II, Ch. IV, 3 (277).

hands and feet, being angry and repenting, if taken literally, he thought blasphemous. Some of the narratives of the Old Testament seemed to him immoral. There could be no profit in reading of the intercourse of Lot with his daughters, the two wives of Abraham, the two sisters married to Jacob, the two handmaids who bore him children.[1] Many details carefully narrated in the Old Testament such as the furnishing of the tabernacle or the genealogies seemed to him trivial if taken at their face value; [2] and some seemed impossible, such as the command not to eat vultures, which no one would ever think of eating, or the command to offer a "goat-stag" or unicorn,[3] when no such animal exists.[4] Concerning the Mosaic legislation Origen not only said that "many of the laws manifest the irrationality, and others the impossibility, of their literal observance," but he thought some laws positively barbarous, as, for example, the law which he understood as a command to kill uncircumcized children.[5] Surely, said Origen, the fault was the parents', not the children's. And turning his attention to the New Testament, Origen said that the Gospels taken literally contained discrepancies, contradictions, and impossibilities.[6]

Such were the difficulties of a great Christian

[1] Ibid., Book IV, Ch. I, 9 (357).   [2] Ibid. (357-358).

[3] Origen's misunderstanding of a Septuagint word not found elsewhere.

[4] De Principiis, Book IV, Ch. I, 17 (366).

[5] Genesis 17:14; Origen: De Principiis, Book IV, Ch. I, 17 (366).

[6] Commentary on John, Book X, 2-3, in The Ante-Nicene Fathers, Vol. IX, 382-383; Ibid., 4-6 (383-385); De Principiis, Book IV, Ch. I. 18 (367).

scholar and apologist at the beginning of the third century. And allegory was the solution. Unworthy ideas of God, inapplicable laws, outgrown customs, and patent contradictions were all read away by means of the mystic sense. The letter was but the body of a passage; the allegorical interpretation was the soul. Indeed, Origen used the mystic sense to defend the mystic sense. When on the first Palm Sunday the ass and the ass's foal stood tied and the Master sent two disciples to loose them and bring them to him, Origen saw in the event a Biblical defense of his whole method of exegesis. The ass was the letter of the Old Testament, and the ass's foal was the letter of the New Testament, and they both were tied, but two apostles were sent to free them and bring them to Jesus, and these two were the moral and the mystic sense.[1] So by allegory Origen supported allegory.

Indeed, when once you start this process there is no end to it. In the Levitical law we read that the meal offering may be baked in an oven, fried in a pan, or toasted on a plate.[2] Surely, said Origen, we cannot imagine that God cares for such trifles. What the passage really means is this: the meal offering is the Scripture and, since an oven, a plate, and a pan are mentioned, it is clear that the Scripture must have a three-fold sense.[3]

It would be difficult to exaggerate the influence of this method of interpretation upon the preaching of

[1] Commentary on John, Book X, 18, same volume as above, 396–398.
[2] Leviticus 2:4–7.
[3] Henry Preserved Smith: Essays in Biblical Interpretation, 53.

the church. When once it had gotten under weigh
there were scarcely any limits to its use. The lifeless
page was helpless before the living man for he could
make it stand and deliver any sense he chose. To be
sure, the great allegorists like Clement or Origen would
indignantly have denied that allegory was guesswork.
They did their best to construct scientific canons to
govern it and to chasten its extravagance. They endeavored to create a methodology. When, however,
allegory once has been allowed, no canons can keep
an eager man from using it, however honestly, to
make the Scripture support what he thinks true.
Gfrörer has said the best that can be said of allegorizing even in the hands of a master like Philo,
by applying to it Polonius' words, "Though this be
madness, yet there is method in 't." [1]

Moreover, allegory, while arising in the first place
from the serious need of accommodating an ancient
book to a new situation, appeals to other motives
also. For one thing, it makes great preaching. By
that fact the luxuriance of allegory can in large
measure be explained. Many a passage, dead as the
moon for homiletic purposes if taken literally, becomes
vital if one is allowed to allegorize it. Augustine
could find little provender for preaching in the garden
of Eden literally taken, but by allegory he opened
up an almost limitless possibility of sermons there.
He said that no one denied that Eden might signify
the life of the blessed; its four rivers the four virtues;
its trees all useful knowledge; its fruits the customs

[1] August Gfrörer: Philo und die alexandrinische Theosophie, Vol.
I, 113.

of the godly, and its tree of life wisdom herself; and the tree of the knowledge of good and evil, the experience of a broken commandment. But in the selfsame chapter he has another allegorical interpretation altogether. There Eden signifies the church; its four rivers the four Gospels; its fruit trees the saints, and the fruit their works; the tree of life Christ. And Augustine adds this revealing comment: "These and similar allegorical interpretations may be suitably put upon Paradise [Eden] without giving offense to any one, while yet we believe the strict truth of the history confirmed by its circumstantial narrative of facts." [1]

Obviously, allegory here has gotten far away from its serious motive of accommodating an old Book to a new age and has become a homiletical device. Indeed, Augustine frankly confesses what he is doing. In a passage very interesting to a preacher he says:

> "Why is it, I ask, that if any one says that there are holy and just men whose life and conversation the Church of Christ uses as a means of redeeming those who come to it from all kinds of superstitions, and making them through their imitation of good men members of its own body; men who, as good and true servants of God, have come to the baptismal font laying down the burdens of the world, and who rising thence do, through the implanting of the Holy Spirit, yield the fruit of a two-fold love, a love, that is, of God and their neighbor;—how is it, I say, that if a

[1] The City of God, Book XIII, Ch. XXI, in The Nicene and Post-Nicene Fathers, First Series, Vol. II, 256.

man says this, he does not please his hearer so much as when he draws the same meaning from that passage in Canticles, where it is said of the Church, when it is being praised under the figure of a beautiful woman, 'Thy teeth are like a flock of sheep that are shorn, which came up from the washing, whereof every one bears twins, and none is barren among them?' . . . And yet, I do not know why, I feel greater pleasure in contemplating holy men, when I view them as the teeth of the Church, tearing men away from their errors, and bringing them into the Church's body with all their harshness softened down, just as if they had been torn off and masticated by the teeth. It is with the greatest pleasure, too, that I recognize them under the figure of sheep that have been shorn, laying down the burdens of the world like fleeces, and coming up from the washing, i. e., from baptism, and all bearing twins, i. e., the twin commandments of love, and none of them barren in that holy fruit." [1]

Ah! Augustine! Even you found the allurements of picturesque rhetoric too strong for a careful and restrained exegesis!

Let us guard ourselves against misunderstanding here. No one should condescend to Augustine because he thus used methods no longer possible to us. Fortunately, efficiency in preaching has never been absolutely dependent on correct canons of exegesis.

[1] On Christian Doctrine, Book II; Ch. 6, in The Nicene and Post-Nicene Fathers, First Series, Vol. II, 537.

Indeed, I call you to witness that if we really believed as Augustine did that the four rivers of Eden could mean the four cardinal virtues, prudence, temperance, fortitude, and justice, and if we could make our audiences believe it too, as he could, we could preach far more useful sermons on those four rivers than we can now. Allegory is thoroughly vicious as a means of getting at what the Bible originally meant to say, but allegory, when honestly believed, is not necessarily ineffective as a means of communicating important truth from one ardent mind to another. I presume that when Augustine preached his tremendous sermon to the Mauritanians against the practise of the feud, he used allegory. I cannot imagine him failing to use it. But how one wishes that with all our modern knowledge we could preach with like effect! Augustine writes:

> "I strove, with all the vehemence of speech that I could command to root out and drive from their hearts and lives an evil so cruel and inveterate; it was not, however, when I heard their applause, but when I saw their tears, that I thought I had produced an effect. For the applause showed that they were instructed and delighted, but the tears that they were subdued. And when I saw their tears I was confident, even before the event proved it, that this horrible and barbarous custom . . . was overthrown; and immediately that my sermon was finished I called upon them with heart and voice to give praise and thanks to God. And, lo, with the

blessing of Christ, it is now eight years or more
since anything of the sort was attempted here." [1]

In the face of such preaching only a small mind will
be tempted to any complacency because we have
outgrown allegory.

At any rate, the whole ancient and medieval church
used it constantly. Even when the light of the new
time began to dawn out of the shadows of the medieval
age, so bold, fearless and unconventional a preacher
as Wyclif never dreamed of surrendering allegory.
His treatment of the parable of the Good Samaritan
is famous. The man who went down from Jerusalem
to Jericho represents our first parents; the robbers
are the fiends of hell; the priest and Levite who went
by on the other side are the patriarchs, saints, and
prophets who failed to bring salvation; the Good
Samaritan is Jesus, pictured as of another nation
because of his heavenly origin; the wine which he
pours into the wounds is sharp words to prick men
from sin, and the oil is hope; the Samaritan setting the
man on his beast means Christ bearing man's sin in
his body; the inn is the church, and the help received
there sacraments and heavenly gifts; the following
day, when he left the inn, is after the resurrection; the
inn keeper is the clergy to whose care needy man is
committed; and the twopence given to him represent
Christ's Godhead and manhood to feed mankind to
the day of doom. [2] The entire scheme of the old the-

[1] On Christian Doctrine, Book IV, Ch. 24, ¶ 53, in The Nicene and
Post-Nicene Fathers, First Series, Vol. II, 593–594.

[2] Select English Works of John Wyclif, ed. by Thomas Arnold,
Vol. I, 31–33, Sermon XIII.

ology is found in the Master's story of a serviceable
deed. Yet not on that account will a wise man under-
estimate the extraordinary character and influence
of Wyclif, who, as an ancient woodcut pictures him,
struck from the flint the spark which John Huss
caught in his tinder, from which in turn Luther
lighted his flaming torch.

So, too, Savonarola was an inveterate allegorist.
His biographer tells us that he devoted a whole series
of sermons to the allegorical exposition of Noah's
ark. The saving of Noah's family was symbolical of
the ingathering of the righteous, and as for the ark
itself, its length was faith, its width charity, its height
hope. "He enlarged upon this strange allegory," we
are told, "during the whole of Lent, 1492, and giving
each day a different interpretation of the ten planks
of which the Ark was composed, again expounded the
virtues good Christians were bound to possess and
the duties they should fulfil." [1] A strange homiletical
method that would seem to most of us but, for all that,
what a preacher Savonarola must have been! How
futile it makes much of our thin piping seem when we
picture him at a sermon's close holding aloft the
crucifix and crying, "Florence, behold! this is the
Lord of the universe, and would fain be thine. Wilt
thou have him for thy king?" And all the people
cried with shouts and tears, "Long live Christ our
king!" [2]

[1] Pasquale Villari: Life and Times of Girolamo Savonarola, in
translation by Linda Villari, 186.
[2] Ibid., 419.

IV

If in the modern church this old method of interpretation is largely discredited, although often surrepti-
tiously used even among intelligent Protestants, we
probably owe that fact more to John Calvin than to
any other man. "For the first time in a thousand
years," writes Gilbert, "he gave a conspicuous example of *non-allegorical* exposition." [1] His attitude
toward the ancient method is indicated at the very
beginning of his treatment of Genesis. "We must
. . . entirely reject the allegories of Origen, and of
others like him," we read, "which Satan, with the
deepest subtlety, has endeavored to introduce into the
Church, for the purpose of rendering the doctrine of
Scripture ambiguous and destitute of all certainty
and firmness." [2]

Calvin, in a word, was a stern and exact literalist.
He hated the vague and insecure renderings of Scripture which allegory made possible. When he appealed
from the Pope to the Bible for his authority, he had
to know with steady certainty what the Bible meant
to say. He would have applied to allegory Jeremy
Taylor's figure of a coin held before a multiplying
glass; "For one piece of good money," he said, "you
shall have forty that are fantastical; and it is forty
to one if your finger hit upon the right." [3] So Calvin

[1] George Holley Gilbert: Interpretation of the Bible; A Short History, 209.

[2] Commentary on Genesis, Vol. I, Ch. II, 8, in translation by John
King, 114.

[3] Sermon, Via Intelligentiæ, in The Sermons of the Right Rev.
Jeremy Taylor, D. D., Robert Carter & Bros., publishers, 455.

believed that every passage in Scripture had but one original and true sense, which allegory only travestied, and that one sense he passionately desired to know. At times his scorn of the prevalent allegorizing flamed out in heat. "Frivolous, and obnoxious to ridicule and calumny" he called one flagrant specimen that aroused his ire.[1] And even when he dealt with the famous promise of Genesis 3:15, "I will put enmity between thee and the woman, and between thy seed and her seed," he refused to follow closely the footsteps of Paul and make it primarily a prophecy of Christ. He was too strict a literalist for that. To be sure, the serpent represents Satan, so that the story has universal application to man's moral trials, but the story itself is rigidly literal. "I interpret this simply to mean," he wrote, "that there should always be the hostile strife between the human race and serpents, which is now apparent; for, by a secret feeling of nature, man abhors them." [2]

To-day Calvin's name suggests rigid and settled orthodoxy. There were plenty of people in his own time, however, who did not so conceive him. Caroli accused him of Arianism and called on him to subscribe to the Athanasian Creed, which he roundly refused to do, saying, "We swear in the faith of the one God, not of Athanasius, whose creed no true Church would ever have approved." [3] Especially did his renunciation of allegory disturb his contemporaries. Dr. F. W. Farrar has gathered such specimens

[1] Commentary on Genesis, Vol. I, Ch. XVIII, Sec. 2, (470).
[2] Ibid., Ch. III, 15 (167).
[3] Williston Walker: John Calvin, 197.

of criticism as these: one of his fellow Protestants accused him of wresting their weapons out of the hands of Christian athletes; another said that he expounded oracles about the Trinity or the Messiah like a Jew or a Socinian; Hunnius, a Protestant, said that he had corrupted Scripture in a detestable manner and that he ought to have been burnt; and, not to be outdone, the Roman Catholics called him a Muhammadan.[1]

So far as theory was concerned Luther, like Calvin, rejected allegory. His language on the subject was picturesquely characteristic of the man. "Origen's allegories are not worth so much dirt," he wrote; "Allegories are empty speculations, and as it were the scum of Holy Scripture"; "Allegory is a sort of beautiful harlot who proves herself spiritually seductive to idle men"; "To allegorize is to juggle with Scripture"; "Allegory may degenerate into a mere monkey-game"; "Allegories are awkward, absurd, invented, obsolete, loose rags." [2]

Indeed, the fundamental principle of Biblical exegesis to which the Reformers gave their theoretical consent and tried to give their practical allegiance was that every passage in Scripture has but one meaning— the original native connotation of the words—and in the practise of that principle no one succeeded so well as did John Calvin. The church never has been able altogether to escape his influence and return peaceably to the old use of allegory. Protestant preachers and theologians have plentifully indulged in the vicious practise, but the best of them have generally done it

[1] Frederic W. Farrar: History of Interpretation, 346.
[2] Ibid., 328.

with an inner sense of exegetical sin. Even Jonathan Edwards, for example, fell from grace when he dealt with the book of Esther. There is not a word of religion in it; yet religion must be there. Even the name of God is not mentioned; yet how could the book be in the Bible if God were not meant? So Edwards stretched his familiar use of typology away over into allegory. The banquet of Ahasuerus is the Gospel feast; Vashti is the rejected church of the Jews; Esther is the accepted church of Christ; Mordecai is the Gospel ministry; and Haman is Antichrist.[1]

Nevertheless, in spite of all lapses, the exegetical principle of the Reformation has never been completely lost. This principle implied scientific investigation. It demanded that we get back to the original sense of the Book. The result was often deadly literalism. The student wishes at times that he could escape from it into the freedom of allegory which did at least give scope to spiritual insight and imagination. So far as profitable teaching is concerned, the license of Origen's mystical sense is often superior to the painful barrenness of passages supposed to be verbally inspired and interpreted as signifying nothing but their first intention. This arid literalism, however, provided the indispensable transition from allegory to modern methods of using the Bible. The reformers did the church a momentous service by their insistence on seeking for the Bible's original meanings. Sometimes their principle was

[1] Notes on the Bible (46), in 1830 edition of President Edwards' Works, Vol. 9, 328-331.

stated with indubitable clarity. So Luther said concerning the understanding of the Hebrew prophets: "It is necessary if one will understand the prophecy, to know what the situation was in the land, what events were happening, what the people thought, what the relationships were which they sustained to their neighbors, friends, and foes, and especially what their attitude was toward their God and toward his prophets." [1] Could a better statement be made today of what we mean by a historic approach to the Scripture?

But the reformers little guessed to what ends the principle they so believed would lead the church. True to their principle in theory, they still in practise were the children of their age, and, lacking instruments of historic knowledge and investigation, they could use eisegesis instead of exegesis on many a passage which they thought they were literally interpreting. Calvin drove allegory out the door, but its first cousin, typology, came in through the window. When Calvin wished to prove the deity of Christ, he took fourteen key-passages, eight from the Old Testament and six from the New. Judges 13:2-25, Psalm 45:6, Isaiah 9:6, Jeremiah 23:6 are some of the proof-passages he chose.[2] As for Luther, when he commented on Psalm 3:5, "I laid me down and slept; I awaked; for Jehovah sustaineth me," he was entirely true to his method. "Christ, by the words of his verse, signifies his death

[1] Præfatio Doctoris Martini Lutheri in Esaiæ Lectionem, 2d ¶, in Exegetica Opera Latina, Vol. 22, 4, Erlangen Edition.

[2] Institutes of the Christian Religion, Book I, Ch. XIII, Secs. IX–XI, in translation by John Allen, 124–128

and burial," wrote Luther. ". . . For it is not to be supposed that he would have spoken so importantly concerning mere natural rest and sleep."[1] So he lifted the Psalm out of its historic setting altogether and regarded it as dictated throughout by Christ.

What has happened between the Reformation and our day is clear. One searchlight after another has been turned on the historic sense of Scripture. Once men could read the Book asking, What does the Bible say? and, not being encumbered by precise historic information concerning the mental categories of Biblical times, could read their own highly developed theologies into almost any passage of the Old Testament they chose. Now, however, the question has changed. We are not asking first, What *does* the Bible say? but, What *did* the Bible say? In terms of the generation in which it first was written, as understood by those who first produced it and read it, what did the Bible say? The consequence is that we face the Biblical world made historically vivid over against the modern world presently experienced, and we cannot use the old method of accommodating the one to the other.

That is the nub of our difficulty. We cannot honestly allegorize. We face the old problem but we cannot use the old solution.

We meet the same kind of difficulties that troubled Origen, accentuated immeasurably by our knowledge of the past and by the newness of our world, and yet we cannot use Origen's way of overcoming it. We have been brought up, whether we know it or not,

[1] Commentary on Psalm III, v. 5, 5th ¶.

on Calvin's literalism. We have been taught that in Eden the serpent literally spoke, that God made woman literally out of man's rib, that into the ark the animals literally went, that God literally promised divine strength to Samson, however silly and brutal he turned out to be, if he never shaved his head, that all the details of the tabernacle were literally revealed to Moses on the Mount, that God with his finger literally wrote the ten commandments upon stone, and that hiding Moses in the cleft he revealed to him his back though not his face, that God literally commanded the massacres of whole populations, and literally arranged the intricate rituals of bloody animal sacrifice. Our allegorizing fathers did not have to believe that. They could either throw the literal sense away or else, neglecting it, read into the passage Platonic philosophy or Catholic theology. From that we are estopped. We know now that Calvin's principle was right. Those passages have but one meaning, and that meaning is what they literally say.

When one thinks not simply of narratives involving gross anthropomorphisms or belated ethics, but of passages involving mental categories which we no longer use in ordinary life, like demonology, angelology, Semitic cosmology, or miracles, the problem becomes even more difficult. At times the preacher tries to abandon his modern world-view and go back to ancient categories, but he cannot. At times he tries by violence to harmonize the ancient and the new, but they will not agree. He is facing Protestantism's third attempt to accommodate the Scriptures to the use of the church. First, Protestantism tried to harmonize the Scriptures with the traditional theology and failed. To imagine Jesus holding the Nicene theology is an intolerable strain on any well-instructed mind's credulity. Then, Protestantism tried to harmonize the Scriptures with themselves, since an infallible Book must be unanimous in all its teaching. But these Scriptures came from too many ages, out of too many diverse experiences, and bore the imprint of too many varied influences to be a book of unanimous dogma. Last of all, Protestantism tries to harmonize the Scriptures with modern thought. She labors to make the science of the Bible our science, the psychology of the Bible our psychology; she endeavors to see in the apostles the favorite attitudes and emphases of a twentieth-century clergyman, and even divests our Lord of that special framework of thought without which he could not have been understood by his own generation and so never could have been handed down to any other generation. But the attempt is all in vain. The whole harmonizing process is wrong in principle and impossible in practise. At last the modern minister sees clearly the correctness of Balfour's words: "The mental framework in which we arrange the separate facts in the world of men and things is a new framework." And because we use new ways of thinking, they are diverse from the corresponding ways of thought in which the Scriptures state their truth.

This then, is the gist of our difficulty: we face here a very old problem but we cannot use the old solution any more.

V

What we can do, however, is to find a new solution. We ought to be encouraged to seek it because the problem which we face was the Master's problem also and he never resorted to allegory. He came with a new revelation into a religious world where an ancient Scripture was revered alike by his people and by himself. At every turn in his ministry he met the towering problem of Biblical interpretation. At last the scribes and Pharisees crucified him, primarily because they saw in his fresh and vital use of the Bible the ruin of their legal system. The Master has rightly been called "the first free spiritual expounder of the Scriptures."

Consider the way he used the sacred Book on which his own spiritual life had been nourished and in whose divine inspiration he ardently believed. First of all, he distinguished himself from the rabbis by appealing to the Book, not in favor of, but against the oral traditions of law and ritual which the scribes had built up. Not for him the clever sophistries of exegesis, the ingenious allegories by which the vast legal system was defended as Scriptural. He knew that the legal system in its minute applications was not in the Scripture and he said so. He discredited the oral law, said that it was a plant which his father had not planted, and that in time it would be rooted up.[1]

In the second place, having thus appealed to the Old Testament against the clever and sophistical interpretations that had been fathered on it, he distin-

[1] Matthew 15:1–9, 13.

guished in the Old Testament between significant and
negligible elements.   He rated ceremonial law low
and ethical law high.   The Mosaic laws of clean and
unclean foods were plainly written in the Book, but
Jesus abolished them from the category of the ethical.[1]
No laws in Scripture were more obvious and more ex-
acting than those relating to the sabbath, but from
Scripture insisting on observance of sabbath laws
Jesus appealed to Scripture insisting on the superior
rights of human need, and said that the sabbath was
made for man, and not man for the sabbath.[2]   Did
not David break the letter of the law, he said, when
in need he ate the showbread from the altar to satisfy
his hunger?[3]   So always the Master put human need
above ritual requirement, quoting moral Scripture
against ceremonial Scripture to prove that God pre-
fers mercy to sacrifice.[4]

In the third place, having appealed from the oral
law to the written law, and within the written law
having appealed from ceremonial elements to ethical
principles, he went on to recognize that some ethical
principles in the written law had been outgrown.   The
easy system of Mosaic divorce was not to be the law
of his disciples.[5]   Eye for eye, tooth for tooth, hand
for hand awakened only his brave and uncompromising protest.[6]   His whole Sermon on the Mount, starting with its assurance that the old law is to be fulfilled
and not destroyed, is a definite endeavor to see that

[1] Mark 7:15–23.   [2] Mark 2:27.
[3] Leviticus 24:9; I Samuel 21:1–6; Mark 2:25–26.
[4] Hosea 6:6; Matthew 9:13, 12:7.   [5] Mark 10:2–12.
[6] Exodus 21:23–25; Matthew 5:38–39.

it is fulfilled, carried to completion, with its outgrown elements superseded and its abiding ideals crowned and consummated.

What the Master did, in a word, was to plunge deep beneath the sophisticated exegesis of his time, the timid literalisms which bound men by a text instead of liberating them by a truth, and in the abiding experiences and principles of the Old Testament find a revelation of God that was fruitful and true.

Let it be clearly noted that this attitude of Jesus involved the recognition of the fact that the Scriptures did contain outgrown elements. No one could have said that more explicitly than he did. He did not try to conceal the situation by strained interpretations and skilful allegories. The church had to wait a long time for men who dared to follow in his steps. Once in a while, in the heat of the Reformation, you catch an accent of his freedom. So Luther, facing the appeals of men like Karlstadt to the laws and morals of the Old Testament, came back like thunder:

> "This we will not stand. . . . We will not have Moses any longer as a law-giver, and God will not have him either. Moses was the law-giver of the Jewish people alone. . . . When they say, Moses says so, it is written in Moses, and so on, answer them: Moses has nothing to do with us. . . . Moses is dead; his rule is obsolete since Christ came. . . . Say to them: Go to the Jews with your Moses; I am no Jew; don't bother me with Moses." [1]

[1] Kemper Fullerton: Prophecy and Authority, 129.

This has Luther's brusque and bristling tone in it, but, surely, one has only to read the Sermon on the Mount to see that his basic position is much more like Christ's than are all the allegories of the ancient church or all the devious devices by which, in accommodating the Scripture to our own age, we try to harmonize the irreconcilable.

Let us then frankly take our stand with the Master on this basic matter! Of course there are outgrown elements in Scripture. How could it be otherwise in a changing world? We are crying for the moon when we ask for a Scripture that does not speak to us in the language and out of the moral and mental categories of the generations when it appeared. Nor is this really a serious problem save as our superficial thinking makes it one; it is to be taken for granted. What does matter is that when we plunge deep beneath such changed settings of thought and speech into the experiences and convictions for which the Book essentially stands, we find spiritual truths there which in themselves are permanently valid. Indeed, one who for long years has preached those truths with joy cannot content himself with so cold a phrase as "permanently valid." He would rather say that in the course of that religious history whose record is the Bible, truths were wrought out without which no man can really live; truths essential to man's health in character, to man's hope in service, to man's triumph in death; truths that for the sake of the life here and the life hereafter must be preached and repreached and preached again as long as the world stands. I am not concerned now to explain this strange thing that men who shared so thoroughly the thought of their time could make their truth permanently essential to the spiritual life of man. Our best explanations do not go far; the residue of mystery is great. He who long can ponder the fact and not perceive that God was speaking there does not earnestly believe in God at all. Not of the explanation, however, of the fact I am thinking, and it is a fact immeasurably important to the preacher.

Here, then, is the first essential of intelligent Biblical preaching in our day: a man must be able to recognize the abiding messages of the Book, and sometimes he must recognize them in a transient setting. No man will ever do this well if he does not divest himself of vanity and pride and clothe himself with humility as with a garment. He must see that many of our ways of thinking are very new; that they, too, are transient, and that many of them will soon be as outmoded as our forefathers' categories are. He must see that just because our ways of thinking are new, the garnered riches of the world's thought have been stored up for us in other forms of thought than ours and in other ways of speaking. If he sees this clearly he will see also what a pitiably provincial life a man must live whose appreciations are shut up to that truth only which is expressed in modern terms. Such a man is a prisoner in the thought-forms of the present age. He cannot get out of that narrow world. He is robbed of all the treasures of spiritual life which were amassed before our modern age came in and therefore were of necessity stored in other mental receptacles than ours.

A man of catholic culture should know how to be
at home in all ages, to appreciate wisdom and spiritual quality in all forms of thought; he should drink
the water of life from Greek vases and Jewish water-
jars as well as from modern faucets, and whoever
lacks such culture robs himself of his racial inheritance of experience and truth.   This, I take it, is
one of the chief accusations against our fresh, young
intellectual life in religion and elsewhere.   Many of
us who call ourselves liberal are not liberal; we are
narrow rather, with that most fatal bigotry of all: we
can understand nothing except contemporary thought.

Let us then turn to the testing of this matter.   Let
us see what it means to find in Scripture abiding experiences set in changing categories.

BIBLIOGRAPHY

Interpretation of the Bible; A Short History, George Holley
    Gilbert.   Macmillan.
Prophecy and Authority, Kemper Fullerton.   Macmillan.
Essays in Biblical Interpretation, Henry Preserved Smith.
    Marshall Jones.
He Opened to us the Scriptures, Benjamin W. Bacon. Macmillan.
Allegorical Interpretation, Louis Ginzberg, in The Jewish
    Encyclopedia, ed. by Isidore Singer.   Funk and Wagnalls.
Allegory, J. Massie, in A Dictionary of the Bible, ed. by James
    Hastings.   Scribner's.
Allegory, Allegorical Interpretation, Johannes Geffcken, in the
    Encyclopædia of Religion and Ethics, ed. by James Has-
    tings.   Scribner's.
General Introduction to the Study of Holy Scripture, Ch.
    XVIII, History of the Interpretation of Holy Scripture,
    Charles Augustus Briggs.   Scribner's.
History of Interpretation, F. W. Farrar.   Dutton.

LECTURE IV

ABIDING EXPERIENCES AND CHANGING
CATEGORIES

I

We have been endeavoring to describe the problem presented to the modern preacher by the contrasts between Biblical thinking and our own. Our first need as preachers is not that scholars should be easy on us, obscuring the contrasts of which we have been speaking. Our chief need is that scholars should make us so familiar with the contrasts that we shall take them for granted. These divergencies between the Scripture and modern thinking should become so thoroughly the commonplaces of our thought that in our preaching they will not be paraded, exploited, oracularly announced, but assumed. There doubtless was a time when a brave, progressive, young preacher, impressed by the fresh fact that the earth revolves around the sun, must have been tempted to announce it upon all occasions. He was self-conscious about the great discovery. It was a brand-new fact and had an irresistible fascination for the mind. If he preached on "Love not the world, neither the things that are in the world," he almost certainly would take advantage of the text to allude to the fact that the world is not stationary; it moves. But we have long ceased that, not because we are ignorant of the fact or afraid of it,

97

but because we are so familiar with it that we take it for granted.

So some preachers are impressed by the truth, vividly presented to us with fresh and startling illustrations, that the Bible has ways of thinking that are no longer ours. The cure of their obsession and bewilderment is not ignorance; it is familiarity.

With this conviction in mind let us consider certain typical contrasts between Biblical thinking and our own. For example, I believe in the persistence of personality through death, but I do not believe in the resurrection of the flesh. Many of our forefathers could not conceive immortality apart from a resurrected body. The resurrection of the flesh was a mental setting in which alone they supposed that faith in life everlasting ever could be found, and they believed in that setting, argued for it, and fought all doubt about it with the vehemence of those who were sure that if the setting went the jewel would be lost. With what vividness popular Christianity used to visualize judgment day and the resurrected bodies of the dead rising from the sea, restored from dust and ashes, or even reintegrated by the assembling of far-scattered members, you know well. When one goes back to early apologists like Justin Martyr, one finds immortality inextricably associated with what the Apostles' Creed calls "resurrectionem carnis." They put it boldly and unequivocally: "We expect to receive our bodies again after they are dead and laid in the ground." [1]

The basis for this physical phrasing of immortality

[1] Quoted by George Foot Moore: History of Religions, Vol. II, 162.

is plainly laid in the Bible. In the first place, the earliest conception of man's nature which meets us in Scripture would logically necessitate a physical resurrection if there were to be any restored life after death at all. For, at the beginning, what we would call the physical and spiritual elements in man were not distinguished, much less regarded as separable.[1] Man was as yet an undifferentiated unity, so that the continuity of a man's spirit apart from his preserved or restored flesh was an inconceivable idea. One of those strands of development in the Bible most rewarding to the student is the gradual differentiation between the flesh and the spirit, until Paul at last can say that flesh and blood cannot inherit the kingdom of God.[2] At the beginning, however, such an idea would have been incredible. When Enoch was translated or Elijah went to heaven in a chariot of fire, the whole man went. Our rarefied conception of a soul had not yet arisen.

In the second place, the earliest idea of the abode of the dead necessitated the phrasing of immortality in terms of resurrection. For the dead went to Sheol, a definite place below the surface of the earth where, ghosts of their real selves, they yet retained material form. This empty and meaningless existence of Sheol, however, was not immortality. Sheol was a barren dread, not an eager hope. The hope which gradually arose was of restoration to the earth, and that expectation inevitably took the form of resurrection

[1] H. Wheeler Robinson: The Religious Ideas of the Old Testament, 83.

[2] I Corinthians 15:50.

from Sheol. We never should have used the word resurrection in expressing hope of life eternal if such had not been its history.

The development of Israel's expectation of a resurrected life makes a fascinating narrative. The eager dream of a Messianic kingdom here on earth grew vivid among the Jews; the question arose whether any one should enjoy it save those who happened to be alive when the consummation came; the sense of justice demanded that at least the eminently righteous should be restored to share the victory; [1] and finally the scene was completed by the expectation that the eminently wicked would also be restored in order that they might be adequately punished for their sins. Only in the late book of Daniel do we find in the Old Testament this fully developed way of thinking: "Many of them that sleep in the dust of the earth shall awake, some to everlasting life, and some to shame and everlasting contempt." [2]

With such a view of man's nature and with such a picture of the estate of the dead, bodily resurrection would have been an inevitable phrasing of life after death even if Zoroastrian influence had not come in. As it was, during the Exile Zoroastrianism became the mold into which the Hebrew expectations of life beyond death were run. The result is familiar: an intermediate state between death and judgment day, then a general resurrection, a gathering of restored body-souls before the throne of God, and the pronouncement of final destinies.[3]

[1] Isaiah 26:19.　　　　　　　[2] Daniel 12:2.
[3] See George Foot Moore: History of Religions, Vol. II, 55, 75.

This mental framework in the minds of New Testament folk is revealed in passage after passage. The new and vivid hopes of life eternal which came with Christ still clothed themselves in a familiar category. In the book of Revelation the whole Zoroastrian-Jewish paraphernalia was employed with picturesque effect. To be sure, the new Christian meaning was beginning to burst through its archaic phrasing. In John's Gospel, addressed as it is to Hellenists, the old apocalyptic is largely replaced by eternal life which begins here; and Paul, while he kept the picture of the general resurrection and the judgment day, definitely altered the old tradition by insisting that the resurrection body is not the old flesh restored, but is as different from the old as new grain is from the sown seed.[1] Never in the New Testament, however, does the hope of life eternal altogether escape from the influence of the inherited framework.

This, then, is the question which the modern church must face: are we forever bound to the old category as an expression of our living faith in immortality? A great deal of water has flowed under the bridge since the days when those first disciples thought of life everlasting in Zoroastrian terms. Historically the major agency in crowding out the older ways of thinking has been the Greek philosophy. Its basic premise was the evil of the physical body and the desirability of the soul's escape from its fleshly imprisonment to the realm of eternal spirit. It did not want a bodily resurrection; it wanted to escape from the body altogether. When Origen, for example, expressed his

[1] I Corinthians 15:35–38.

faith in life everlasting, he frankly dematerialized it,[1] and thus became one of the first of that long succession of Christians who, believing earnestly in immortality, have not associated it with the resurrection of the flesh.

Personally, I do not pretend to know the details of the future life. I am sufficiently sense-bound so that I do not easily imagine a completely disembodied existence. I wonder just what we mean by the persistence of personality if we do not include in our thought some such idea as Paul's "not for that we would be unclothed, but that we would be clothed upon." [2] But I am likewise sure that the old Scriptural framework with its background of a Hebrew Sheol and a Zoroastrian judgment day is not in my mind.

To-day there are two parties in the churches. They are in active controversy now, and every day their consciousness of difference becomes more sharp and clear. The crux of their conflict lies at this point: one party thinks that the essence of Christianity is its original mental frameworks; the other party is convinced that the essence of Christianity is its abiding experiences. To one party a mental category once worked out and expressed in Scripture is final. Men must never carry the living water in any other receptacle than that; to do so is to forego the right to call oneself a Christian. As a recent writer put it: "The originators of the Christian movement . . . did have an inalienable right to legislate for all genera-

[1] Origen Against Celsus, Book VI, Ch. XXIX, in The Ante-Nicene Fathers, Vol. IV, 586.
[2] II Corinthians 5:4.

tions that should choose to bear the name of 'Christian.'" [1] To the other party nothing in human history seems so changeable as mental categories. They are transient phrasings of permanent convictions and experiences. They rise and fall and pass away. To bind our minds to the perpetual use of ancient matrices of thought just because they were employed in setting forth the eternal principles of the New Testament seems intellectual suicide. What is permanent in Christianity is not mental frameworks but abiding experiences that phrase and rephrase themselves in successive generations' ways of thinking and that grow in assured certainty and in richness of content.

The matter of immortality is simply one illustration of the crucial difference between these two conceptions of Christianity. If the majority of Christians in America would face the facts, they would have to confess that they do not believe in some of the mental frameworks in which Scriptural faith in immortality first arose. Yet for all that they do believe in life everlasting. The two things are separable. Many of us for years have been preaching the Christian hope of life eternal with certitude and joy. We have been comforting the bereaved, solemnizing the frivolous, rebuking the sinful, and undergirding the strong, by the message of life's abiding issues. We have helped to make youth's struggle for character and maturity's devotion to spiritual aims more worth while, and to render the "patient continuance" of old age more joyful by the gospel of everlasting life. We believe it with assurance; we have seen its power.

[1] J. Gresham Machen: Christianity and Liberalism, 20.

But we no more believe in some of the mental categories from which that gospel first emerged like a fine flower out of a green cusp, than we believe that the earth is flat.

II

Consider another illustration of this same principle. I believe in the victory of righteousness upon this earth, in the coming kingdom of God whereon Christ looking shall see of the travail of his soul and be satisfied, but I do not believe in the physical return of Jesus. Multitudes of our fathers never thought of separating the two. All history to them was a drama whose dénouement was a literal return of Jesus in the clouds of heaven.

Let us not forget the world-view which possessed the mind of the church when this phrasing of expectancy grew up. It was a world-view in which the literal second coming of our Lord was easily picturable. Cosmas, for example, in the sixth century A. D., gave a precise and detailed statement of the cosmology which with only minor alterations had held the consent of the church from its beginning. The earth, according to Cosmas, is a parallelogram; it is flat; on every side of it are seas; it is four hundred days' journey long and two hundred broad; beyond the seas are massive walls which enclose the whole structure and support the heavenly vault; above the vault are the celestial dwellings.[1] In such an easily picturable world the farewell of Jesus to the earth could be

[1] Andrew D. White: A History of the Warfare of Science with Theology in Christendom, Vol. I, 93.

imagined literally as a physical levitation until he was received into heaven a definite distance above the ground, and his return could be literally imagined as a physical descent from the place where he had gone. The marvel is not that such a picture of the Master's going and return should arise in the setting of such a world-view; the marvel is that after that world-view has been so long outgrown, after we have known for centuries that this earth is a globe whirling through space with no ups nor downs any longer meaningful in the old sense, so that if one man ascend from Melbourne and another from London they go in opposite directions, many folk should still retain the old picture of our Lord's ascent and descent from the sky and should regard that picture as a test of a standing or falling church and an indispensable item in the evan- gelical faith.

The reason for the persistence of this special phras- ing of Christian confidence in God's final victory lies of course in the fact that this phrasing is to be found in the Scriptures. The rise of it is not difficult to trace. Given the passionate belief of the Hebrew people that they were Jehovah's chosen race; given the high hopes associated with the Davidic kingdom and the stirring words of prophets predicting a glo- rious future; given the catastrophes which one by one fell upon the nation, crashing in upon its fortunes as Persia succeeded Assyria, Greece succeeded Persia, and Rome succeeded Greece; and, clearly, if the He- brews were to cherish hope at all they would cherish it in terms of divine intervention. In some writers, although not in all, this expectation of supernatural

help took Messianic form.   At first the Davidic kingdom and dynasty were to be restored; then the personality of the Messiah assumed more definite and
more glorious importance, until finally the Day of the
Lord was to come when the Son of man should appear
upon the clouds of heaven.   The full flower of this
hope is not found in the Old Testament.   Only fore-
shadowings of it are there.   The full development of
the Messianic expectation came between the Testaments and is now laid bare to us in the apocalyptic
writings.   They differed in innumerable details but
in their world-view and their philosophy of history
they were unanimous.   They were utterly pessimistic
about the present; there was no good in it and no hope.
They were all concerned about a future which would
not be an outgrowth of the present but a catastrophic
upsetting of it, its final calcining and annihilation.
The Day of the Lord would come suddenly with a
Messianic invasion from heaven.

   Such was the popular phrasing of hope in the en-
vironment where Christianity began, and the effects
of that phrasing, the outlines and implications of it,
are visible in passage after passage of the New Testament.   It is present in some sayings attributed to
our Lord, and unless one accepts Matthew Arnold's
principle, "Jesus over the heads of all his reporters,"
at least some elements of it were in the background
of his thought.   A few years ago Jesus was widely
interpreted by scholars as an apocalyptic thinker; to-
day the swing of scholarly opinion is rather the other
way and the Master's thought of the victorious future
is seen to be rooted in the prophets and psalmists and

not in the apocalyptists. Certainly, he never indulged in fanciful pictures of the established kingdom,
as the Jewish apocalyptists did. He had no interest
in their carnal materializations of the coming era of
God's sovereignty over man; he made the kingdom
thoroughly moral, a life of filial fellowship with God
and fraternal relations between men. Moreover, he
emphasized inward preparation for the kingdom's
coming. His expectation of God's triumph was not
primarily an occasion for proud joy, but for humble
penitence. Purity, self-forgetting love, sincerity—
such are the attributes of life in the coming kingdom,
and a man should repent and seek inward cleansing and
renewal when he hears that the Day of God is coming.

More important still, the Master made no such gulf
between the present and the future ages as the Jewish
apocalyptists did. In his thought the kingdom of God
already was throwing foregleams of the new day into
the life of man. There was a spiritual sense in which
the kingdom was in the earth now—"The kingdom of
God is within you." [1] One could feel its power when
divine strength and goodness overcame evil—"If I
by the finger of God cast out demons, then is the kingdom of God come upon you." [2] It was possible for a
man by the quality and spirit of his life to enter the
kingdom now—"Thou art not far from the kingdom
of God "; "Blessed are the poor in spirit: for theirs
is the kingdom of heaven"; "Suffer the little children to come unto me . . . for to such belongeth the
kingdom of God."[3] The kingdom, therefore, was not

[1] Luke 17:21.   [2] Luke 11:20.
[3] Mark 12:34; Matthew 5:3; Mark 10:14.

something merely to be awaited in the future, but to be sought now in spirit like a pearl of great price or a treasure hidden in a field.[1] In this spiritual approach to the idea of God's coming sovereignty over life one loses the apocalyptic way of thinking altogether, and the kingdom, already here, like a grain of mustard seed will grow into a great tree, or like a bit of leaven will gradually transform the whole lump.[2]

Finally, the Master denationalized the kingdom. It was to be no triumph of the Jews over their enemies, but the rule of God over all mankind, and when he lifted up the eyes of his faith he saw men coming into the kingdom from east, west, north, and south.[3] Thus the Master took a current category in which all his people phrased their hope of God's victory on earth, and transformed it. In his hands its fantastic features were stripped away, its deep spiritual requirements were exalted, its present meanings were put to the front, and its narrow national boundaries were broken down.

Nevertheless, the outline of the old thought-form meets us constantly in the New Testament. John's Gospel is one notable exception. That was a brave attempt to reinterpret the Christian hope. It asserted Christ's second coming, but it spiritualized the event. John was addressing his Gospel to Hellenistic readers. They did not understand Jewish apocalyptic; they did not like it; its dramatics, its catastrophic arrival of the day of judgment, its physical resurrections were alien from Greek thought. Just

---

[1] Matthew 13:45–46; 13:44.   [2] Luke 13:18–19; 13:20–21.
[3] Matthew 8:11, Luke 13:29.

as John's Gospel, therefore, presented Christ, not primarily in terms of Jewish Messiah, but of Greek Logos, so it presented the Christian hope on earth, not in terms of an apocalyptic kingdom, but of an immediately possessed eternal life. Even upon the lips of Jesus at the last supper is put the reiterated teaching that his second coming is now, in the hearts of his true disciples, and that he dwells in them.[1]

Elsewhere in the New Testament, however, the old framework is the familiar setting of hope. The book of Revelation is built upon it. When Paul lets his imagination dwell on God's coming victory he draws the familiar picture with which his Jewish training had acquainted him long before he had known Jesus: the sudden, physical coming of the Messiah upon the clouds, the ascension of the living saints to meet him in the air, the resurrection of the righteous dead, the day of judgment, and the final destinies.

Once more, then, the church faces an issue: are we bound to continue forever expressing in this ancient category our living hope of God's victory on earth? Even John reinterpreted the form of expectation that he might preach God's coming sovereignty in terms that his Hellenistic hearers could understand. Must we then retrace our steps, give up what have seemed to us the gains of centuries, go back to the ways of thinking which developed among Jewish apocalyptists between the Testaments, and become premillenarians that we may be Christians?

[1] John 14:19–23. Cf. Ernest F. Scott: The Fourth Gospel, its Purpose and Theology, Ch. X, The Return of Christ.

Many of us for years have been preaching the victory of God's purpose on earth. We have not surrendered to that superficial modernity which thinks that man, blowing upon his hands, can tackle the task of transforming human character and society and can win against the dead-weight of a materialistic universe. Our hope has been in God. We believe that his purpose undergirdles human life, that his providence directs it, that his victory lies ahead. The proudest title that we can think of is found in Paul's phrase, "God's fellow-workers."[1] To be ourselves of such a spirit that God can work his victory in and through us; to persuade others to be transformed by the renewing of their minds; to strive for the better organization of society that the divine purpose may be furthered, not hindered, by our economic and political life; and then to await the event in his way and time—such have been our attitude and our preaching, and they have seemed to us Christian.

Those first disciples were expressing in terms of thought familiar to their generation this fundamental hope which we are preaching still. A changed category does not mean an abandoned conviction. At any rate, an increasing number of Christian ministers will go back to the New Testament as the fountainhead of their faith in God and of their assurance that his kingdom will come and his will be done on earth, without its occurring to them to expect the physical return of Jesus on the clouds of heaven.

[1] I Corinthians 3:9.

III

Consider still another illustration of this principle. Belief in demons as the source and explanation of life's manifold evils has been one of the most universal and prevalent ways of thinking that Christendom has ever known. Of course, it is no specialty of Christendom; it is one of the primitive ways of thinking common to all mankind. In particular, the Græco-Roman world was permeated with belief in demons. There was little difference in this regard between the many conflicting schools of thought; men everywhere explained cosmic evil and the multitudinous mishaps of daily life by demonology and, so far as the basic outlines of this way of thinking are concerned, the Stoic philosopher and the common peasant were alike. When Christianity, therefore, went into the Græco-Roman world, there was no dispute between Christian and non-Christian as to the existence of demons. Origen and Celsus, or any other debaters of the Gospel versus paganism, started in their controversies with the same premise: the reality, power, and malignity of demons.[1] One of the chief sources of the Gospel's influence in the early centuries lay in the fact that, advancing triumphantly into a demon-ridden world, it announced a power to cast the demons out and to redeem men from their sway. The early Christians entered deliberately into a war on evil spirits, in whose existence and machinations both pagan and Christian unanimously believed. The result was two-fold:

[1] Cf. Origen Against Celsus, Book I, Ch. VI, and Book II, Ch. LI, in The Ante-Nicene Fathers, Vol. IV, 398–399 and 451–452.

first, a fine sense of victory on the part of multitudes of folk who through faith in Christ cast off their fear of devils; but, second, a new reality, a fresh vividness, an expanded importance contributed to that demoniacal world by the very efforts that were made to overcome it. What is treated so seriously becomes increasingly serious, and Christianity did treat demons with tremendous earnestness.

The evidence of this is inexhaustible. Not because it is in the least unique, but to help our minds more vividly to think in those early Christian terms, we choose almost at random this typical passage from Tertullian:

> "We affirm indeed the existence of certain spiritual essences; nor is their name unfamiliar. The philosophers acknowledge there are demons; Socrates himself waiting on a demon's will. Why not? since it is said an evil spirit attached itself specially to him even from his childhood—turning his mind no doubt from what was good. The poets are all acquainted with demons too; even the ignorant common people make frequent use of them in cursing. In fact, they call upon Satan, the demon-chief, in their execrations, as though from some instinctive soul-knowledge of him. Plato also admits the existence of angels. The dealers in magic, no less, come forward as witnesses to the existence of both kinds of spirits. We are instructed, moreover, by our sacred books how from certain angels, who fell of their own free-will, there sprang a more wicked demon-brood, con-

demned of God along with the authors of their
race, and that chief we have referred to. It will
for the present be enough, however, that some
account is given of their work. Their great business is the ruin of mankind. So, from the very
first, spiritual wickedness sought our destruction. They inflict, accordingly, upon our bodies
diseases and other grievous calamities, while
by violent assaults they hurry the soul into sudden and extraordinary excesses. Their marvelous
subtleness and tenuity give them access to both
parts of our nature. . . . Invisible and intangible,
we are not cognizant of their action save by its
effects, as when some inexplicable, unseen poison
in the breeze blights the apples and the grain
while in the flower, or kills them in the bud, or
destroys them when they have reached maturity;
as though by the tainted atmosphere in some
unknown way spreading abroad its pestilential
exhalations. So, too, by an influence equally
obscure, demons and angels breathe into the soul,
and rouse up its corruptions with furious passions
and vile excesses; or with cruel lusts accompanied
by various errors, of which the worst is that by
which these deities are commended to the favor
of deceived and deluded human beings, that they
may get their proper food of flesh-fumes and
blood when that is offered up to idol-images. What
is daintier food to the spirit of evil, than turning
men's minds away from the true God by the
illusions of a false divination?" [1]

---

[1] Apology, Ch. XXII, in The Ante-Nicene Fathers, Vol. III, 36.

This vivid reality of demons in the faith of the church continued with unabated prevalence for centuries. Demons were indeed regarded as superhuman, but, for all that, they were supposed to be amenable to much the same sort of influences as those which affect us. Gregory the Great, Pope of Rome and one of the four supreme doctors of the Western church, relates that a nun ate some lettuce without making the sign of the Cross and thereby swallowed a devil; when commanded by a holy man to come forth, the devil replied, "How am I to blame? I was sitting on the lettuce, and this woman, not having made the sign of the Cross, ate me along with it." [1] With such a view of devils in the minds of the church's foremost doctors, popular methods of exorcism can be easily imagined. In the manuals one finds speeches that seek to cast the devils out by flattery, directions for smudging them out by burning asafetida and sulphur, tremendous and disgusting curses fitted to weary the devils and to make them leave; and sometimes the victims were beaten to the point of death that the devils might find them undesirable habitations. Go back to the early church and you find Saint Jerome in his life of Saint Hilarion giving a graphic account of how the saint exorcised a demon from a possessed camel,[2] and come down to the Protestant church and you find John Bunyan describing a scene which he himself witnessed where they smudged a man to get the

[1] Andrew D. White: A History of the Warfare of Science with Theology in Christendom, Vol. II, 101.

[2] ¶ 23, Bruta animalia curata, in Patrologiæ Latinæ, ed. by J. P. Migne, Vol. XXIII, 39.

demon out of him, and almost smothered him in the process.[1]

Everywhere in the life of the church up to the very threshold of our own time demonology was rampant. Demons caused thunder-storms, and Romanists guarded against them by carrying little pieces of holy wax stamped with a lamb,—the Agnus Dei,—and other charms to ward off their power. Luther insisted that the repetition of the first verses of John's Gospel uttered with faith were of unfailing efficacy in stopping the assaults of the most obstinate devils.[2] The very church bells were used not simply to sound far and wide their call to worship, but to drive devils from the thunder-clouds, and great cathedral bells in Europe were anointed with holy oil, blessed with sacred benedictions, and stamped with special mottoes, that they might achieve this purpose.[3]

Consider the architecture of Christendom with its embellishment of demons, the early drama in which Satan and his hosts play so indispensable a part, the painting where the devils are as real as men, the literature where, as in Robert Burns, one sees reflected prevalent primitive beliefs, and the universal sway of demonology becomes impressive. Consider more sinister facts—persecutions for witchcraft and the long, unutterable horror of Christendom's treatment of insanity—and the old belief becomes more than

[1] James Anthony Froude: Bunyan, 6.

[2] Auslegung des ersten und zweiten Kapitels Johannis, in Werke, Kritische Gesammtausgabe, Weimar, Vol. 46, 628.

[3] Andrew D. White: A History of the Warfare of Science with Theology in Christendom, Vol. I, 342–347.

impressive; it becomes terrific. Even John Wesley held that many diseases were caused by demons, that the gods of the heathen were actual existences and were demons, that dreams are often caused by demons, that most lunatics are demoniacs, that to give up witchcraft would be to give up the Bible, and that diabolic possession is too valuable a testimony to the reality of the invisible world for Christians ever to surrender it.[1]   And if all this is considered popular superstition rather than intellectual conviction, read St. Thomas Aquinas' highly wrought doctrine of devils and learn with him to discuss the nature of their sin, their present estate and future prospects, their powers and limitations, their number, and the conditions of their knowledge.[2]

All this has gone from the minds of most of us. Little by little the realms where demons used to oper-ate have been invaded by scientific knowledge.   In-sanity, which once was universally ascribed to demons, is now known to be the result of a disordered brain.   Epilepsy, once familiarly regarded as an evi-dence of demoniacal possession, has been diagnosed and described, and the nature of its attendant lesions is at least partially understood.   Dreams, melancholia, hysteria, and other ills are dealt with in terms of pathological psychology and are not treated as the mischievous work of devils.   Strange freaks of second

[1] Cf. sermon, Of Evil Angels; A Letter to the Rev. Dr. Conyers Middleton; Preface to a True Relation of the Chief Things Which an Evil Spirit did and said at Mascon, in Burgundy.

[2] Summa Theologica Part I, Second Number, Treatise on the An-gels; Third Number, Treatise on the Divine Government.

sight, clairvoyance, telepathy are put in the realm of psychic activity. Thunder-storms, formerly thought of as the vivid and picturesque manifestations of diabolic activity, are now classed under meteorology, and Luther, whose conversion took place in a terrific thunder-storm which frightened him because he thought the devil was doing it,[1] would now be shocked to learn that scientists are making thunder-storms of their own. Moral temptation is generally looked upon, not as inspiration from an outer world of demons, but as the fruit of our own evil impulses. In a word, the attack upon the vast and picturesque demoniacal world in which our forefathers believed has not been theoretical, but practical. Nobody in our intellectual world stops to explain anything as the result of its activity. Devils may exist, but their functions are gone.

To be sure, demoniacal possession continues on mission fields, but only where demons are believed in. Wherever the modern doubt of demons comes in the phenomena of demoniacal possession go out. The result is that demonology has gradually faded. Some still carry rabbits' feet, knock on wood, and cross their fingers, but they do not really believe in demons as their fathers did. As a matter of fact, if we did so believe in them and acted accordingly, the public authorities would at once take charge of us. We read with antiquarian interest, not with understanding sympathy, the early chapters of The Toilers of the Sea, by Victor Hugo, where the old ideas are described operating in full blast in the nineteenth century.

[1] Arthur C. McGiffert: Martin Luther; The Man and His Work, 17.

Let us, however, frankly face the fact that when
we surrender demonology we surrender a Scriptural
category. Demonology is in the Bible. To be sure,
many of its exaggerations, its ludicrous applications,
its cruelties and grotesque enlargements are not there.
The Bible dignifies everything it touches. Nevertheless, belief in demons, their multitude, malignity,
activity, and power is unquestionably a Biblical
framework of thought.

There are few developments in Hebrew religion
much more easy to trace, at least in outline, than the
growth of this particular category. In the background is the universally prevalent belief in evil
spirits which the Hebrews shared with their Semitic
fellows. Azazel, a wilderness demon, even retained
his place in one of the temple rituals.[1] An important
addition was made to this original demoniacal world
when the divinities of other people, denied godhead
by the Hebrews, were not denied existence but were
demoted to the rank of devils. As gods of the Sanskrit
classics became the dævas of Zoroastrianism, as the
gods of the old Arab tribes became the jinn of Muhammadanism, as the gods of the Græco-Roman world
became the devils of the early Christians, and as the
Teuton deities were turned into demons by the medieval church, so the Hebrews regarded foreign divinities as demons.[2] Later, the story of Genesis 6:2–4,
where heavenly beings married earthly women, was
elaborated until a previous rebellion of angels in

[1] Leviticus 16:10; J. F. McCurdy, K. Kohler, and I. Husic: article
on Azazel in The Jewish Encyclopedia, ed. by Isidore Singer.
[2] Psalm 106:37–38, Deuteronomy 32:17.

heaven was posited and their unholy union with the daughters of men was supposed to have issued in demoniacal births.[1] This became orthodox Christian doctrine. Justin Martyr spoke of angels who trans-gressed the divine appointment and by sinful inter-course with women produced offspring who were demons.[2]

The mold into which Hebrew demonology at last was run and from which it took its final shape was Zoroastrianism. When the Persian influence was com-plete, the hitherto inchoate demonic world of the Hebrews was a well-organized hierarchy of evil with a chieftain, Satan, at its head. He never appeared in the Old Testament until after Persian influence had begun its work, and then he was spoken of in only three connections.[3] Long before Christianity appeared, however, the Hebrew people had a highly developed demonology. In practical life demons surrounded them on every side. As we believe in the almost omnipresent danger of destructive bacilli, so they believed in the multitudinous hosts of evil spirits which everywhere invaded their life and caused all manner of misery and sin. Said one rabbi: "They are more numerous than we and surround us as the mounds of earth (thrown up by the plow) surround the furrow." Said another rabbi: "Each of us has a thousand on his left hand and ten thousand on his right." Still another said: "Whoever wishes to be-

[1] Cf., e. g., The Book of Enoch, Sec. I, Chs. VI and XV.

[2] The Second Apology of Justin for the Christians, Ch. 5, in The Ante-Nicene Fathers, Vol. I, 190.

[3] Job 1:6–12 and 2:1–7, Zechariah 3:1–2, I Chronicles 21:1.

come acquainted with them, let him take sifted ashes
and strew them around his bed and in the morning he
will see the footprints of a cock." [1] If one believed
thus in demons, he could not live if he took them too
seriously, and one suspects that many people used
exorcising prayers or employed incantations and
amulets for guarding against demons with the same
cheerfulness with which we use paper cups and liquid
soap in our campaign of sterilization against the
microbes.

Nevertheless, it still remains true that this gigantic
host of evil spirits was supposed to be the source of all
things terrible. Insanity, individual wickedness, deafness, dumbness, blindness, epilepsy, power of evil
emperors, were all the work of demons; and the source
of that cosmic warfare against God of which the
earthly struggle was a counterpart was to be found in
the rebellion of Satan and his hosts against the Almighty.

This method of explaining human sin and misery
is thoroughly characteristic of the New Testament.
Demons entered into the working ideas, habitual
explanations, and common terminology of all New
Testament folk. There is a notable absence of folk-
lore in the Book; there are no charms and incantations; Paul and John especially sublimate the whole
idea, but when the mind of the New Testament dealt
with physical ills like dumbness, deafness, blindness,
epilepsy, or with moral ills whether individual or

---

[1] I Tractat Berachoth, in Der Babylonische Talmud in Seinen Hag-
gadischen Bestandtheilen, ed. by Aug. Wünsche, 23, Erster Halb-
band, 12.

cosmic, that vast realm of experience was inevitably phrased in terms of demonology.

Does that mean, then, that Christians must always so phrase their experiences of human evil and their convictions about it? To answer in the affirmative is to shut the door of Christianity against intelligence, for while an intelligent mind may well refuse to claim omniscience by denying the theoretical possibility that evil spirits exist, no intelligent mind can possibly go back across the centuries and enter into demonology as an habitual, inevitable, comprehensive category of explanation for human sin and misery. What we have in ancient demonology is a transient phrasing of abiding experiences. Once men explained eclipses of the sun by saying that a dragon swallowed it. We know better now, but because we no longer believe in that old explanation we have not thereby gotten rid of the sun's eclipses. So we surrender the old category of demonology as a means of scientific explanation but, for all that, the age-long eclipse of man's life in sin and misery is as much of a fact and as terrible a fact as ever it was. Everything the devil and his hosts ever meant is with us yet.

Having frankly recognized, therefore, the outgrown nature of the category, we need not be troubled by it when we read the Bible. What we should seek to understand is the abiding experience. "Then was Jesus led up of the Spirit into the wilderness to be tempted of the devil" [1]—surely no one needs another to tell him what that experience was. "Satan entered into Judas who was called Iscariot, being of the num-

[1] Matthew 4:1.

ber of the twelve" [1]—is there any one of us who does
not know the peril of a privileged place such as Judas
had and from which he fell? "Get thee behind me,
Satan" [2]—did none of us ever face temptation clothed
in the alluring voice of a friend and feel as Jesus felt
about Peter? "He [the devil] is a liar" [3]—have any
of us so escaped the deceitfulness of sin that we cannot
preach on that? "Even Satan fashioneth himself
into an angel of light" [4]—indeed he does and by it
he has fooled us all!

Nothing that the devils ever stood for has yet gone
out of human life. Personal temptation; various
aspects, allurements, and results of sin; disease, especially diseases with spiritual rather than physical
origination; and the ever present mystery of human
suffering and death—all this is with us still. For
years many of us have been trying to bring the Christian message to bear upon life's sin and evil. We
have found the Gospel that men need in the New
Testament. We return to the New Testament to
refind it when its meaning eludes us, to refresh it if
ever it grows dim. To cast the devils out of human
life is our commission, too, as it was that of the first
disciples, but it never occurs to us literally to hold in
our minds the ancient framework of demonology.

IV

An important part of the modern preacher's responsibility is thus to decode the abiding meanings

[1] Luke 22:3.   [2] Matthew 16:23.
[3] John 8:44.   [4] II Corinthians 11:14.

of Scripture from outgrown phraseology. Some of the
Bible is written in a cipher which the mind of our
time finds it difficult if not impossible to read. We
have always recognized this in minor ways. When
the psalmist makes God say, "Upon Edom will I
cast my shoe," [1] it requires a knowledge of ancient
Hebrew legal customs to grasp the meaning. Such
information has been the commonplace of our Sunday
School instruction, but the decoding demanded by
the facts which we are now considering is more serious.
The contrast here is not between transient customs
but between elemental forms of conception, a manifest divergence between our habitual presuppositions
of thought and those used in Scripture. Yet all the
more because the letter of the Bible often grows
cryptic as our modern categories prevail must the
mind of the church be made familiar with its abiding
sense.

Consider angels. From the time Jehovah himself
walked in the garden in the cool of the day and familiarly conversed with man, through the stages by which
his figure grew in dignity and transcendence until he
dealt with men by means of angels, the development
of angelology can be traced through the Old Testament. At first it was not easy to distinguish between
Jehovah and the angel of Jehovah [2] but soon the separate individuality of angelic beings became clear,
and finally, when Zoroastrianism had done its work,
the flexible and fluid Hebrew angelology had been
frozen into Persian form. During the Exile angelic
beings became increasingly important; they assumed

[1] Psalm 108:9.   [2] See, e. g., Genesis 16:7, 13; 31:11, 13.

definite rank; they were arranged in a great hierarchy; seven archangels were at their head and these chieftains were known familiarly by name.[1] Read Daniel's tenth chapter and observe the definite and picturesque conception of the angels, the literalness with which their activities were imagined, the organization of the nations under their jurisdiction after the manner of Persian satrapies, and the mention of one archangel's name.

When we turn to the New Testament, angels are the common phrasing of God's ministry to man. They form an innumerable host; they serve men by causing useful dreams, by strengthening the spirit in temptation, by opening prison doors, by giving peace and power in time of stress.[2] Not only do they surround the heavenly throne and attend the divine Majesty, but they appear corporeally on earth, glorious in splendor.[3]

This is a phrasing of experience which we folk of the twentieth century do not naturally use as an explanation of our blessings either material or spiritual. The typical modern mind does not habitually think of angels as the cause of events in his life. Nobody knows enough to assert that angels do not exist. That statement, however, is of small importance in dealing with our practical problem as interpreters of the Bible. We may believe it entirely reasonable to sup-

[1] K. Kohler: article on Angelology, sec. on A Heavenly Hierarchy, in The Jewish Encyclopedia, ed. by Isidore Singer.

[2] E. g., Luke 2:13, Matthew 26:53, Hebrews 12:22, Revelation 5:11; Matthew 2:13; 4:11; Acts 5:19; Luke 22:43.

[3] Matthew 16:27, 28:2–3, Acts 12:7.

pose that the unseen world is populous, that multitudes of beings exist, angelic in character and estate; certainly we may refuse to claim omniscience by denying it; but, for all that, we know well that we do not think about angels in the Zoroastrian fashion. Gabriel has no real place in our explanation of events. We cannot think with Jude of Michael and the devil fighting over the possession of Moses' body.[1] We do not practically ascribe helpful dreams or anything else to the beneficent activity of individual angels. Indeed, we must confess that as a category of scientific explanation actually applied to daily life we are not Biblical in our thinking about angels.

Here, then, is a way of thinking and speaking that needs to be decoded for the use of well-instructed folk. Surely it is not difficult to do it. Angels represent our fathers' profound and practical consciousness of the reality, friendliness, and availability of the spiritual world. Pick up at random passages about angels and consider their significance: "He said, Surely, they are my people, children that will not deal falsely: so he was their Savior. In all their affliction he was afflicted, and the angel of his presence saved them"; "The angel of Jehovah encampeth round about them that fear him, and delivereth them"; "He will give his angels charge over thee, to keep thee in all thy ways. They shall bear thee up in their hands, lest thou dash thy foot against a stone"; "Even so, I say unto you, there is joy in the presence of the angels of God over one sinner that repenteth"; "Thinkest thou that I cannot beseech my Father, and he

[1] Jude 9.

shall even now send me more than twelve legions of angels?" [1]

Looking at such passages from the standpoint of literal fact with modern psychology as standard, we get one kind of judgment; but, looking at them from the standpoint of experience to see what vital truth all this was about, we must perceive that our fathers here were speaking of the essential principle of religion—the presence, providence, directing care, and constant availability of that unseen friendship whose source is in God. Moreover, as one sees how real, vivid, and easily picturable angelology made this experience, one begins to suspect that we have lost something with our lost angels.

Indeed, if any one has been tempted to look with condescension on benighted minds that once believed in them, he would better see how shallow that attitude is. R. J. Campbell I suspect does not use the category of angelology any more literally than most of us, but listen to his wisdom when he deals with it:

> "Often I pause and smile as I think what an enormous contrast there is between such a character as, say, Louis IX—St. Louis of France— and the average member of the Stock Exchange at the present day, in general outlook upon life. And yet which is the higher? The advantage is not all on the side of the stockbroker. St. Louis lived, or so he thought, in habitual intercourse with invisible beings, saints and angels, and in a world which was continually being acted upon

[1] Isaiah 63:8-9; Psalm 34:7; 91:11-12; Luke 15:10; Matthew 26:53.

from the unseen—in fact he believed that unseen powers had far more to do with the shaping of his life than had the people whom he saw around him in the flesh. Was he wholly wrong? And was he the worse or the smaller man for extending his perspective beyond the horizon of things material? I do not think so; and, notwithstanding the evils wrought by unreasoning superstition in the hands of an unscrupulous priesthood, I am sure we shall have to recover that old-time consciousness of the nearness and activity of the invisible world." [1]

For myself, I would far rather believe in angels and so have the spiritual world real and near than be as some modern men who live in a gross world of carnal things and never in their lives have felt upon their souls anything that resembles the "brush of an angel's wing." Angelology has rightly been preserved in our poetic utterance. Some things cannot easily be said without it. Read the poets and see how naturally the sense of the Spirit's reality, nearness, and availability pours itself out in terms of angels:

> "Around our pillows golden ladders rise,
>   And up and down the skies,
>   With wingéd sandals shod,
> The angels come and go, the Messengers of God." [2]

Not superstition only kept alive that ancient category through so many centuries in so many souls great and wise; it was rather their way of conceiving and expres-

[1] The Ladder of Christ and Other Sermons, 212–213.
[2] Richard Henry Stoddard: Hymn to the Beautiful.

sing their utter confidence in, assurance of, experience with, the reality, nearness, friendship, and availability of the spiritual world.

To be sure, it is notable that in the supreme souls one overpasses this need of angels. The Master, for example, so far as we know never spoke of his experience in terms of their ministry. Others might speak of divine help mediated to him through divine messengers, but the angels of whom the Master himself speaks are always in heaven; they never come into his experience to intervene between his soul and his immediate access to God. When he prays he goes into the inner chamber and speaks to the Father in secret. Most of us in this are seeking to follow Christ. We find it more congenial to our ways of thinking to pray as he prayed and to conceive of God's immediate approach to our souls as he conceived it. But the man who has difficulty in understanding what the saints and prophets meant by their belief in angels must have a shallow and provincial mind.

Indeed, something has happened in this realm which is typical of our modern spiritual loss. Our fathers enshrined their sense of the divine nearness in angels who were close at hand; they carried the living water of a real experience in old-fashioned water-buckets. Then, their children, seeing how out of date the buckets were, threw them quite away, water and all, and now we wistfully are missing the necessary thing they spilled. We are not clear gainers by our shift of thought away from angelic categories. We cannot go back, to be sure; but in other and deeper ways we

must regain our fathers' sense of the reality and nearness of God; we must see for ourselves and help our
generation see

> those angel faces smile,
> Which we have loved long since, and lost awhile.

V

This, then, is the conclusion of the matter. It is impossible that a Book written two to three thousand
years ago should be used in the twentieth century
A. D. without having some of its forms of thought
and speech translated into modern categories. When,
therefore, a man says, I believe in the immortality of
the soul but not in the resurrection of the flesh, I believe in the victory of God on earth but not in the
physical return of Jesus, I believe in the reality of sin
and evil but not in the visitation of demons, I believe
in the nearness and friendship of the divine Spirit but
I do not think of that experience in terms of individual
angels, only superficial dogmatism can deny that that
man believes the Bible. It is precisely the thing at
which the Bible was driving that he does believe.
Life eternal, the coming of the kingdom, the conquest
of sin and evil, the indwelling and sustaining presence
of the Spirit—these are the gist of the matter once
set forth in ancient terms, but abidingly valid in our
terms too, and valid also in other terms than ours in
which our children's children may express them.

BIBLIOGRAPHY

The Christian Doctrine of Immortality, Stewart D. F. Salmond. T. and T. Clark.

The Christian Hope, William Adams Brown. Scribner's.

A Critical History of the Doctrine of a Future Life in Israel, in Judaism, and in Christianity, R. H. Charles. A. and C. Black.

The Kingdom and the Messiah, Ernest F. Scott. T. and T. Clark.

Eschatology of the Gospels, Ernst von Dobschütz. Hodder and Stoughton.

A Symposium on Eschatology, Members of the Society of Biblical Literature and Exegesis. Yale University Press.

The Messianic Hope in the New Testament, Shailer Mathews. University of Chicago Press.

Toward the Understanding of Jesus, Vladimir G. Simkhovitch. Macmillan.

Demons and Spirits, H. L. Pass, George A. Barton, and others, in the Enclyclopædia of Religion and Ethics, ed. by James Hastings. Scribner's.

Angelology, Ludwig Blau and Kaufmann Kohler, in The Jewish Encyclopedia, ed. by Isidore Singer. Funk and Wagnalls.

Demonology, Kaufmann Kohler, in The Jewish Encyclopedia, ed. by Isidore Singer. Funk and Wagnalls.

A History of the Warfare of Science with Theology in Christendom, Ch. XI, From "The Prince of the Power of the Air" to Meteorology, Ch. XV, From "Demoniacal Possession" to Insanity, et passim, Andrew D. White. Appletons.

The Expansion of Christianity in the First Three Centuries, Ch. II, Excursus: The Conflict with Demons, Adolf Harnack. Putnam.

LECTURE V

MIRACLE AND LAW

I

We have saved for a special lecture that contrast between Scriptural methods of thinking and our own which more than any other perplexes modern minds. Dr. James Moffatt of Scotland has said that when students discuss the New Testament their questions generally turn upon two subjects, miracles and money.[1] Any one who deals intimately with students will recognize that in this regard the puzzled thinking of young people in Great Britain and America is much alike. They are anxious about the application of New Testament ethic to modern economic conditions, and in a world where natural law seems regnant they are bewildered by religion's classic belief in miracles.

The failure of religious teachers to speak candidly about this latter subject, their timidity in dealing with so crucial a perplexity, is surprising and sometimes shocking. One example of the sort of thing we have been doing is supplied in the English translation of Sabatier's Philosophie de la Religion. In the original French are straightforward, illuminating passages on miracles, characterized by the lucidity of French thinking in general and by the candor of Sabatier in

[1] Approach to the New Testament, 9.

particular, which in the English translation have been deliberately omitted. Evidently our Anglo-Saxon theological sensitiveness must be preserved from shock, even at the cost of pious fraud.

The time for such evasion and equivocation long since has passed if it ever existed. Unless the church is to content herself with a blind, unreasoning dogmatism, which in the end will alienate intelligent minds, she must face this crucial matter of miracles, state the involved difficulties just as frankly as her enemies can state them, and handle them with unimpeachable frankness and devotion to the truth.

A familiar question to-day is the inquiry, Do you believe in miracles? but too often in asking it the one consideration is neglected on which an intelligent answer must depend: the meaning of miracle. If we use miracle in a general and popular sense to signify marvelous events transcending known means of ordinary explanation, there have been in the history of human thought at least four different connotations to the idea of the miraculous—so different that a man could believe one of them and yet disbelieve the others. There are some mountains that can be climbed from only one point of approach, and the discussion of the miraculous is like them, for the road that leads us over the defiles and past the chasms starts from one point only—a clear idea of miracle. The swiftest way to reach that starting point is to make, however briefly, a survey of the various meanings through which, in the history of human thought, the idea of the miraculous has passed.

That the conception of miracle is bound to have had

a history, to have passed from one significance to another, should be clear. For the way in which a man will understand and describe marvelous events in his world-order will always depend on what he thinks about the world-order as a whole. A savage in the heart of Africa to-day has one idea of miracle— anything done, as he conceives, by superhuman powers, demonic or divine—and his life is full of such activities. A college man in America, however, has another idea of miracle altogether: with him the conception, if he harbors it at all, involves either the suspension of natural laws or the extraordinary use of law-abiding forces. Obviously, the African savage and the modern college man hold very different ideas of miracle, and the difference lies primarily in the world-view which occupies the background of the mind. Miracle, that is, is a relative term; its meaning changes as the world-view changes, and in the development of human thought it has changed radically at least four times.

II

The earliest form of conceiving miracle which we can discern in the dimness of antiquity was associated with the animistic view of the world. According to that conception, everything which was not the deliberate act of man was the act of spirits other than man's. All nature's movements were looked upon as the direct activity of extra-human wills. Winds and waves, thunder and lightning, strange noises and odors, the rising sun and the changing constellations,— everything, from the phases of the moon to so intimate an occurrence as the conception of a child, whose natural causation was not understood, was looked upon as due to the direct agency of spirits. In such a world-view, notable for the absence of the slightest idea of regularity, with whimsical individual wills as the explanation of everything, a miracle would be any occurrence which men did not deliberately cause. Of course, with such a world-view, life would be mostly miracle. Breathing, for example, would be regarded as man's act, but sneezing is so unaccountable, sudden, and irresistible, that it was universally regarded as specially inspired by a spirit—a miracle, that is—and to this day many civilized people cross their fingers or utter some cabalistic incantation when they sneeze.

This, then, was the earliest idea of miracle. Any event which was not obviously man's own action was regarded as the action of some extra-human will and so belonged to the miraculous realm.

The way out from this earliest view to its successor lay through the development of a long experience of dependable regularity in the world. The Bible sometimes gives lyric expression to confidence in the standardized activities of nature. In Genesis 8:22 we read, "While the earth remaineth, seedtime and harvest, and cold and heat, and summer and winter, and day and night shall not cease," and in Psalm 148 the psalmist sings of the heavens,

> " He hath also established them for ever and ever:
> He hath made a decree which none shall transgress." [1]

The old whimsical world of animism, filled with the

[1] Marginal translation for verse 6.

unpredictable activity of spirits, had been at least in part supplanted by the trusted regularities of nature.

Never in the Bible, however, do we deal with any such idea as is represented in our phrase "natural law." In all the Old Testament there is not even a word that can be translated "nature" and in the New Testament the word so rendered means not the cosmic order, but the specific constitution of some particular thing as, for example, an olive tree, wild by nature.[1] Few things could make us feel more vividly the difference between Biblical categories and our own than the simple fact that the very word "nature," without which we could not do our ordinary thinking, and the idea of natural law, without which our view of the world would be unimaginable, are not once to be found.

What had happened to differentiate the Scripture from the preceding form of thought was the growth of a large body of experience as to many reliable regularities in man's dealing with the world. In much the same way a child starts in infancy with no idea of habitual and dependable processes in nature. You can startle an infant, but you cannot surprise him. He has no idea of what is usual against which you can project the experience of the unusual. "Extraordinary" has no meaning to him because he has not achieved any conception of what is ordinary. Throw a ball into the air and if it stays suspended the infant will not be surprised. But when childhood has come on and a body of experience has been built up as to what usually happens, a ball which stayed in the air

[1] Romans 11:24.

would be amazing. The extraordinary nature of the event would stand out against the background of ordinary experience. Nevertheless, the child, however able to distinguish usual and unusual, and to be surprised at the marvelous, would not yet know the law of specific gravity nor even suppose that such a law exists.

This experience of habitual regularity in the world without any accompanying idea of involved laws which could be discovered and stated was the background of the Biblical idea of miracle. What we would call gravitation, for example, was a constant experience; men had come to depend on it, but no one had ever thought of it as a law-abiding force or had supposed that it could be stated in a mathematical formula. To the writers of the Book God was the ultimate actor in all good events. His providence undergirdled and penetrated all life. Some events he did in a usual way, others in an unusual. A miracle was simply an extraordinary event which surpassed or transcended the ordinary course of God's procedure. God was free to do anything he wished to do in any way he wished to do it. For the most part he had standardized his activities; one could depend on an established and familiar regularity. But he might at any moment choose an abnormal instead of the normal way of acting. An axe-head might usually sink in water but there was no reason why God should not make it float if he wished to do an extraordinary thing. It was surprising when he did it, but it presented no intellectual problem whatever. No laws were broken because no laws were known. No He-

brew had ever dreamed of such a thing as a mathematical formula of specific gravity in accordance with
which an axe-head in water ought invariably to sink.

Wherever one turns in the Bible he finds this simple
idea of miracle as an extraordinary activity of God
standing out from his ordinary habit of procedure.
There are three Hebrew words and three Greek words
in the Bible that connote miracle and they are variously
translated wonders, wonderful things, strange things,
glorious things, works, mighty works, signs.[1] Without
the slightest idea of laws to be suspended or broken,
the writers of the Bible described the unusual activities of God and indiscriminately treated as miracle such
things as the Red Sea held back by a wind and God's
restoration of sinners to his favor,[2] resurrection from
the dead and God's sending rain upon the soil,[3] a fish
swallowing a man and the exaltation to safety of those
who mourn,[4] walking on the sea, commanding a tem-
pest to cease, and the healing of some distracted mind.

Indeed, so easy and unembarrassed by any intellectual difficulty was this idea of usual and unusual events,
that not God alone and his representatives, but Satan
and his satellites were supposed to work miracles continually. To the contemporary thought of Biblical
times miracles did not necessarily argue divine power.
The Pharisees thought that even the Master in his
mighty works might be acting for Beelzebub,[5] and

---

[1] מוֹפֵת‎, פֶּלֶא‎, אוֹת‎, δύναμις, τέρας, σημεῖον. See Maurice A. Canney:
article on Wonders, in the Encyclopædia Biblica, ed. by Cheyne and
Black.

[2] Psalm 107:17–21.   [3] Job 5:9–10.
[4] Job 5:9, 11.   [5] Matthew 12:24.

in passage after passage the marvelous invasion of the ordinary course of things by the extraordinary activity of evil powers was taken for granted.

This, then, was the second conception of miracle: unusual events which stand out with surprising effect from the background of usual procedure.

The next change in the understanding of miracle was precipitated when the Hebrew-Christian tradition moved out into the world of Greek thought. For the first time in its history that tradition faced in Greek philosophy an impressive concept of cosmic order. The solemn words of Prometheus,

> " Necessity doth front the universe
> With an invincible gesture,"

are a summary of one aspect and that not the least significant of Greek thought. In Hebrew thought necessity never confronted anything. In Jeremiah's figure, God could make and unmake and remake his earthly vessels, whether men or nations, as a potter does his pots.[1] Everything was free, anything could happen, and hope had wings. But in Greek thought the Fates were in control and even the father of the gods was vassal to their irresistible decrees. Not by the path of inductive science but, none the less surely, by the flight of speculative philosophy, the Greek mind came to a lofty, majestic, and sometimes terrific idea of an all-comprehensive and dominant cosmic order.

Soon or late it was inevitable that this masterful idea should raise an intellectual problem with refer-

[1] Jeremiah 18:1-8.

ence to miracles. To be sure, the conception was too ponderous to be well assimilated in popular thought and, even if it had been assimilated, there always have been ways of making predestination in general lie down in peace with miracles in particular. Yet, for all that, the simple Biblical idea of God's usual and unusual ways of acting could not long go unquestioned in a world where belief in a vast cosmic system had once taken possession of man's imagination.

The conflict came to the surface in Augustine. So far as our records go, he was the first man in our Hebrew-Christian tradition who ever felt the need of presenting an intellectual defense of the miraculous. As you read him you can feel in the background of his mind the influence of the cosmic order of the Greeks. "We say that all portents are contrary to nature," he wrote, "but they are not so. For how is that contrary to nature which happens by the will of God, since the will of so mighty a Creator is certainly the nature of each created thing? " [1] That is to say, there is an all-inclusive cosmic order in which from God's point of view there are no breaks nor interventions, and what seems miracle to us is simply the fulfilment of deeper powers and purposes than we yet have fathomed.

If the church had followed Augustine's lead, how different the course of subsequent thought would have been! As a matter of fact, however, the church went off on another road. It, too, accepted into its think-

[1] The City of God, Book XXI, Ch. 8, in The Nicene and Post-Nicene Fathers, First Series, Vol. IJ, 459.

ing much of the Greek contribution, which heightened greatly the idea of a cosmic order, but instead of making that cosmic order include everything, even miracles, as natural in God's eyes, the medieval church used the cosmic system to set off miracles in sharp contrast, to make them more exceptional than they had ever been before. For the first time, miracles were regarded as an intervention in a regular world-order. There was a cosmic system—so thought the church—but God was more powerful than that system, vast and impressive though it was. He transcended it, broke through its regularities, disrupted its habitual procedures. Miracle to the Biblical writers meant God's working in an extraordinary way, whereas he usually worked in an ordinary way; miracle in the middle ages was understood to mean the sovereign power of God intervening in the established methods of a cosmic order. Miracle thus was heightened and given a specific uniqueness that never had been there before.

The next stage in the development of the understanding of miracle we need not at length elaborate, for we ourselves are in the midst of it. Modern science came upon the scene. It took the Greek philosophic concept of a cosmic order and brought it down from heaven to earth. Regularity in nature was no longer left as a vague impression made by the general order of the universe; nature's habitual procedures were now dealt with one by one and set in mathematical formulas as irrevocable laws. The result is that the modern mind finds itself in a cosmic system which is regular with a vengeance. Many of its established

procedures can be put into mathematics and tested
by repeated experiment. From chemistry to psychology we are living every day more confidently
upon the basic idea that this is thoroughly and unin-
terruptedly a law-abiding universe.

What happened to the idea of miracle when this
onrush of inductive science overtook it is clear. Miracle had been defined as God's intervention in a cosmic order. It was redefined as God's intervention in
mathematically stated law. When a word is headed
strongly in one direction it is hard to stop its momen-
tum, and miracle, having come to mean God's irrup-
tion into established order, kept on meaning that even
when established order was defined with the partic-
ularity of Newton's formula of gravitation. The consequence has been disastrous. Many have concluded
with brusque finality that miracles do not happen.
And if we were compelled to accept the idea of miracle on which the church stranded in the eighteenth
and nineteenth centuries, most of us, however unwil-
lingly, would have to accept that dictum.

If, then, we use the word miracle to mean marvelous
events transcending known means of ordinary explanation, the idea has had four major formulations
in human history. It started by meaning all activities
in the world which man did not deliberately cause;
it went on to mean unusual events which rose above
the level of the ordinary; it then fell under the sway
of a philosophic idea of cosmic order and began to
mean intervention in an established system; and at
last it faced modern science and was redefined to
mean the rupture or suspension of demonstrable laws.

III

With this historic background in our thought we turn to picture the resultant state of mind in many of our well-instructed auditors when on Sunday we read a passage in the Bible involving miracle. Let us put the matter without the mitigations and reverent asides that our ministerial instincts would suggest, but with the brusqueness and unsparing candor that often find expression in private on the lips of an impatient modern man. However much he may adore Christ, believe in the basic principles of Christianity, and support the church, what is this typical twentieth-century man feeling to-day about stories of miracles?

For one thing, he feels that miracles are a priori improbable. Something radically transforming happened to the minds of men when Newton first set down in a demonstrable formula the law of gravitation. That formula eliminated chance and irregularity from a wide area of human experience. Lawlessness and whimsicality were banished from the relationships where that formula applied, and a regular procedure was established which could be stated in figures and verified by anybody who intelligently experimented with the phenomenon at any time and under any circumstances. Realm after realm has thus been redeemed from irregularity. Once the fact that we see the flash before we hear the roar was given the very childlike explanation that "sight is nobler than hearing." With such an explanation it is conceivable that some day for special purposes the arrangement might be reversed and hearing dignified above sight.

But when light-waves and air-waves have been differentiated and their habits studied and formulated, no such changeableness is any more imaginable. We feel sure that men always and invariably have found sight swifter than hearing, and that they always will. This sort of thing has deeply transformed men's thinking. They are convinced that this is a thoroughly law-abiding world.

When, therefore, our modern friend faces in the Bible a story which seems to involve a ruptured law of nature, his first and very strong impression is that the story is antecedently improbable.

For another thing, our modern friend feels that stories of miracles are historically unreliable. Indeed, the farther he goes in the study of the documentary evidence, the more he is likely to feel that way. In estimating the life of Francis Xavier, for example, we have many personal letters of his own and, as well, accounts written by his fellow missionaries who accompanied him upon his travels. In addition to these first-hand documents we have the early lives of Xavier and then later lives written centuries after his death. The growth of miracle-stories up through these successive documentary strata is amazing. In all Xavier's letters and the accounts of his companions not a miracle is mentioned, but the biographies of Xavier are full of them. St. Francis himself tells us of the struggle he had in learning the simplest elements of the Japanese tongue; but in the later lives he spoke Japanese so fluently, never having studied it, that his hearers thought he was a Japanese himself, and, moreover, other nationalities present heard him

miraculously in their own tongues. When one re-
calls that the ample, first-hand documents contained
not a single miracle, it certainly is astonishing to find
that when St. Francis was canonized Cardinal Monte
described ten great miracles wrought by the saint,
including making sea-water fresh, raising the dead,
levitation, transfiguration, causing an earthquake and
burying a town under cinders, and even having a crab
restore a crucifix which had been lost at sea.[1]

To one who is familiar with the successive documents involved in the development of miracle-stories,
this kind of thing is a commonplace. One stands in
wonder now in Canterbury Cathedral on the bare
stone floor where innumerable throngs once came on
pilgrimage to see and experience miracles at the tomb
of St. Thomas à Becket. The early stories of the
dead saint's power describe easily explicable healings,
but in the end there is no limit to the credulous acceptance of marvels. Canterbury water was turned
to milk, leprosy was cured, amputated members were
restored, a baby eight months old sang the Kyrie
Eleison, a starling seized by a kite invoked St. Thomas
and was saved, a cow dead and flayed, whose skin had
been sent to the tanners, was restored unharmed to
the owners, and a boy dead seven days was brought
back to life.[2]

Wherever we possess successive renditions of miracle-workers' lives we find this tendency to give

[1] See Andrew D. White: A History of the Warfare of Science with
Theology in Christendom, Vol. II, 5–23.

[2] See Edwin A. Abbott: St. Thomas of Canterbury, His Death and
Miracles

entirely explicable events a miraculous twist, to
heighten the effect of marvels by astonishing additions, and to invent miracles of which the earlier
records bear no trace. Muhammad distinctly dis-
claimed all possession of miraculous powers and when
pressed for a "sign" pointed to the weight and truth
of his words as the only evidence of his prophethood.
His followers, however, soon told a different story.
He was credited with having made the sun stand still,
with having obtained water from a flinty rock, with
having fed thousands by the multiplication of a little
food.[1]

The endless repetition of this sort of thing in documents involving miracles has seriously limited the
credulity of modern minds when they face stories of
the marvelous in ancient literature. Nor is it surprising that men should turn to the Bible, wondering
if the same process is at work there.[2] We have, for
example, three sets of documents about the early
church: the epistles, the "we-sections" of Acts,—a
diary in the first person written by some companion of
Paul,[3]—and the rest of Acts. In all of the epistles no
miracles are recorded—only references to them as
among the gifts of the Spirit;[4] in the "we-sections"
of Acts we have explicable events such as revealing
visions, a healing of fever, the recovery of Eutychus

[1] George Foot Moore: History of Religions, Vol. II, 476.

[2] On the following point see J. M. Thompson: Miracles in the New
Testament.

[3] Acts 16:10–17, 20:5–15, 21:1–18, Chs. 27–29:16.

[4] I Corinthians 12:8–11, 28–29, Galatians 3:5, Hebrews 2:4, Romans
15:19.

stunned by his fall from a window, and the escape of
Paul from the poison of the viper's bite.[1] When,
however, one steps back from these two sets of first-
hand documents into the other material of Acts, he
faces such marvels as these: a man lame forty years
is instantaneously healed; Peter, as he passes down a
street full of sick folk, heals "every one"; Philip is
miraculously caught up from the Jerusalem-Gaza
Road and is set down miles away at Azotus; Peter
raises a dead woman to life, and is released from
prison, the iron gate opening of its own accord.[2] It
looks on the face of it as though the farther we get
away from the first-hand documents the more marvelous the stories become.

When one turns to the Gospels, if one considers
Mark the earliest, as the consensus of scholarly opinion does, with Matthew and Luke each using Mark
and other material of their own, and with John coming last of all, the same heightening process appears.
It appears in spite of the fact that Mark could not
have been written before 65 A. D. Mark traditionally
is not a first-hand document; it is full of miracles, a
few of which are omitted by Matthew and Luke; and
there must have been comparatively little time between its composition and the writing of the later Gospels. The chance of discovering development in the
successive narrations of the same miracles does not
seem promising. Nevertheless, comparing Mark and
Matthew, we find that in the earlier Gospel there are
no birth-stories while in Matthew Jesus is virgin-born

[1] Acts 16:10; 28:8; 20:9-12; 28:3-6.
[2] Acts 3:1-8, 4:22; 5:15-16; 8:26-40; 9:39-41; 12:10.

and the star of Bethlehem miraculously leads the
Magi to the manger; that in Mark only Jesus walked
on the water, while in Matthew Peter tried it too;[1]
that in Mark a fig tree denounced in the evening was
wilted the next morning, while in the later record the
fig tree was cursed in the morning and "immediately
. . . withered away;" [2] that Mark recorded no other
marvels at the crucifixion than the rending of the
temple veil, but that Matthew added the resurrection
of "many bodies of the saints that had fallen asleep,"
who "entered into the holy city and appeared unto
many"; [3] that at Gadara, according to Mark, Jesus
healed one demoniac while according to Matthew he
healed two; [4] that at Jericho in Mark's Gospel he
gave sight to one blind man, in Matthew's Gospel to
two.[5]

When we compare Mark and Luke we get the same
impression of heightened effect and added detail. In
Luke, though not in Mark, are the stories of the
virgin birth and of the angelic apparition to the
shepherds.[6] In Mark, where "one of them that stood
by drew his sword, and smote the servant of the high
priest, and struck off his ear," no miracle is recorded.
In Luke, however, the ear is restored—the only
example in Scripture of the restoration of an amputated member.[7] Luke is especially rich in dramatic

[1] Mark 6:45–51, Matthew 14:22–33.
[2] Mark 11:12–14, 20–21, Matthew 21:18–19.
[3] Mark 15:38, Matthew 27: 51–54.
[4] Mark 5:1–20, Matthew 8:28–34.
[5] Mark 10:46–52, Matthew 20:29–34.
[6] Luke 1:26–35; 2:9–14.
[7] Mark 14:47, Luke 22:51.

additions to the narrative. Although not so specified
in Mark, in Luke we learn that Jairus' daughter was
an only daughter and the demoniac boy was an only
boy.[1] Where in Mark Jesus "healed many," in Luke
"he laid his hands on every one of them, and healed
them";[2] and whereas in Mark the story of the de-
scending dove at Jesus' baptism is easily interpreted
as a symbolical description of a spiritual experience,
Luke makes the event indubitably physical—" in a
bodily form, as a dove." [3]

When we turn from the Synoptic Gospels taken as
a group to compare them with the later Gospel of
John, once more we face a heightening of the miraculous element. In particular, among miracles that the
Synoptists do not mention we find some of the most
astonishing wonder-works attributed to Jesus: turning water into wine, curing a man born blind, raising
Lazarus from the dead after he had been four days
entombed.[4]

Consider such facts as this, increasingly well known
to thoughtful minds, and surely it is evident that we
would better come to serious grips with the problem
that is here presented.

In the Old Testament as well as in the New appears
this same tendency to heighten marvels as one retreats
from first-hand documents. All the records of the
prophets whose writings we have are notable for the
absence of miracle. Even the book of Jeremiah, which
contains not only his sermons but his life compiled by

---

[1] Luke 8:41–42, Mark 5:22–23; Luke 9:38, Mark 9:17.
[2] Mark 1:34, Luke 4:40.   [3] Mark 1:10, Luke 3:22.
[4] John 2:1–11; 9:1–7; 11:1–44.

his nephew Baruch, has not a miracle in it. In Amos, Hosea, Ezekiel, where biographical elements are present, no miracle is to be found, and in Isaiah only the retreating shadow on Ahaz' dial. But when from the records of those prophets whose first-hand documents we possess we step back to Elijah and Elisha, the first great figures of the prophetic line, who left no first-hand documents at all, we are in another realm. With Elijah's name are associated such miracles as these: the unfailing cruse of oil, the resuscitation of the widow's son, the feeding by the ravens, the heaven-lighted sacrifice on Carmel, the dividing of the Jordan when smitten with the prophet's cloak, the slaying of two troops of soldiers by fire from heaven, the ascension in a fiery chariot.[1] Around Elisha's name cluster such marvels as these: the dividing of the Jordan, the embassy of bears to eat up mocking children, the raising of the Shunammite's son, the increase of the widow's oil, feeding a hundred men with twenty loaves, curing Naaman's leprosy, making an axe-head swim, smiting a whole Syrian army blind, and the raising of a dead man to life by the efficacy of the prophet's bones.[2] Surely, it does look as though the farther we get from first-hand documents the more marvelous the stories are.

Indeed, one of the most interesting illustrations of this fact in Scripture still remains. If ever miracle-stories might a priori have been expected, one might

[1] I Kings 17:8–16; 17:17–24; 17:6; 18:38; II Kings 2:7–8; 1:9–12; 2:11.

[2] II Kings 2:13–14; 2:23–24; 4:18–37; 4:1–7; 4:42–44; 5:1–14; 6:5–7; 6:18; 13:21.

look to find them associated with the establishment
of David's kingdom. That was the beginning of
Israel's greatness; it was regarded as the act of God;
around it the dearest memories of the nation centered:
but not a miracle is told in connection with David's
life.[1] The narratives are plainly first-hand documents
written by a contemporary who was intimately con-
versant with events. When, however, one steps back
from these records of the foundation of David's kingdom to the ages of the judges and the desert-wander-
ings, miracle at once begins: the sun stands still,
Jericho's walls magically fall, the Jordan parts and
waits with piled-up waters while the people cross,
water flows from rock, and plagues in swift succession
come and go in Egypt as Moses and Aaron with up-
lifted wand command.[2]

Our modern friend who looks upon miracle-narratives as historically unreliable may be to us exceed-
ingly bothersome. We may wish he were not here and
we may cry to be free from his harassing questions
and his embarrassing facts, but when we ourselves
face the documentary evidence we must admit that in
general the nearer we get to first-hand sources the
fewer and simpler are the miracles, and that the
farther we get away into tradition and report the
more complex, elaborate, and inexplicable they become. That is the second item in the attitude of the
modern mind.

There is a third item, however, which, so far as

[1] Cf. II Samuel, Chs. 1–7, 9–20, and I Kings, Chs. 1–2.
[2] Joshua 10:12–14; 6:20; 3:15–17; Numbers 20:11, Exodus, Chs.
7–10.

prevalence and popularity are concerned, is probably
more influential still: the conviction that miracles
are practically undesirable. The modern man does
not regard the ages of miracles with any wistful desire
to have them back again. He knows that once everybody, saint and sinner alike, believed in miracles, took
them for granted, relied on them in business, politics,
and jurisprudence, regarded them not as matters of
pious belief in past events but as contemporary factors
in daily life. He knows that no kind of miracle is
related in Scripture the counterpart of which cannot
be found and found repeatedly in the records of other
religions. What is still more important, miracles of the
most extraordinary sort, healings, exorcisms, resurrections from the dead, and physical prodigies of
every kind were the familiar events of the most intelligent European Christianity up to the gateway of the
eighteenth century. "All this," writes Lecky about
the church's miracles, "was going on habitually in
every part of Europe without exciting the smallest
astonishment or scepticism." [1]   Scores of saints have
to their credit on the official records miracles like
raising the dead, speaking with tongues, miraculous
appearance and disappearance, instantaneous transfer
from one spot to another, and all manner of healing,
even to the restoration of amputated limbs. When
our forefathers discussed miracle they were not, like
us, playing the limelight of attention upon a small
area of history nearly two thousand years ago; they
were discussing a contemporary expression of God's

[1] W. E. H. Lecky: History of the Rise and Influence of the Spirit
of Rationalism in Europe, Vol. I, 158.

providence and power in which they believed and on
which they practically relied as much as ever the New
Testament disciples did.

The typical modern man does not regret that that
old world of thought has gone and that the new world
has come in. He is not unaware of the history of the
change that has passed over man's mind since the
Reformation. First, doubt fell on the contemporary
ecclesiastical miracles, and Protestants even developed
a theory which, not denying their occurrence, ascribed
them to the devil. Then doubt fell on the miracles of
the patristic age and the frontier of the miraculous
was pushed back to apostolic times.[1] In consequence
of this elimination of the church's miracles from intelligent credence, the miracles of the Bible became the
only ones in which Christians any more believed, and
they were thereby lifted into an absolute uniqueness
which they had not before possessed. Increasingly
they became a mainstay of apologetics. The divinity
of the Christian revelation was vouched for by the
miracles which uniquely attended it. Indeed, at this
point an idea of miracle was brought to the front, so
important that much of the eighteenth century's
discussion of religion centered about it and is unintelligible without it. Miracles, as Tillotson taught, were
not simply marvelous events, however astonishing

[1] Cf., for example, Conyers Middleton: A Free Inquiry Into The
Miraculous Powers, Which are supposed to have subsisted in the
Christian Church, From the Earliest Ages through several successive
Centuries. By which it is shewn, That we have no sufficient Reason
to believe, upon the Authority of the Primitive Fathers, That any
such Powers were continued to the Church after the Days of the
Apostles. 1748.

and inexplicable; they were signs wrought with an apologetic aim for the purpose of bearing testimony to a person or a doctrine.[1] Transubstantiation, said Tillotson, inasmuch as it is never visible to the senses, would not be a miracle, even if it were a fact. Then, under the assaults of men like Hume, this apologetic use of the miraculous began to give way. Doubt fell at last upon the Biblical miracles themselves and, instead of proving the truth of Christianity by miracles, men began arguing for miracles because Christianity was true. Believing in the divine nature of the Christian revelation because of its spiritual quality, folk were urged to regard as reasonable the miracles which adorned it like spangles on a royal robe.

One inevitable issue followed from this process of thought: *miracles ceased being a contemporary matter.* To discuss them became more and more an argument for a post-mortem case. The only miracles to be considered had happened very long ago. The theologians were hard put to it to explain why they should have ceased happening. Some who still believed in the patristic miracles said that God withdrew miraculous powers when Constantine became a Christian because they were not needed any more, and some Catholics set the date of the Inquisition's establishment as the time when God stopped miracles because the "secular arm" could take their place. Various and often skilful were the explanations, for men found the fact which they were trying to explain hard to handle.

[1] John Tillotson: sermon, The Miracles wrought in Confirmation of Christianity, in Tillotson's Works, Vol. III.

If miracles had happened in the Bible and had not happened since, then God had changed his way of running the world. At some definite date he had changed gear from one method to another. Such was the dangerous position in which the church was cornered in the eighteenth century when the idea of miracles as the rupture of demonstrable law led to a disbelief in all miracles except those recorded in the Bible.

This constitutes almost the nub of our modern difficulty. We are desperately trying to believe in events two thousand years ago the like of which we no longer expect in our experience nor regard as reasonable in our world. We are trying to project our minds back over a date when God changed his method of running the world into a previous age when things were done that no longer have any part in our reliance or our expectation. The result is deadly unreality in our thought of miracle. As Mr. A. G. Hogg put it, miracle is "the most depressing and lifeless of topics," when it is "approached as a question concerning events of an unrepeatable past."[1]

This is the more so because the modern man does not want the age of miracle repeated. He glories in the achievements and possibilities of the age of law, and prevalent religious thought has taught him to put miracle and law in contrast. In practical living he does not miss miracle at all. He knows that we are doing by means of law what the most successful miracle-workers in history never dreamed.

Miracle is sporadic; it helps some one occasionally:

[1] Redemption from This World, 3.

law is reliable and a law-abiding force is the most dependable servant that the race ever had. Miracle is aristocratic; it helps a few favored individuals: law is democratic; when once it has been put to work it serves all men who will avail themselves of its gifts. A few special blind folk in the New Testament recovered their sight through miracle, but innumerable multitudes of folk are saved from blindness and cured of blindness by modern scientific medicine. Miracle is curative; it comes in as a deus ex machina when the damage has been done: law is preventive. A miracle in Elijah's hands may save one widow from famine, but irrigation plus scientific agriculture can in time forestall famines altogether. Far more than strictly intellectual difficulties, this practical love of a law-abiding world, this distaste for the whimsicalities and the irregularities of the age of miracle makes the narratives of miracle unreal to the modern man. It might be easier for him to believe in miracles if he really wanted to.

Such is the state of mind in an increasing number of our auditors on Sunday. To them miracles are antecedently improbable, stories of them seem in general unreliable, reliance on them seems practically undesirable, and so in the end the whole matter becomes pretty much unbelievable.

IV

Personally, I do not think that this sweeping negation adequately deals with the problem of miracle, but, surely, there is no escape from the problem by the

denial of such facts as we have been considering. The
way out lies in another direction altogether. It lies in
the endeavor to discover what, if any, was the vital
spiritual experience that our forefathers were trying
to express by their category of miracle.

If miracles are to have any vitality whatever in the
faith of men to-day, they must be a contemporary and
not simply a historic matter. Jesus never called on
his followers as a test of discipleship to believe in narratives of other people's marvelous deeds, but he did
insistently call on them to manifest in their own
lives superhuman power, so that they might not have
to scale down their expectations and achievements to
the level of ordinary life. He did not expect them so
much to believe in miracles as to work them. The
church to-day, in wide areas of her teaching, is de-
manding something else altogether. She is making
it a test of discipleship that men should give credence
to miraculous events sixty generations old while generally she takes it for granted that nothing even remotely similar to them can be expected now. She has
pushed miracle to a remote antiquity. She has largely
surrendered to the futile position which Bishop Spratt
expounded. Said the Bishop:

"God never yet left himself without a witness
in the world; and it is observable that He has
commonly chosen the dark and ignorant ages
wherein to work miracles, but seldom or never
the times when natural knowledge prevailed; for
He knew there was not so much need to make
use of extraordinary signs when men were diligent

in the works of His hands and attentive to the impressions of His footsteps in His creatures." [1]

This endeavor to believe in miracles and to make faith in them significant, when all the time we are thinking of miracles as indissolubly associated with ancient ignorance and as vanishing when intelligence arrives, is not Christian faith at all. Religiously it is the essential denial of the superhumanly empowered life which Jesus demanded and demands still of his disciples, and intellectually it leads to hopeless confusion. Straining to believe miracles nearly two thousand years old if miracle means nothing to us now is vanity. Unless the miracle-idea has some contemporary significance, Biblical miracles will more and more become unreal ghosts lost in antiquity and, gradually becoming dimmer, will disappear in utter incredulity.

What, then, was the abiding conviction which our forefathers at their best were expressing when they thought and talked in terms of miracles? They were believing in the providence of God and in his immediate presence and activity in his world. They were saying that life so divinely ordered never can be ironed flat, reduced to the rigid limitations of the ordinary, but that always expectation must include events of "luminous surprise." [2] They were saying that in actual experience life like a vast and varied

[1] W. E. H. Lecky: History of the Rise and Influence of the Spirit of Rationalism in Europe, Vol. I, 161.

[2] William Adams Brown: Dudleian Lecture on The Permanent Significance of Miracle for Religion, in The Harvard Theological Review, Vol. VIII, 305 (July, 1915).

continent has lowlands and lofty peaks; that to the eye of spiritual insight life is full of events, not ordinary but special, not tame but exciting, not familiar but marvelous. They were saying that superhuman power is here, available for use, and that when men are open to its inrush and control it is not easy to set limits to the results that may ensue. Granting all the associated aberrations and credulities of the miracle-idea, it was nevertheless our forefathers' way of saying that they believed in the living God, whose ways of working are not bound within the narrow limits of man's little knowledge.

Unless it is willing to be denatured, religion cannot get on without this exciting aspect of its thought, this real and expectant faith in God, this consciousness of superhuman power, this experience of luminous events. The crucial question for modern Christianity to face is not first the credibility of this or that narrative nearly two thousand years old, but the possibility of retaining in our modern scientific thought such a vital and vivid expectancy of divine action as our fathers often phrased in terms of miracles.

Personally, I think that it can be done, and while an adequate presentation of the case would involve the statement of one's whole philosophy, I venture to put a modern Christian view of the world into three brief propositions.

First, the concept "law" does not exhaust reality. This does not mean that everything is not law-abiding. I presume it is, although it was a modern scientist and not a preacher who said, "The Uniformity of Nature which the legalists hold over us as a sacrosanct prin-

ciple is a big assumption. For who shall define its
tenure in a world of æonic flux?"[1] What one does
want to say is that the popular idea of natural law as
a receptacle into which can be poured the entire universe with none of it spilled over is a false idea. State
all the laws we know about a man and then guess at
all we can imagine, and we have not yet gotten the
whole man. We have merely gotten everything except the man. For law may express life; it never can
explain it. The more one deals at first hand with
really great scientists the more one sees how much less
they themselves think they know than popular opinion credits to them. Said Professor J. H. Poynting
at the British Association in 1900:

> "We must confess that physical laws have
> greatly fallen off in dignity. No long time ago
> they were quite commonly described as the
> Fixed Laws of Nature, and were supposed suffi-
> cient in themselves to govern the universe. Now
> we can only assign to them the humble rank of
> mere descriptions, often erroneous, of similar-
> ities which we believe we have observed. . . .
> A law of nature explains nothing, it has no govern-
> ing power, it is but a descriptive formula which
> the careless have sometimes personified."[2]

Surely, such descriptive formulas do not shut out
vital belief in a provident and active God. To modern Christian thought what we call laws are our partial plottings of the ways in which creative Spirit acts.

[1] J. Arthur Thomson: The System of Animate Nature, Vol. I, 24.
[2] Ibid., 9.

Our second proposition is that law is not a means of imprisonment to personality, but of release. To immature thought the first vision of the reign of law is overwhelmingly oppressive. Imagination builds a prison-house whose stones are material things and whose bars are rigorous laws. This is a strangely mistaken impression, however, for the plain fact is that the more we know about nature's laws the more free we are to act. We learn a new law and we can do a new thing. Why can we tunnel our rivers and bridge our gulfs, ride on the wings of the wind, speak in New York and be heard in San Francisco, if not because of the liberated creativeness which we have gained through the knowledge of natural law? Personal initiative and control are not hampered by law; law-abiding forces are the supreme medium for their freest expression.

So Boutroux, approaching the problem from the standpoint of philosophy, stated the truth about natural law's effect on man:

> "Modern science showed him physical law everywhere, and he imagined he saw his freedom being engulfed in universal determinism. A correct idea, however, of the natural laws, restores him to true self-possession, and at the same time assures him that his freedom may be efficacious and control phenomena. . . . The mechanical laws of nature, . . . instead of being a necessity, . . . set us free; they enable us to supplement, by active science, that state of contemplation in which the ancients were plunged." [1]

[1] Emile Boutroux: Natural Law in Science and Philosophy, 218.

If, therefore, we were to consider God in the most anthropomorphic way, we should have to credit him with freedom to create and control at least as much as we can. And when we enlarge our thought of God, see him as the ideal-realizing Capacity in the universe or the creative Spirit at the heart of it, what we call laws may be standardizations of his activity but certainly not limitations of it.

Our third proposition is that existence is not a closed system into which nothing new can come. The rigid, mechanical interpretation of all life, which looks on it as a predetermined affair with past, present and future potential in the primeval star-dust and automatically unfolding, is not a necessary implication of modern science. Personally, I do not think it a permanently tenable implication of modern science. Read J. Arthur Thomson's System of Animate Nature, and see! Certainly, the swing of prophetic modern thought is away from a mechanistic toward a vital conception of the universe. Whatever may be the philosophic terms in which we choose to put it, this seems to be a live cosmos, endlessly creative, constantly introducing factors not mechanically predictable from what went before, full of unexpected issues and unforeseeable events.

Such, then, in briefest outline, is a modern Christian outlook on the world. When one gathers up its total meaning it assures us that God is the immanent life of the universe, whose familiar ways of acting are partially plotted in what we call laws and who by them and others unknown to us is working out his eternal purposes.

If, now, this be the truth about our world, I can see that miracle may have a modern meaning. None of the previous meanings which the word has had are adequate for our purposes. Certainly, I do not believe that all actions not our own are the work of spirits; I am sure that the simple category of usual and unusual divine activities does not cover the case; I cannot think of a miracle as intervention in a philosophically conceived cosmic system; and I do not believe that miracles are the suspension or rupture of universal laws. Once more miracle must be redefined. It has passed through four previous meanings; it should easily endure decoding into a fifth. At any rate, if miracle is to have any meaning at all to modern minds I venture it will have to be reinterpreted from its old phrasings into some such terms as this: a miracle is God's use of his own law-abiding powers to work out in ways surprising to us his will for our lives and for the world. Unless the whole Christian Gospel is false, miracles in that sense are happening all the time. If I had not experienced them and seen them I should not be a Christian at all.

V

With such an idea let us turn back to the Bible and consider the credibility of the miracle-narratives there. Let us not talk about believing them as though historical questions could be or ought to be settled by any leap of faith. Credence of ancient miracles in the Bible or out of it is not properly a matter of faith; it is a matter of evidence. Antecedently I am pre-

pared to acknowledge that anything is possible.
There is no telling in advance what God may do or
may not do when he sets out to use his law-abiding
power to consummate his purposes. Even Huxley,
agnostic that he was, said: "Whoso clearly appre-
ciates all that is implied in the falling of a stone can
have no difficulty about any doctrine simply on account of its marvelousness."[1] Surely, a Christian
who believes in God and who thinks of God as working in and through human life will not close the doors
of his mind against the acceptance of evidence just
because it is evidence for something marvelous. Nevertheless, we do not accept Biblical narratives of the
miraculous as an act of faith. We do it, if we do it
at all, because we are historically convinced. Approaching the Bible so, there are some narratives of
miracles there which I do not believe. To suppose
that a man in order to be a loyal and devout disciple
of our Lord in the twentieth century A. D. must
think that God in the ninth century B. C. miraculously sent bears to eat up unruly children or made
an axe-head swim seems to me dangerously ridicu-
lous. Folk who insist on that kind of literal inerrancy
in ancient documents are not Fundamentalists at all;
they are incidentalists. Joshua making the sun
stand still may be poetry and the story of Jonah and
the great fish may be parable; the miraculous aspects
of the plagues in Egypt and the magic fall of Jericho's
walls may be legendary heightenings of historical
events; the amazing tales of Elijah and Elisha may

[1] In a letter to Charles Kingsley quoted in Life and Letters of
Thomas Henry Huxley, by His Son, Vol. I, 234.

be largely folk-lore; and, in the New Testament, finding a coin in a fish's mouth to pay the temple tax, or
walking on water, or blasting a tree with a curse,
may be just such stories as always have been associated with an era of outstanding personalities and
creative spiritual power.   Certainly, I find some
of the miracle-narratives of Scripture historically
incredible.

Others puzzle me.   I am not sure about them.
What does the story of the miraculous draft of fishes
mean?   Is it, as some think, a sermon on the failure
of evangelism when carried on without Christ and the
success of it when Christ directs, so that the nets of
the church are full to breaking when the fishers of
men cast in at his command?   Our Occidental minds
probably miss many symbolic literary devices in an
Oriental book and this may be one of them.   Or what
shall we say about the physical aspects of the resurrection of Christ?   We believe that he is not dead but
is risen; that we have a living Lord.   And yet we
may not know what to make of narratives about his
eating fish after his resurrection, passing through
closed doors, and offering his hands and feet to the
inquiring touch of Thomas.   Is it the Hebrew necessity
of associating continued life with a physical resurrection that made these stories, or is Frederic W. H.
Myers on the truer track when, speaking from the
standpoint of a psychic investigator, he says: "I
predict that, in consequence of the new evidence, all
reasonable men, a century hence, will believe the
Resurrection of Christ, whereas, in default of the new
evidence, no reasonable men, a century hence, would

have believed it." [1]   There is no use in pretending
that we know more than we do, and about many an
ancient miracle-narrative a man may well suspend
judgment awaiting light.

There are, however, many miracles narrated in the
Scripture which I cannot help believing. To be sure,
they often are told in language that the representative of a New York newspaper would not have used
if he had been covering the case. They are often
robed with the marvelous drapery which ages when
miracles were part and parcel of men's common
thought habitually employed in their imagination of
events, but, for all that, the abiding experience involved in them is clear and it is as true and as possible
for our day as for theirs.

For this is the principle on which alone can Biblical
miracles have a vital part in our faith. Wherever a
narrative in Scripture describes an experience in terms
of miracle so that we recognize that the same kind of
experience is open to us or would be open if we were
receptive of God's incoming power, that narrative is
fundamentally credible and useful.

At once, when this approach is made, wide areas of
Biblical miracle rise, not only into credence, but,
what is more important, into challenge, calling us in
our generation to explore the possibilities of divine
resource released in marvelous ways through faithful
men. It is not simply true that from the leadership
of Moses to our Lord's healing of the sick I see not
the slightest reason to doubt many recorded miracles;
it is more significantly true that this same kind of

[1] Human Personality and its Survival of Bodily Death, 351.

miracle ought to be among the signs of religion's reality to-day. Providential guidance of men and nations, as in Israel's release from Egypt, divine calls and commissions, as when God spoke to Samuel in the temple, conversions like Paul's on the Damascus road, and endowments of the church with power as on Pentecost, answered prayers where men let in the waiting Spirit and came off more than conquerors, healings where men proved that Spirit is mightier than flesh—all through the Scripture such activity of divine power is presented in terms of miracle. Such experiences, however, are among the inevitable fruits of vital religion in any generation, and the Bible in such narratives does not so much call on us to stretch back our minds and believe in ancient events as to gird up our souls and reduplicate them in our own time.

It is this aspect of miracle that alone seems to me exciting and worth while. God guides men and nations as much now as he ever did; he empowers men, commissions them, opens to them possibilities of abundant life, and has at his disposal and ours resources of which we have hardly touched the shallows. He is as ready now as ever to use his law-abiding powers to work out in ways surprising to us his will for us and for the world. Belief in miracles, therefore, is not first of all an historical matter; it is a contemporary challenge. To learn anew the power of prayer, to release through our lives a superhuman Spirit into human affairs, to do things which cannot be done, until men find it easy to believe in God because of the evident marvels of his presence in us and through us— this is what it really means to believe in miracle.

Faith in the miraculous is not primarily mental credence of past events; it is spiritual adventure into the
release and use of divine power in our own day.

To you, therefore, who are going out to preach, I
say, Make men believe in miracle. But do it by leading them into the experience of God's power in their
own lives now. Teach them so to find conversion,
direction, commission in their fellowship with God,
so to explore the possibilities of prayer, so to believe
in God's providence for a willing nation and an
obedient world, that they will find their minds at
home when in other terms than theirs the Bible
presents them with the same experiences. Never let
the mechanistic philosophy imprison your mind. Keep
the doors of hope and expectancy open. Above all,
believe in the living God until you see him, in ways
surprising in your eyes, working out his will for you
and for the world.

BIBLIOGRAPHY

La Notion Biblique du Miracle, E. Menegoz, in Séance de
    Rentrée des Cours . . . 5 Novembre, 1894.
Esquisse d'une Philosophie de la Religion d'apres la Psycho-
    logie et l'histoire, Ch. III, Du Miracle et de l'Inspiration,
    Auguste Sabatier. Librairie Fischbacher.
The Permanent Significance of Miracle for Religion, (Dud-
    leian Lecture for 1915 at Harvard University), William
    Adams Brown. The Harvard Theological Review, Vol.
    VIII (July, 1915).
Miracles and the New Psychology, E. Romilly Micklem. Ox-
    ford University Press.
Miracles in the New Testament, J. M. Thompson   Edward
    Arnold.

The Christian Hope, Ch. VII, The Effects of the Resurrection upon the Christian Hope, William Adams Brown.
Scribner's.

The Resurrection in the New Testament, Clayton R. Bowen.
Putnam.

The Virgin Birth, Frederic Palmer. Macmillan.

The Virgin Birth of Christ, Paul Lobstein; trans. by Victor
Leuliette. Putnam.

A Critical Examination of the Evidences for the Doctrine of
the Virgin Birth, Thomas James Thorburn. Society for
Promoting Christian Knowledge.

The Virgin Birth of Christ, James Orr. Scribner's.

The Virgin Birth of Jesus, G. H. Box. Isaac Pitman.

LECTURE VI

PERILS OF THE NEW POSITION

I

We have been endeavoring to deal candidly with the contrasts in mental category between Biblical times and our own. In every case we have found that the category which at first seemed outgrown was in fact the transient phrasing of a permanent experience. We have seen that the true way to understand the Bible's vital message is to go through the ephemeral category into the repeatable experience. This lesson is one which not only theological reactionaries but, perhaps even more, liberals need to learn. Out of an early training in which literalism was in control, many a mind, accepting new ways of thinking, has come to the conclusion that older mental frameworks are untrue. The revolt from credulous acceptance of ancient categories in their youth throws them into impatient rejection of them in their maturity. To them angelology, demonology, apocalyptic, and miracle simply are not so and that is the end of it. As a matter of fact, for all their assurance of increased knowledge, they are in danger of missing more truth than they gain. For they have not traveled the whole road until they have gone on to see that the thought-forms which they reject were old ways of framing experiences and convictions which are true and always will be. Not

till a man has taken for granted the changed frameworks and is rejoicing in the abiding truth has he
finished his course.

If the essential value of the Bible thus lies in its
abiding and reproducible experiences, even when one
has to get at them through altered categories, how
much more when there are no outmoded frameworks
to be displaced at all! Wide areas of Scripture deal
with abiding experiences set in timeless and universal
terms. The elemental needs of man's spirit for peace,
stability, comfort, and divine saviorhood; the meaning of temptation, sin, remorse, penitence, pardon,
and reconciliation with God; the basic virtues of
honesty, sincerity, courage, charity, magnanimity,
love; the great hopes of a kingdom of righteousness
here on earth and of life hereafter—these are the
fundamental matters in Scripture, and in Scripture
they always were gotten at by way of actual experience and they cannot now in any other way be understood.

In this lies one of the distinct characteristics of the
Bible. All its attitudes and its whole course of thought
were arrived at experimentally, not theoretically; they
were the result, not of philosophic speculation, but of
practical living reacting on thought. The idea of
God in characteristic Greek or Indian philosophy was
under the sway of an impressive speculative theory—
God was the Absolute; he was Pure Being. Everywhere in the best thinking of India and Greece one
finds that speculative concept in control. When,
however, one turns to the Bible, he finds himself in
another realm. The Hebrews were not philosophers;

their thinking was practical, imaginative, dramatic. Abstract theory never dominated their minds about anything, and in particular never laid the rails on which the idea of God must willy-nilly run to its logical conclusion. Rather, in the Bible, the idea of God developed as a man walks, following the grade as it comes, up hill and down dale, going across lots when that seems shorter, and encountering alike the unexpected beauties and the unforeseen obstacles of a pedestrian journey close to mother earth. In consequence, the idea of God in the Bible may be less consistent—certainly it is less abstract and theoretically determined in its development—but it is immeasurably closer to human life. It never loses contact with that. The writers of the Book did not call God by abstract names. The Absolute, Pure Being— no such words and no such ideas are in the Bible. Father, Mother, Husband, Friend,—such are his names in Scripture. The writers rose to think of him as Hosea did out of the experiences of his own domestic tragedy, or as Jesus did out of his filial fellowship. Every thought of God in the Bible came warmly out of actual experience; every stage in its development was associated with practical factors in the people's life that called it forth.

This experimental quality of the Bible at first may give it a feeling of homeliness and childlikeness in comparison with the lofty and majestic speculations of Plato, but it has helped immeasurably to give the Scriptures their abiding appeal. Plato has been very influential, but largely by indirection; few now read him and fewer still profit by him as a guide when they do. The Bible, however, never wears out; it never loses its appeal; it claims a wider audience with every century; the plain man who knows life at first hand often understands it better than the philosopher; and all of us get more vital help from it than from all the philosophers we ever read. One reason is this: philosophers make mental frameworks determinative; they erect abstract theoretical concepts as essentials of truth, when, as a matter of fact, nothing is so ephemeral as these forms of our thinking. All philosophies, therefore, are bound in time to be outgrown. Some super-Darwin, some ober-Einstein will arrive and be the death of them. But life is not outgrown. In its basic needs and fundamental experiences life is the most constant thing we know. And the Bible builds on that. In the Bible mental frameworks are secondary; the creative force is always experience, and one may challenge the inquirer to point out many passages in Scripture where the pulse of the living experience is not still beating strong.

History furnishes many examples of this ephemeral nature of mental frameworks. Milton's Paradise Lost illustrates it. Milton set himself to write a poem that would last forever. He deliberately chose a theme which should be timeless and universal. He was sure that in his setting of the fall of man with its cosmological background and its contemporary theological categories he had lighted on a mental receptacle so essentially permanent that into it he could pour his truth, confident that it never would be lost. What actually has happened we all know. The one thing that Milton thought permanent has turned out to be ephemeral.   His system of mental categories has utterly collapsed.   Nobody reads Paradise Lost for its setting, where, as Sidney Lanier sings,

> "Immortals smite immortals mortalwise
> And fill all heaven with folly."

We read it, if we read it at all, partly because of its nobility of cadence and style, and partly because its characters, especially Satan, depict so much abiding human experience.   For it is only experience that lasts; the mental phrasings of it are temporal.

If, therefore, cosmology, demonology, angelology, apocalyptic, and old forms of the miracle-idea had been speculatively controlling elements in Scripture, then the Book would be doomed to lose its hold on modern minds.   But because they are the incidents, not the essentials, the stream's flotsam and jetsam, not the stream's banks, and because the basic and creative factors in Scripture are always the living experiences of the human soul in its deepest needs, direst struggles, noblest aspirations, and finest hopes, the heart of man turns tirelessly back to the Book. So rich, fruitful, and indispensable are these normative experiences with God and man which the Bible thus sets forth, that the main business of the Christian preacher can be defined as the endeavor to reproduce them in the lives of men to-day.   Preaching is primarily the endeavor not to get men to accept a formula, but to get them to reproduce a life.

The ultimate purpose, therefore, of all our discussion of changing categories is to get the matter out of the way.   Changing categories are important only because we make them important by being perplexed about them. When once we have looked squarely at them, been honest about them, taken them for granted, then we are free to launch out on the Bible like those who go down to the sea in ships, and do business in great waters.

II

Nevertheless, there are perils associated with this modern use of the Scripture and fairness demands a frank facing of them. For one thing, spiritual values often are discerned by a naive and childlike faith when they are invisible to a critical and analytic mind. It is a pity that these two attitudes, appreciation and criticism, both of which are indispensable to fully rounded personality, should be set over against each other. In actual experience, however, they often are not confederate, as they should be, but hostile, and many a man to whose open and unquestioning soul the Scriptures came in youth with their authoritative and appealing message, has paid for his later critical intelligence about the Book by surrendering the far-too-precious coin of spiritual insight and appreciation.

Keat's complaint that the rainbow never could be so beautiful again, now that science had analyzed it, has had its replica in the disillusioned attitude of many souls toward the Bible, modernly interpreted. Nor is the reason difficult to see. No man easily keeps his mind analytic and reverent at the same time. The botanist and the poet do not often co-exist in the same person. The botanist and the poet have very different business with the flowers. The first must pull them apart, dissect them, and describe their component elements, while the second wants to see them whole and appreciate them.

> "And then my heart with pleasure fills,
> And dances with the daffodils,"

is a poet's attitude, rather than a botanist's.

Our modern mind in its scientific attitude toward the Bible, as toward everything else, is largely botanical. We want to see the facts stripped bare and subjected to merciless analysis. We positively fear poetry, sentiment, emotion, "as a tight-rope walker fears the wind," because they are unbalancing. Nor can any one who knows the incalculable contributions to knowledge made by this habit of mind fail to respect it. Even toward flowers we need Luther Burbank's attitude as well as Wordsworth's; he will make better flowers for other Wordsworths to sing about, just because of his clear-cut, hard-headed analysis of facts. Nevertheless, it is a pity that folk who have only one life to live should get from life only what critical dissection gives and not at all the values which come from appreciation and reverence.

In Yosemite Valley the waterfalls tumble from the lofty cliffs in such diaphanous and delicate tracery of spray and mist that one might imagine angels weaving on those watery looms the garments they will wear before the throne of God. Ask a chemist, however, what a waterfall is and as a chemist he will answer H_2O. That is the truth; moreover, it is important truth; but, surely it is not all the truth. Something is there for those to see who have more than analytic eyes; something is there visible only to insight, appreciation, reverence.

Not only with reference to the Bible, but in wide ranges of human interest, the modern age needs to learn this lesson. In particular, students of religion, no longer withheld by false taboos from fearless investigation of sacred things, are analyzing everything that ever has made religion rich and fruitful. They analyze prayer. They decompose it into its psychological processes. They pick it to pieces and study its works as a boy might take his father's watch apart and strew upon the table wheels, ratchets, pivots, and jewels, saying, That is the watch. Moreover, that process applied to prayer is useful. We are learning more about prayer as a law-abiding, reliable, psychological activity than we ever knew before. But when one's attitude toward prayer stops with analysis one has lost out of praying all that ever made it worth analyzing. Paul had never heard of modern psychology, but when in the midst of his conflict he cried, "Strengthened with power through his Spirit in the inward man," [1] he knew the might of prayer. Henry M. Stanley never had studied the analysis of mental states, but returning from Africa, he said:

> "On all my expeditions, prayer made me stronger, morally and mentally, than any of my non-praying companions. It did not blind my eyes, or dull my mind, or close my ears; but, on the contrary, it gave me confidence. It did more:

[1] Ephesians 3:16.

it gave me joy, and pride, in my work, and lifted me hopefully over the one thousand five hundred miles of Forest tracks, eager to face the day's perils and fatigues." [1]

Whatever else he knew about prayer, he knew the power of prayer itself. If one can know prayer only one way, he would better know it so. Far better a boy who uses a watch to tell time by than a boy who picks one to pieces and then lacks wit to put it together again!

Many modern minds crucially need the capacity to gather up their split and scattered analyses and to see steadily and whole the things men live by. The application of this truth to our modern treatment of the Bible is plain. The process from which the new views have come is the same ruthless facing of facts, unobscured by any haze of sentiment, that has given us our other sciences. We have analyzed the Book into its constituent documents; we have catechized each fact that might bear witness to the truth about the ancient writings, their authors, times, and circumstances; we have let no sentiment of reverence, no time-sanctioned taboo deflect our search. We have gone at this investigation of our sacred books counting courage a duty and hesitant sentimentality a sin. "Truth! though the heavens crush me for following her," as Carlyle said. "No Falsehood! though a whole celestial Lubberland were the price of Apostasy." [2]

[1] The Autobiography of Sir Henry Morton Stanley, 519.

[2] Thomas Carlyle: Sartor Resartus, Book II, Ch. VII, Centenary Edition, 131.

All this is admirable. A religion that is afraid of the facts is doomed. But, after all, what is the use of analysis without appreciation? What is the use of dissecting the world's supreme book of religion if in the end we do not find it a more vital inspiration to our religious life than it was before? What is the use of laying bare the transient thought-forms of the Book if we do not in spiritual adventure go past them to lay hold on the Scripture's abiding experiences? This is the first peril of the modern attitude toward the Bible. Folk analyze the Book and think that they know it, whereas the Bible at its heart cannot be known save through spiritual insight.

When one sees the intellectual eagerness, coupled with spiritual superficiality, with which new views of the Bible are accepted by some minds, he wishes that he could make this deeper matter clear. You who all too readily acclaim the new truth, one would say, remember that the heart of the Bible is not in its outgrown forms of thought, but in its reproducible experiences which can be phrased in other ways of thought. From Genesis to Revelation these are the abiding glory of the Book, and here lies its unassailable spiritual authority. "In the beginning God created the heavens and the earth"[1]—that faith in creative Spirit is reproducible; never let mechanistic interpretations of the cosmos steal it from you. "The Lord is my shepherd; I shall not want"[2]—that fellowship with God is reproducible; never let the pressure of a pagan world despoil you of that glory of the soul.

[1] Genesis: 1:1.　　　　　　　　　　[2] Psalm 23:1.

"Let justice roll down as waters, and righteousness as a mighty stream"[1]—that passion for the social good is reproducible; God give us more of it! "Come unto me, all ye that labor and are heavy laden, and I will give you rest"[2]—that retreat of the soul on Christ is reproducible; alas for the ship on stormy seas that knows no such harborage! "If any man is in Christ, he is a new creature"[3]—that regeneration of the life by the influx of the Divine, forgiving, reconciling, reinstating, and empowering, is reproducible; he that does not know it is spiritually barren and bereft. "To me to live is Christ"[4]—that devotion to the Lord of all great living is reproducible and in its repeated exhibitions across the centuries lies the chief glory that Christendom can claim. To know the Bible is to enter through its open door into such experiences as these.

The Bible is a book of vital personal religion. The reality, friendliness, and unescapableness of God are its dominant themes. In a Psalm like the 139th, where God besets a man behind and before and lays his hand upon him, where neither the heights of heaven nor the depths of Sheol can hide a man from God, nor any wings of the morning bear one to such distance as to escape him, where night and day are alike to the all-encompassing Presence so that when one awakes he is still with God, we have the experience full blown and beautiful toward which the whole Old Testament has been aspiring. And in the New Testament this experience is perfected in the filial fellow-

---

[1] Amos 5:24.
[2] Matthew 11:28.
[3] II Corinthians 5:17.
[4] Philippians 1:21.

ship with the Father which was the glory of the Master's life and with which he sought to inspire his followers.

How futile, then, is the idea that one can know the Bible who does not know what this experience means! And no analytic, critical faculties can win through to it. One may know all about the various "Isaiahs" and still lose it; one may handle the "Synoptic problem" with an expert's skill and yet miss the vital matter which created the Gospels in the first place. To get at the Bible's transforming experiences is an adventure of the whole soul. A chemist's formula in the Yosemite is no more futile to grasp the beauty of the falls than is documentary analysis to comprehend the meaning of the Book when, for example, it calls a man to fellowship with God realized in secret prayer. This ideal of praying which Jesus gave us in the Sermon on the Mount and to which the whole development of Biblical thought about prayer leads is not simple and easy. Rather, of all ideals of prayer it is the most searching and difficult. When one by one, in the inner chamber, with the door shut, we try to talk with the Father in secret, how all too few have thoughts of God and a life with God which make the experience real and fruitful!

In this regard the church is like the sea. The sea as a whole is blue: deep blue, light blue, with changing tints of green. But when you dip up its drops one by one they are not blue. Blue is only the way they look in the mass. So the church as a whole, with its venerable history, its ancient institutions, its rituals, creeds, and anthems, its innumerable worshiping as-

semblies, looks very God-conscious. But when you
take its members one by one, they often are not God-
conscious at all; that is only the way they look in the
mass. One by one they too often lack vital personal
religion.

When, then, one has said all that needs to be said
about the new views of the Bible, about critical processes of study and their results, and in particular
about the obvious changes in mental categories between Biblical times and our own, how empty is the
issue of it all if it does not liberate our minds from
handicaps and summon our souls the more clearly to
the spiritual adventures for which the Scriptures
stand! Being a "Bible Christian" in this sense is a
great matter. Too often it is made a small matter.
To be a Bible Christian must we think, as some seem
to suppose, that a fish swallowed a man, or that the
sun and moon stood still at Joshua's command, or
that God sent she-bears to eat up children who were
rude to a prophet, or that saints long dead arose
and appeared in Jersualem when our Lord was crucified? Is that what it means to be a Bible Christian?

Rather, to be a Bible Christian is a more significant
affair than such bald literalism suggests. To believe
in "the God and Father of the Lord Jesus," creator,
character, comforter, consummator,—that is to be a
Bible Christian. To know moral need which our wit
and will could not meet, and inward salvation from
it through the power of the Spirit, and to live now in
undying gratitude that overflows in service,—that is
to be a Bible Christian. To have found in Christ,

revealer of God and ideal of man, one who calls out
our admiration, captivates our love, centralizes our
ambition, and crowns our hopes,—that is to be a Bible
Christian. To be led by him into a victorious life
which rises above anxiety and fear, is made con-
queror over sin, and which, laboring for the kingdom of heaven here, is assured of the kingdom
of heaven hereafter,—that is to be a Bible Christian.

If some of us rejoice in the modern use of the Bible
and are thankful for it when we pray, it is because by
it we have been set at liberty from mental handicaps
to pass through transient forms of thought into these
abiding experiences which are the glory of the Book.

III

Another peril, however, springs out of this very
release from literalism in which we have been rejoicing.
An editorial in a New York paper hit the matter off
with alliterative cleverness when it said that in the
present controversy the Fundamentalists lacked
charity and the liberals lacked clarity. Not being
Fundamentalists we may leave the first part of the
charge to the serious consideration of those for whom
it was meant, but the latter part belongs to us and we
would better take it in earnest. Theological liberalism
to-day does lack clarity and the reason lies in the very
attitude which we have been thankfully describing.
It is possible to be emancipated from the bondage of
ancient categories without undertaking the mental
toil of constructing new ones, and the issue of that is

obscurity and confusion.   Liberals often are accused
of being rationalists.   That is largely absurd.   If
liberals were taunted with being sentimentalists, the
charge would come far nearer the truth.   The liberal
emphasis rests upon experience; we regard that, rather
than mental formulas, as the permanent continuum
of the Gospel; we proclaim our freedom from bondage
to the mental formulas of the past; and often the
total result is that our unformulated religious experience, refusing the discipline of older thinking and
shirking the discipline of new thinking, lands in
chaos.   It is often much easier to discover what
liberals do not think than to discover what they do
think.

How fatal this is should be obvious.   Safety and
assurance lie in having the deep experiences of the
soul enshrined in accepted ways of thinking.   Let the
experience of redemption through Christ once get
itself expressed in a mental formula which is generally
believed and confidently proclaimed, and the truth
gains both vital and intellectual impact difficult to
resist.   Men feel free to rejoice in the experience because they are so widely supported in their acceptance
of the mental formula which is its vehicle.   Mental
and spiritual satisfaction alike come to them in their
religion, and that way lies power.

Moreover, that way lies clarity.   At this point the
defenders of ancient theologies have an incalculable
advantage over the modernists.   To the sponsors of
old forms of thought Christianity is indissolubly
associated with an historic system of logically interrelated ideas to be accepted by the mind.   Some-

times this system is regarded as laid down in Scripture. Sometimes the classic creeds are exalted as the authoritative and final formulas. A recent defender of this type of thought insisted that a true Christian must accept every word of the Apostles' and Nicene Creeds in the sense in which those words were meant when they first were written. One may rebel against the obscurantism of this attitude, its utter blindness to the history of human thought, but the strategic advantage inherent in it is clear. These defenders of old theologies know exactly what they think. Their formulas have been wrought out and written down for a long time. They can state with embarrassing exactitude their precise opinions on the great facts of Biblical history and the great articles of Christian faith. They, too, plead for the abiding experiences of the soul with God, but they confidently present them in clearly visualized mental formulas which, when they are credible to their hearers, give to their appeal penetration and power.

Turn, now, to our liberal preaching. How much of it is intellectually chaotic and obscure! We have liberated ourselves from older ways of thinking, bondage to which had become mentally intolerable, but too generally we have shirked the difficult yet necessary task of restating in mental categories which modern minds can confidently use the central experiences of the Christian soul. We have indeed called men to the life which the Gospel offers, but we have too often been content to do it through mental formulas very disordered and confused.

The primary reason for this lies in the nature of the

situation. All doctrines spring from life. In the first
instance men have experiences with their own souls,
with their fellows, with their God, which, involving
mental elements as all sane experiences must, are
nevertheless primarily valued for their contribution
to the practical richness of life. Unable, however, to
deny their intellectual necessities, men carry these
experiences up into their minds and try deliberately
to explain, unify, organize, and rationalize them.
They make systematized doctrines out of their experiences. And when the formula has been con-
structed, they love it because the experience for which
it stands is precious. Their affections and loyalties
gather around the formula and the church swings
down the centuries with a shining formula like a
banner at its head.

The days come, however, as they have come now,
when the church moves out into a new generation,
with new ways of thinking and new outlooks on the
universe. Ideas never dreamed of before, such as
scientific law and evolution, become the common
property of well-instructed minds. Then men begin
to have trouble with the old formula. Once they
followed it as though it were their flag. Now they are
troubled and hesitant concerning it. Once they
fought for it; now they fight about it. They do not
understand it, they cannot believe it, because it was
made in times when man used other ways of putting
things. Then comes a period of theological discord
and controversy with all the trouble centering in the
formula. The way out leads inevitably through
liberalism. Some men, to be sure, impatient with the

incredible formula, throw over all religion and go out from it crying like Clifford, "The Great Companion is dead," but other souls cannot do that; religion means too much to them. They discover that their religion does not consist in the formula but in the experience of which the formula was a transient phrasing. They become liberals by retreating from the formula into the experience behind it, by translating the formula back into the life out of which it came.

In this they are like Paul. Brought up a Jew, indoctrinated in the strictest sect of Hebrew orthodoxy, he discovered that much of the religious framework in which he had trusted was for him untenable. He gave up his old interpretation of the Scripture, dropped circumcision, clean and unclean foods, and the burden of ceremonial requirement. He gave up his old view of worship and left the temple behind. A more radical transition in mental framework and practical religious expression it would be hard to find. Paul, however, did not give up religion. He went deeper into it. His casting off of old forms sprang from the positive expansion of his religious experience. Cramped and prisoned in Judaism, he sought more room for his enlarging life. He became a liberal, from the standpoint of his older thinking, not because he was less religious, but because he was more religious. He struck out for air to breathe and he found it in the central regenerative experiences which lie at the heart of the Gospel. And when he was through he was sure that he understood the depths of the Old Testament as he never had understood them before This is the very genius of liberalism. Its first step is to go through old formulas into the experiences out of which all religious formulas must come. In Phillips Brooks' figure, it beats the crust back into the batter.

Consider, for example, the "divinity of Jesus." As a formula it is not in the New Testament, but the New Testament is full of the abounding experience out of which it came. The early Christians found God in Christ. They entered into this experience with the aid of the mental categories of their time, but they primarily desired it because of the moral renewal and abundant life which it so richly brought to them. "We beheld his glory, glory as of the only begotten from the Father; full of grace and truth," [1] "the light of the knowledge of the glory of God in the face of Jesus Christ" [2]—such exultant affirmations have intellectual elements in them but they sound more like hymns than creeds. Systematic doctrine, however, inevitably ensued, and now, when the formulated doctrine, stated, let us say, by the Nicene fathers, is presented to a modern man, he often does not get it, cannot understand it, finds it difficult to believe or else quite incredible, because he habitually uses ways of thinking that the Nicene fathers never used. It may even be that impatiently he throws away the formula and the experience which it enshrines.

The typical Christian liberal, however, takes another course. He believes in the divinity of Jesus, not because he is content with ancient formulas, but because he has translated them into the experience from which originally they came. He makes his discovery of God in Christ more a matter of spiritual

[1] John 1:14.   [2] II Corinthians 4:6.

insight than of systematized formulas. Many of us
have found at least a temporary refuge in this attitude. The deepest question which man's mind asks
and man's life at its very center depends upon,
What is the truth about God? has been answered for
us in Christ. He is the best we know and we will not
interpret God in terms less than that. We see that
truth so clearly, believe in it so triumphantly, are so
sure that God is immanent in his world and in his
people and is best seen where spiritual life is clearest,
that we know well enough what old formulas were
trying to say when they cried that "very God of very
God" was in Christ. We admit that our new age
needs new ways of expressing the same experience,
but we are not troubled by that. We have translated
the doctrine back into the vital discovery of the
Divine in Christ from which all formulas must come.

Or consider the doctrine of the Trinity. Many are
puzzled by it, and who can blame them? As preached
in our Protestant churches the Trinity has often been
little more than a mathematical formula about three
being one and one three. Let it be said to the credit
of the early fathers who introduced the church to the
philosophical treatment of the Trinity, that they did
not deal in such arithmetical absurdity as has characterized our modern pulpits in their identification
of one person with three persons. If, then, any one
is troubled about this formula of the Trinity, the
liberal prescription is familiar: translate the formula
back into the experience from which it came. The
Trinity that matters is the Trinity of experience. To
know God as Father of all, God as revealed in the

historic Son, and God as the unseen Friend in our hearts—that is to know the Trinity of the New Testament: "the grace of the Lord Jesus Christ, and the love of God, and the communion of the Holy Spirit." [1]

This appeal from outgrown mental categories to the experiences which they were trying to express is the keynote of liberalism. All doctrine comes from life, it says; all doctrine is the endeavor to understand life, and, if it be true, can be taken back to life and tested there.

Nevertheless, this much liberalism and no more is incomplete. It is not difficult (every year it grows more easy) to dispossess modern minds of old frameworks in religion. It is more difficult (how much more every earnest preacher knows) to lead souls into the deep experiences which the old frameworks endeavored to express. But perhaps the most difficult task of all remains: building up constructive statements of what we positively do believe in new formulas endowed with the same persuasiveness and penetrating power which the older mental categories once possessed. One acute peril of our modern use of the Bible is found at this point. We take away old formulas. What do we put in their place? To say that we put vital experience in their place is not enough. A deacon in one of our churches told his minister that when he said "God" the picture in his mind was "a kind of an oblong blur." [2] Deeper experience alone will not meet this man's need; he must have an intelligible

[1] II Corinthians 13:14.

[2] Quoted by James Bissett Pratt: The Religious Consciousness; A Psychological Study, 200.

conception of God or else even the experience which he does possess will grow unconvincing and unreal.

Thoughtful modern minds, with increasing consciousness of our lack, face us to-day saying in effect, You give up old ways of thinking about God's relationship with us and with the world; very well! but how, then, do you conceive that fundamental matter? what is your way of putting the truth so that we can see it, understand it, organize our faith around it, and live triumphantly on the basis of it? We cannot positively live either on negations concerning old ways of thinking or on experiences expressed in them, enjoyed but not thought through nor understood. We want a reasonable faith, and that means a life of spiritual wealth and fruitfulness set in mental frameworks that are congenial, convincing, and communicable.

In every realm where the passage of centuries has broken down man's confidence in ancient categories, and in particular has made untenable for us Scriptural ways of thinking around which some of the dearest associations of man's soul have gathered, the modern world is facing us with this challenge to a positive formulation of our faith. It is the crux of the whole matter for liberalism to-day. It is a challenge to some of the most serious thinking that ever has been done on this planet. We do well to retreat from old categories into the experiences behind them, but we must also enshrine those experiences in positive formulations even though that means building up a new orthodoxy which in time will be dissolved by a new liberalism.

Into this wide field this course of lectures obviously cannot go. But it is well to chasten our delight in modern views of the Bible by depicting the sobering challenge which liberalism faces in consequence of their arrival. We do have new ways of thinking about the universe, about man's origin and nature, about the law-abiding regularity of everything, from stars to thoughts. We have often said that in these new categories the Christian Gospel in its essential meanings and abiding experiences can be persuasively expressed. But with more thoroughgoing earnestness we must set ourselves to prove that by doing it. To be sure, the result will not come from swift and facile efforts. The great Nicene Creed did not arrive until the church had been thinking for three hundred years. But with all the work which already has been done, one suspects that we soon could get a much more intelligible and presentable statement of modern Christianity if we keenly realized the need and with serious cooperative thinking undertook to meet it.

IV

Such are two major perils associated with the new position: analytic criticism may smother reverent appreciation, and unformulated experience may degenerate into sentimentality. But another danger plunges even deeper. This peril is not intellectual, but moral. It is one thing as a matter of theory to say that the continuum of Christianity lies in its reproducible experiences; it is another thing seriously to face what the reproduction of the spirit and quality of Scriptural living actually involves. That ethical challenge must be faced supremely in Jesus himself. The test of our sincerity and earnestness in claiming the repeatable experiences of the Bible as the centers of our faith and devotion comes when through the open door of our investigations, past the formulas in which first-century Christianity visualized him, we come into the presence of the historic Jesus himself and face the demands of his teaching and his character. The most far-reaching and prophetic influence playing on the church to-day is this rediscovery of Christ. Whatever else happens now, we Christians, if we are to be sincerely Christian, must take Jesus in earnest.

Moreover, taking Jesus in earnest is the most searching ethical enterprise ever undertaken on earth. The Master bore down with tremendous insistence on moral reality. Never under any circumstances would he let a theoretical dispute keep him away from an ethical issue. A lawyer came to him with a controversial question: "Teacher, what shall I do to inherit eternal life?" It was a popular question in the schools of the rabbis and the lawyer expected a spirited discussion. What he got was much more than he bargained for. First, the Master forced him back to the central and great commandments of the law, full of moral meaning and demand, "Thou shalt love the Lord thy God with all thy heart, and with all thy soul, and with all thy strength, and with all thy mind; and thy neighbor as thyself." When the lawyer, because of the searching turn which the debate was taking, raised a technicality, asking, "Who is my neighbor?" Jesus lifted the discussion out of the theoretical

realm altogether by telling the story of the Good Samaritan and adding, "Go, and do thou likewise."
That lawyer came in with a theoretical discussion on
his mind; he went out with a moral problem on his
hands.[1]

A group of scribes and Pharisees brought to Jesus a
woman taken in adultery and raised the moot question about the imposition of the Mosaic penalty of
stoning in such a case. Whoever would have dealt
with the situation as he did? He went straight
through all theoretical aspects of the problem, saying,
"He that is without sin among you, let him first cast
a stone at her." And as "they went out, one by one,
beginning from the eldest, even unto the last," what
had happened is clear: they came in with a theoretical discussion in their minds; they went out with a
moral problem on their hands.[2]

We often hear it said that it must have been de-
lightful to have talked with Jesus. I am not sure. I
love him; I adore him; but I stand tremendously in
awe of him. It has been said that a man is like an
island—sometimes one has to row all around it before one finds a place to land. Could any figure more
adequately picture what Jesus always did when he
met a man? He rowed around his life until he saw the
real problem and then he landed. He did that with
the rich young ruler and landed on the money question.[3] He did it with Zacchæus and landed on his
exactions from the poor.[4] He did it with academic,
rabbinical Nicodemus, all whose batter had turned to

[1] Luke 10:25–37.   [2] John 8:3–11.
[3] Luke 18:18–24, Matthew 19:16–22.   [4] Luke 19:1–10.

crust, whose free-flowing streams had frozen into ice, and he landed on the need of spiritual rebirth.[1] He did it with the woman of Samaria and he landed on the moral question in her life.[2] Were he to talk with us he would do the same. There would be no use in raising theoretical discussions. No such device would serve our turn. He would be after our real problem. Once more his terrific emphasis would fall on moral reality.

The Master is very beautiful to think about; he is wonderful to preach about; but there never could have been any one half so searching to face. Women might cry in sentimental praise, "Blessed is the womb that bare thee, and the breasts which thou didst suck," but he came back like thunder : " Yea, rather, blessed are they that hear the word of God and keep it."[3] Men might say, "I go, sir," with facile and polite consent and then go not, but Jesus preferred instead the man who ungraciously said, "I will not," and then went.[4] He wanted people to pray, but above all he wanted moral reality in prayer: "Whensoever ye stand praying, forgive, if ye have aught against any one."[5] He wanted men to worship, but above all he wanted moral reality in worship: "If therefore thou art offering thy gift at the altar, and there rememberest that thy brother hath aught against thee, leave there thy gift before the altar, and go thy way, first be reconciled to thy brother, and then come and offer thy gift."[6] He wanted men penitently to seek the

[1] John 3:1-3.
[2] John 4:7-24.
[3] Luke 11:27-28.
[4] Matthew 21:28-31.
[5] Mark 11:25.
[6] Matthew 5:23-24.

Father's forgiveness, but above all he wanted moral reality in penitence: "If ye forgive not men their trespasses, neither will your Father forgive your trespasses."[1] By any road one travels through the teaching of Jesus, he arrives always at this insistent demand for moral genuineness: "By their fruits ye shall know them. Not every one that saith unto me, Lord, Lord, shall enter into the kingdom of heaven; but he that doeth the will of my Father who is in heaven"; "If ye love me, ye will keep my commandments"; "Ye are my friends, if ye do the things which I command you."[2]

When, therefore, we claim that the heart of the Bible is its reproducible experiences, we are facing a most serious and challenging ethical demand. For as one goes back to the Bible now in search of its repeatable experiences, it is clear that whatever else loyalty to the Book may mean, one element must be put first: the spirit and quality of Jesus were meant to be reproduced in his followers. Nothing is Christian which leaves that out or makes that secondary. In the New Testament the Master's life, like music, was meant to be reproduced. As a score of Bach or Beethoven, into which the composer's love of harmony once was poured, is meant to be caught up by each new generation and played over again, interpreted by organs, orchestras, choirs, by old instruments that may abide and by new ones that may be invented, so the life of Jesus in the New Testament was meant to be reproduced in all sorts of circumstances, by all sorts of temperaments, until the whole earth should be full of it.

[1] Matthew 6:15.   [2] Matthew 7:20–21; John 14:15; John 15:14.

There are types of old-fashioned orthodoxy which can leave this central matter out or dim it down and still have something left to fall back upon. They can retreat upon theological beliefs or sacramental practises in which they think they find salvation, or they can look forward to a cataclysmic second coming of the Christ. But if liberal Christianity neglects or dims the Master's ethical demands, it has lost its reason for existence. For according to liberal Christianity we are here by the grace of God and in the power of God to bring all men's personal and social life under the dominion of the Master's principles of living.

So far as I can see, there was just one thing that the Master's religion was all about: he wanted to bring men into more abundant life. This objective turned out in the end to be no undisturbing aim that he peaceably could prosecute. More than any other one thing this objective brought the Master into conflict with the popular religion of his day. Popular religion had hardened into stiff and established forms. Conventionalities had become set and rigid. Then Jesus appeared. He disregarded the formalities of popular religion. When they grew intractable and obstinate he vehemently assailed them and made himself intolerable to them. Surely the motive behind that is to be found in the fact that Jesus did not think first of usages, institutions, traditions; primarily he thought about people who were missing an abundant life. He regarded people as more important than anything else on earth and thought that to lead people into a larger life was earth's most important enterprise. Therefore, when any usage, institution, or tradition impeded the prosecution of this aim, it had to look out.

Here, for example, was a sabbath rule, set, stiff, and sacred, and here was a needy man crying to be released from disease on the sabbath day. And Jesus crashed through the rule to get at the man in order that, rule or no rule, that man might have a fuller life. Nothing else mattered to the Master.

Or here was a synagogue where they had had for years undisturbed services on the sabbath day, and here Jesus came to preach. "And he opened the book. . . where it was written,

> The Spirit of the Lord is upon me,
> Because he anointed me to preach good tidings to the poor:
> He hath sent me to proclaim release to the captives,
> And recovering of sight to the blind,
> To set at liberty them that are bruised,
> To proclaim the acceptable year of the Lord." [1]

That was the text of Jesus' first recorded sermon. It concerned the bringing of freer, fuller life to people. And before that sermon was through the synagogue was in an uproar and old neighbors were leading him to throw him over the village cliff to kill him.

Or here was a set of regulations honored and meticulously kept concerning the ceremonial cleansing of the hands, and the Master, unable to see what they had to do with a more abundant spiritual life, discarded them for himself and his disciples. Nothing mattered to the Master except those things which ministered to fruitful living.

That this was the major objective of the Master

[1] Luke 4:17–19.

is made clear in every phase of his ministry. How else shall we explain his interest in bodily healing? We should not have expected it from him; he was concerned about the inner life of men. "What is a man profited, if he shall gain the whole world, and lose his own soul?"[1]—that was his emphasis. He was an ascetic, one might say, not concerned about the body. Upon the contrary, he gave himself to healing. Wherever he had the chance he lifted burdens from the disabled bodies and minds of men. It was one of his greatest joys to stand before stricken souls and say, "Wouldest thou be made whole?"[2] And the reason is that he came to bring men fuller life, and, as Amiel says, "Health cut off . . . means life reduced in attractiveness and utility by five-sixths."[3]

Or how else shall we explain the Master's interest in economic conditions? We might not have expected it from him. He did not rate financial affluence high. "Take heed, and keep yourselves from all covetousness: for a man's life consisteth not in the abundance of the things which he possesseth"[4]—that was his emphasis. We might say that he was a teacher with no economic message. Upon the contrary, when he saw folk depressed and hurt by greed and niggardliness, his interest and sometimes his indignation flamed. Victims left unhelped by the roadside, the poor lying untended at rich men's gates, widows robbed of their houses by the rapacity of rulers—

[1] Matthew 16:26.   [2] John 5:6.
[3] Henri Frederic Amiel: Journal Intime, Sept. 1, 1874, in translation by Mrs. Humphry Ward, 217.
[4] Luke 12:15.

wherever he went he was concerned about and was trying to lift all sorts of burdens from depressed lives. And if he were to come into our present economic situation, while, to be sure, he would not be a program builder, a sponsor for economic systems, he would walk through our mills, mines and factories, would lay his hands on wounded personalities and say, "Do you have to do that to men and women, to boys and girls to make your money? I came that they may have life, and may have it abundantly."

If we wish to see this major objective of the Master in full flower, we must turn to his religious teaching. How sharp the contrast is between him and the popular religion of his day! To be sure, in the rabbis are insights and intuitions that are deep and beautiful. A gentile once offered to become a Jew if Rabbi Shammai would teach him the whole law while he stood on one foot, and Shammai in indignation drove him forth with a builder's rod. But Hillel converted him, for while he stood on one foot Hillel said: "What is hateful to thee, do not unto thy fellow; this is the whole law. All the rest is a commentary." [1] While at times, however, we do discover these fine insights, how trivial were the preoccupations of popular religion in Jesus' day! We keep running on them in the background of the New Testament: whether Gerizim or Jerusalem was the proper place to worship; how ceremonially one should cleanse the pots and pans; if one took oath by the temple it was not binding, but if by the gold on the temple, it was; when one swore

[1] The Babylonian Talmud, Tract Sabbath, Ch. II, in translation by Michael L. Rodkinson, 2d edition, Vol. I, 50.

by the altar it was not binding, but if by the gift on
the altar, then it was; if one had a sacred obligation
to support his parents one could say Corban, and be
relieved of the obligation.[1]

From all this one turns to Jesus. It is another
world. He never taught anything in religion except
the great matters that make for a richer life. To trust
in God, to be, as the Scotch say, "far ben with God,"
that is, in the inner room with him,—he did teach
that, for that is a fountain of life. The majesty of
the moral law, the sovereignty of God's will, the beam
of whose eternal justice no man can ultimately tip,—
this he proclaimed with austerity and power. The
possibility of moral reformation so that men, inwardly
cleansed, can go out to live in new interests, with
new powers, for new ends,—he did teach that, for
that is the secret of life. Love for all sorts and
conditions of men, ungrudging, magnanimous, long-
suffering love, he taught. And the kingdom of
heaven on earth, around which if a man organize
his ambition and his work, living no more an aimless,
meandering existence, he finds life indeed,—he did
teach that. Wherever you touch Jesus' ministry,
concerned with health, dealing with practical circumstance, teaching the central messages of his Gospel,
he always is working for one objective only: to bring
fuller, richer life to men, to give them "power to become the sons of God."

Liberal Christianity is committed to this idea of the
Master as to what religion is all about. But liberal
Christianity faces the peril of shrinking from the im-

[1] John 4:20; Mark 7:4; Matthew 23:18; Mark 7:11-12.

plications of that idea and refusing to undertake the revolutionary business which it entails. For the full working out of this idea that the end of religion is a full, fruitful, abundant life for man is revolutionary business.

It is revolutionary for the church. Consider the situation in our modern Protestantism: Lutheranism, the lengthened influence of the great Martin; the Reformed churches, coming up from John Calvin in Geneva or John Knox in Scotland; Episcopalianism, the notable consequence of the hesitant reformation under Henry VIII; Methodism, the prolonged shadow of the Wesleys; the Baptist movement, inheritor of the extreme, revolutionary left wing of the Reformation; Congregationalism, successor of the Puritan tradition; Unitarianism, the intellectual revolt against an incredible metaphysic—all these and others, with their special histories, their accumulated peculiarities, their inherited shibboleths and partisanships, distribute themselves in our modern American communities or in the foreign field confuse the minds of the benighted with their varying theologies and polities. If Jesus should come, what would he say? Surely, it is not hard to guess: *Nothing matters in all this except the things that lead men into more abundant life.* What a revolutionary principle! It does not lead men into a more abundant life to be baptized with more water or less. It does not lead men into a more abundant life to live under this special polity or that. It does not lead men into a more abundant life to have been a vehement Episcopalian and to have become a vehement Congregationalist, or vice versa.

There are just a few things in religion that lead to a more abundant life. To have your sins forgiven, to have the burden of your guilt roll from you as from Bunyan's Pilgrim at the Cross—that does it. To know God in your heart and, as you draw from the physical world the sustenance by which you live so to draw from the eternal Spirit the power by which you live indeed,—that does it. To know Christ, the revelation of the Eternal and the ideal of man, and in a deepening discipleship with him to behold as in a mirror the glory of the Lord and to be transformed into the same image from glory into glory—that does it. To be led up by him into the expanded life of service and the dignity of helpfulness to man, to share his hopes of God's triumph on this earth and the assurance of the everlasting privilege of going on hereafter—that does it. What horizons lift, what deeps unfold, what heights allure through such a faith! These are the things that make life rich and full.

God help the church to see it, for if Christ who walked in the Gospels should walk here now, he would not like the present situation. Once more he would stand in the courts of the temple and call us to those central truths and those great services that make more fruitful life for men.

Moreover, this approach to the understanding of Christianity means revolutionary consequences in our social relationships. When I see the way some poor families in New York have to live, with such conditions of ill health and misery as few people dream; when I walk the city streets thinking of innumerable boys who never will know any other playground than the streets afford, or go into homes where little children who ought to be asleep work until midnight making paper flowers; when I watch the terrific incidence of the city's industry upon multitudes of workers or see the tragedy of the whole world reflected on the faces that come up from Ellis Island, hoping against hope to find here a paradise; and when I think of the thousands in the city who live careless, useless, futile, frittered lives, with time for business, dress, bridge, golf, dance, theater, and automobile, but who never sacrificially think of their brothers living in an earthly hell or of children robbed of childhood's heritage, I sometimes wonder how God Almighty in his infinite patience lets our miserable lives go on. We need to be made Christian, but there is no question that it will be a radically revolutionary performance.

Moreover, taking Jesus in earnest about the major objective of his ministry will involve profound changes in our economic system. So long as profit rather than service is the motive of our industrial life, so long as money rather than personality is its ultimate concern, so long as autocracy rather than democracy is its method of organization, and imperialism rather than international cooperation is its consequence, our economic system cannot be thought Christian. To see clearly yet fairly the unchristian elements in our industrial life, to see also the next step toward a better order, to present it courageously yet convincingly to men, to hold steadily before them the Christian insistence that property was made for man, not man for property, is a task calling for all the wisdom, tact, courage, and skill, that a minister possesses.

As for international and interracial affairs, what taking Jesus in earnest will do with them is becoming increasingly obvious. In our Western world a conflict is on between two traditions. From the days of the cave-men and before, the tradition of war has come up among us. Our Western civilization is built on war; our Western history has been one war after another. We have bred men for war, trained men for war; we have glorified war; we have made warriors our heroes and even in our churches we have put the battle flags beside the Cross. But centuries ago a different tradition came into our Western world. It was not war, but love. Its symbol was not a sword, but the Cross. Its voice was not a battle-cry, but "God so loved the world, that he gave his only begotten Son,"[1] and at the heart of it stood a Personality that has captured the choicest aspirations and loyalties of the race, saying, "One is your teacher, and all ye are brethren." [2]

For nearly two thousand years we have been trying to make those two traditions blend, have been endeavoring to make two antithetical and irreconcilable philosophies of life lie down in peace together. With one corner of our mouth we have praised the Prince of Peace and with the other we have glorified war. So well have we succeeded in blending Christ and carnage, the Gospel and organized slaughter, that recently a missionary in an Oriental country, after an address upon Christian goodwill, was taken aside by a native, who said, "You must know that the educated people of this country look upon Christianity as a warring,

[1] John 3:16.   [2] Matthew 23:8.

blood-spilling religion." Never in the history of the Christian church was there a more clear-cut and crucial issue than this. We cannot go on blending those two alien traditions any more. It is not a question of Christ *and* war; it is a question of Christ *or* war.

The preacher who undertakes to stress the objective of Jesus and to apply his ethical teaching to the personal life, social customs, economic systems, racial problems and international needs of this generation, has undertaken one of the most thrilling, challenging, and dangerous tasks of our day. Samuel Butler was right when he described the Christian church as full of people who would be equally horrified at hearing the Christian religion doubted, and at seeing it practised.[1] The moral avoidance of the kind of ministry which takes Jesus in earnest and makes the reproduction of his life central is the great peril of liberalism. The reactionary who takes an ancient mental formula and calls it Christianity is wrong, but he is logical. A liberal, however, who protests that on the contrary a modern formula is true Christianity instead is neither right nor logical. He has betrayed his own position. Christianity is a way of life, incarnate in Christ, that has expressed itself in many formulas and will yet express itself in many more, and the world will ultimately choose that church which produces the life, whatever the formulas may be in which she carries it. No expectation ever was more credulous than the hope that we can win our case by the mere rationality of our mental categories. The ultimate test of any religious movement is the richness of spir-

[1] The Way of All Flesh, 73.

itual life which it produces and the ethical consequences which flow from it.

Now abide three perils of liberalism—irreverence,
sentimentality, and ethical disloyalty to Jesus—and
the greatest of these is ethical disloyalty to Jesus.

BIBLIOGRAPHY

What is Modernism? Leighton Parks. Scribner's.

The Faith of Modernism, Shailer Mathews. Macmillan.

Religion in the Thought of To-day, Carl S. Patton. Macmillan.

Religion and the Mind of To-day, Joseph Alexander Leighton,
Appletons.

The Religious Revolution of To-day, James T. Shotwell.
Houghton Mifflin Co.

What Shall We Think of Christianity? William Newton Clarke.
Scribner's.

Can We Still be Christians? Rudolf Eucken, trans. by Lucy
Judge Gibson. Macmillan.

Reconstruction in Theology, Henry Churchill King. Macmillan.

Christian Theology in Outline, William Adams Brown. Scribner's.

Some Christian Convictions, Henry Sloane Coffin. Yale University Press.

Social Law in the Spiritual World, Rufus M. Jones. J. C.
Winston.

The Meaning of God in Human Experience, William Ernest
Hocking. Yale University Press.

What and Where is God? Richard La Rue Swain. Macmillan.

The Enlarging Conception of God, Herbert Alden Youtz.
Macmillan.

Man and the Attainment of Immortality, J. Y. Simpson. Doran.

Does Death End All? John Haynes Holmes. Putnam.

Social Idealism and the Changing Theology, Gerald Birney
Smith. Macmillan.

Christianity and the Social Crisis, Walter Rauschenbusch. Macmillan.

Christianizing the Social Order, Walter Rauschenbusch. Macmillan.

The New Social Order, Harry F. Ward. Macmillan.

Social Progress and the Darwinian Theory, George William Nasmyth. Putnam.

The Acquisitive Society, Richard Henry Tawney. Harcourt, Brace & Howe.

Empire and Commerce in Africa; a Study in Economic Imperialism, Leonard Sidney Woolf. Allen and Unwin.

Christianity and Economic Problems, Kirby Page. Association Press.

War: its Causes, Consequences and Cure, Kirby Page. Doran.

LECTURE VII

JESUS, THE MESSIAH

I

When in our discussion of the modern use of the
Bible we come to the problems associated with the
personality of Jesus, we have reached the heart of the
whole matter. The central task and the crowning
privilege of the Christian preacher are to present
Christ. Dr. Burkitt's dictum that "Christianity
stands or falls, lives or dies, with the personality of
Jesus Christ" [1] is one, I should suppose, to which all
evangelical preachers would consent.

Indeed, this follows inevitably from the position
we have been maintaining. The abiding continuum
of Christianity, we have said, lies in basic experiences
which phrase and rephrase themselves in different
forms of thought. But in the New Testament all the
basic experiences are essentially associated with Jesus
Christ. Gautama Buddha apparently thought that
his religion could persist altogether by dint of the
doctrines which he had taught without reference to
his own personality. Christianity, however, has been
too keenly aware of its own nature ever to suppose
that it could escape from vital dependence upon the
personality of Jesus.

[1] F. Crawford Burkitt: The Gospel History and Its Transmission, 284.

No one should understand this more clearly than the preacher. The theologian may be tempted to reduce the Gospel to its implied philosophic postulates and to present a scheme of logically interrelated abstract ideas as the essence of Christianity. But when the preacher stands before his people he knows that this will never do. His task is to win them to a new kind of living whose norms he finds in the New Testament and whose incarnation he finds in Christ. His perpetual endeavor, therefore, must be to keep fresh in his own mind and vital in his own life the experiences of the New Testament, all of which center in Christ. Christian preaching primarily consists in the presentation of the personality, the spirit, purpose, principles, life, faith and saviorhood of Jesus.

To be sure, the preacher's task includes the endeavor to make explicit and reasonable the structural ideas of Christianity, but he, better than most men, should understand that people believe not primarily in doctrine but in life. A Gothic cathedral is inconceivable without architectural doctrine. Every step from a mud hut up means an involved development of structural ideas, until in a Gothic temple we reach the climax of mathematical formulas about balanced thrusts. When, however, we stand in a cathedral subdued by its sublimity until in imagination we hear the very angels singing among its aisles and arches, it is not the involved mathematical formulas that stir us; it is the beauty and grandeur of expanded spaces and aspiring altitudes.

Such is the secret of Christian preaching. We win men to Christianity, not primarily by presenting the involved ideas, but by presenting their incarnation in life. Christ is our great asset. He actually lived the life for which we plead.

I am taking it for granted that we can know this character who so gloriously lived and died in Palestine. That school of thought which endeavored to dissipate his historic existence into myth made much more noise than either its importance or its following justified, and it has, I should suppose, been adequately dealt with. To be sure, on antecedent grounds the life and influence of Jesus might well seem incredible. There is always something unbelievable about the greatest lives, so that if some one in advance had narrated the story of Chinese Gordon or of Adoniram Judson or of Abraham Lincoln it would have seemed impossible. But of all the astounding careers with which we have to deal, where is there anything comparable with Christ's? If some one had told us beforehand that some day a baby would be born in a cattle shed, be brought up in a carpenter's home, working at the household trade until he was a full-grown man; that then he would teach his people at the most for three years, until he died at thirty-three; that he would raise no armies, organize no institutions, write no books, hold no office; that he would be poor and unbefriended, called "beside himself" by his family, a heretic by his church, a traitor by his nation; and that at last he would be taken outside the walls of the city which he loved and there be crucified as a felon between thieves: if anybody had told us that two thousand years afterward there would be no land on earth where men and women were not gladly laying down their lives for the privilege of telling people about him, that men like George Bernard Shaw, rebellious, cynical, would be saying, "I am ready to admit that after contemplating the world and human nature for nearly sixty years, I see no way out of the world's misery but the way which would have been found by Christ's will if he had undertaken the work of a practical statesman,"[1] and that seers like Browning would be singing of him:

> "The very God! think, Abib; dost thou think?
> So, the All-Great, were the All-Loving too "—[2]

if anybody had told us this in advance how impossible it would have seemed! But it is true; it actually has happened; the fact is here. To many of us it is the most considerable fact that ever took place on this planet.

Just here emerges a strange thing. Men who call themselves scientific and who pride themselves on sticking to the facts often interpret the word "fact" in such a way as to shut out from their consideration the major facts of human life. They see that rocks are facts and they build from them the science of geology. They see that stars are facts and they induce from these the science of astronomy. They know that fossils are facts and from them they read a whole chapter in the history of the earth. But after all this building of inductions from physical facts, they will base nothing on the most dominant, towering, influen-

---

[1] Androcles and the Lion: Preface on the Prospects of Christianity, xiv.

[2] Robert Browning: An Epistle, last stanza.

tial, spiritual fact in human history. A life that has changed the whole calendar so that we date everything from the time he came—that ought to be a considerable fact. A life that after sixty generations of searching investigation makes a cautious and critical mind like Matthew Arnold's say, "Nothing will do, except righteousness; and no other conception of righteousness will do, except Christ's conception of it"[1]—that ought to be a revelatory fact. Some men, however, absorbed with subhuman, quantitative facts, neglect as a basis for induction this major fact of man's spiritual history. They base immense conclusions on the heavenly bodies; they base no conclusions on the heavenly character. The primary trouble with that kind of science is not that it is not religious enough. The primary trouble with that kind of science is that it is not scientific enough.

II

When, however, recognizing that the abiding experiences of Christianity center in the Master, we turn back to the New Testament, saying like the Greeks to Philip, "We would see Jesus," we find that even here we are dealing with mental phrasings that no longer are familiar in our ordinary thought. Messiah, Logos, and Kurios[2] are categories in which the New Testament habitually conceives Jesus, but

[1] Literature and Dogma, 373.
[2] Kurios, Paul's word for "Lord," carrying many special connotations familiar to the religious life of the first century. These lectures, for reasons of space, specifically deal only with Messiah and Logos.

they are not our categories. We never use them in any other reference than this. They have to be translated from first-century Judaism and Hellenism before we understand them at all. For so long a time we have taken this situation for granted and have resigned ourselves to its necessity that we have not properly estimated the unreality that it has caused in the church's thought of Jesus. The first Christians faced the Master himself, a towering and tremendous character not yet interpreted, not yet run into the molds of any mental categories whatsoever. And when, forced by the necessity of thinking, they began to interpret his meaning for their lives, they used categories which were immediately at hand, vivid, vital, contemporary ways of thinking that carried with them richly significant connotations. The Jewish Christians naturally used "Messiah," the Hellenistic Christians naturally used "Logos," but they all were using their own familiar ways of thought, not a second-hand, historic, decoded category which they had never thought of using except with reference to Jesus.

The development of the Messianic idea among the Jews had two aspects. The simpler of the two was the hope associated with the glory of the house of David. Beginning with the expectation of a perpetual Davidic dynasty—"kings sitting upon the throne of David," [1] as Jeremiah said—it went on to more definite expectations of one glorious, specially anointed sovereign who should redeem his people. When the first Jewish Christians began interpreting Jesus, they used this

[1] Jeremiah 22:4.

category. They had radically to alter its meaning, but, even so, they used it. It was a phrasing of greatness in personality with which they were familiar. The genealogies in Matthew and Luke tracing the family of Jesus back through David and the many passages where Messiah and son of David are evidently synonymous show how prevalent this mode of thinking was and how inevitably the personality of Jesus was run into its mold.[1]

The second aspect of the Messianic thought was more elaborate. It was associated with the apocalyptic hope which developed between the Testaments. In the New Testament the Messiah became more than an anointed sovereign; he was the Son of man from heaven, pre-existent before all worlds and awaiting the appointed hour when on the clouds of heaven he would appear. In this familiar form of thought the personality of Jesus was naturally set. Scholars differ as to whether, in spite of words ascribed to him, Jesus held this thought of himself or even called himself Messiah at all. Certainly he broke through and overflowed the ordinary meanings of Messiahship and was plainly troubled by the misunderstandings of his mission which the application of the current category caused. But there is no doubt that many first-century Christians, when they interpreted the Master, used this familiar, vivid phrasing of his greatness.[2]

Logos was not a Jewish category at all. It was the most familiar, popular way of interpreting the divine

[1] Mark 10:47, Matthew 9:27, 12:23, 21:9, 22:42.
[2] Mark 8:31, Matthew 10:23, Mark 14:61–62.

approach to man which the Hellenistic world outside of Judaism knew. It was in current use in Stoicism, in Alexandrianism, in Platonism. If one were to be understood in philosophy in that day, one would as inevitably think in terms of that category as to-day one must think in terms of evolution. Hence, when Jesus was preached to Hellenists, the Logos idea was used.

Here are three categories in which the personality of our Lord is enshrined in the New Testament. He is the Messianic son of David, the Messianic Son of man from heaven, and the divine Logos mediating eternal life to men. Were these three categories in their first-century forms infallible? Are we bound to their literal terms and connotations? Can we never think of our Lord except in the categories which the first-century philosophy set up? Were they adequate to interpret him in the first place? Much more, are they adequate to interpret him now? Such questions, I should suppose, any thoughtful preacher must ask himself if he is sincerely eager to make Jesus Christ real to this generation. And in seeking an answer there are at least three factors that are significant.

First, Jesus did not create any of these forms of thought in terms of which he was described. They all had developed before he came, were in prevalent control of men's thinking when he arrived, and had been used to describe others before they were used to interpret him. This is a plain fact whose significance has all too little been appreciated. When we think of Messiah or Logos we think of Jesus. We have no use for the terms, see no meaning in them, except in reference to him. He has absorbed all the significance

which these terms have for us, until his personality
and the interpretative categories have blended into
an indissoluble unity. The very title Christ (the
Greek for Messiah) has in our usage become indis-
tinguishable from a proper name. But the situation
in the first century was as different as possible from
that. The men of that day, like their fathers before
them, had thought from their youth up in terms of
Messianic expectation or of Logos philosophy. Such
thinking was the bread and meat of their daily lives.
It was their native, natural, spontaneous understanding of history and of the world. In Judaism, when
men felt the impact of a powerful personality they
wondered at once if he might not be the Messiah, and
more than once they had followed those to whom they
had given the name. Or, in the Hellenistic world,
men ascribed the greatness of special personalities,
such as Pythagoras, to the presence of the Logos or,
like John's Gospel itself, attributed all wisdom and
greatness everywhere to the "Word" that "lighteth
every man." [1] What we see awaiting the arrival of
Jesus are these prevalent categories of interpretation
in the minds of men.

Then Jesus came. He came with his supreme
personality, and he had to be interpreted. Men did
not have time to ask whether their thought-forms
were adequate for the task. Even if they had asked
that question they could not, on the spur of the moment, have thrown away their working categories of
explanation and gotten new ones. The human mind
never works that way. Always we have in our heads

[1] John 1:9.

a stock of mental frameworks and categories of explanation, and when a new fact rises in our experience we have to do the best we can with any mental apparatus we possess to make sense of the new fact, get it oriented, and explained. It was not otherwise with the fact of Christ. Men used the intellectual forms of thought with which they were equipped. Adequately or inadequately, they did the best they could to see his personality truly, to set it where it belonged with relation to all the other truth they knew, and to present it as worthily as possible to the understanding and acceptance of men.

The second significant fact is that the first-century Christians used about Jesus all the loftiest categories that they possessed. Had you asked a Jew who, next to God himself, was the supreme personality, he would have said the Messiah. Had you asked a Hellenist what was the supreme Principle, or Being, standing with God like his alter ego, revealer, mediator, agent of Deity, or, as Philo said, "the first-born Son of God," he would have said the Logos. But not only one of these, both of them, along with other current categories representing the loftiest ways of thinking that men knew, like incarnation and deification, were used about Jesus. Here was a personality who drew to himself as necessary to his interpretation all the noblest ways of conceiving spiritual greatness which men possessed. This is an important fact. It never had happened before. It never has happened since. It is unique and it argues a uniqueness in the personality who caused it.

The third fact is that within the New Testament

itself we have clearly acknowledged the inadequacy of the categories which the church used at first and the necessity of getting new ones. The first creed of the Jewish Christians was simply the Messiahship of Jesus. But the church outgrew that. She outgrew it, not only because that form of thought was in itself ill adapted to represent the deepest truth about Jesus, but because even if it had been perfectly adapted among Jews it would have been unconvincing among Hellenists. When, therefore, the Gospel moved out from its early Jewish matrix into the Greek world, the personality of our Lord was reclothed in a new interpretation. He was presented as the eternal Son of God, the Logos, who came into our humanity and brought life eternal.

If, now, the apostle who in Ephesus so magnificently preached Jesus as the Logos were preaching, not in Ephesus, but in New York or London, is it conceivable that he would fail to do over again what he did so well before? Would he not reinterpret the personality of Jesus in terms that are native and natural to the thought and speech of the people? In the Fourth Gospel he has given us the charter of our liberty and I do not think that he would go back on it. He has shown us that the personality of Jesus is central but that the mental frameworks by which he is interpreted may change. The New Testament in this regard is no friend of the reactionary with his static philosophy. As Dr. Moffatt has said, that kind of conservatism "has no right to cut wood for its crutches from the forest of Church history, least of all from the historical study of the New Testament." [1]

[1] James Moffatt: The Approach to the New Testament, 28.

III

The preacher, therefore, who above all else is eager
to make Jesus real to the thought and life of this
generation, must be no literalist, reciting words like
Messiah and Logos, as though they were sufficient
vehicles for the Master's personality. Many modern
minds do not clearly see what these words mean.
The first requisite of a real preacher of the Master is
insight to look through not only the church's elaborate
theologies about him, but even the New Testament's
first phrasings of him, and to become acquainted with,
enamored of, the personality himself, around whom so
many frameworks of interpretation have risen, and
yet who himself is greater than them all. Just as soon
however, as the preacher does this, I suspect that he will
make an interesting discovery; he will find that what
he wishes most to say about Jesus to his people now is
at heart the same message which in the mental categories of their own time New Testament Christians were
expressing when they called him Messiah and Logos.

Let the preacher try as thoroughly as he can this
experiment of going back to the historic Jesus. In
the last generation there has been an immense access
of new information from travel, archeology, the discovery of old literatures, that has made first-century
Palestine for us a living place, has lighted up the time
when Jesus was alive, has reconstructed the social
life, home life, schools and religious customs of the day
when he walked the earth, until we can visualize his
historic figure more clearly than our fathers could.
People are still alive who can remember the stir caused

when Dr. Seeley published Ecce Homo. It was one of the first endeavors to recover from the mists of antiquity a clear visualization of Jesus. We regard it now as a classic of our English-speaking Christianity, but it was violently hated when it first appeared, and even the good Earl of Shaftesbury called it the most pestilential book ever vomited from the jaws of hell.[1]

The endeavor to recover the historic figure of the Master, however, has gone on. There is no one of us who can escape its influence. Say "Jesus" to a medieval Christian and he instinctively would think of a king sitting on his throne or coming in the clouds of heaven. Say "Jesus" to a man of to-day and he instinctively thinks of that gracious and courageous Nazarene who lived and worked and taught in ancient Palestine. Once the great pictures of Jesus were of an exalted Judge, like Michelangelo's. Now a modern painter like Tissot goes to live in Palestine and paints the figure of Jesus as he must actually have looked, among people and scenes as they must actually have been. Once Te Deums, calling upon angels and archangels, seraphim and cherubim to fall before the throne, spontaneously expressed the church's imagination of the Master. Now we find it much more natural to sing with Whittier:

> "In simple trust like theirs who heard,
>   Beside the Syrian sea,
> The gracious calling of the Lord,
> Let us, like them, without a word
>   Rise up and follow Thee."

[1] See Edwin Hodder: The Life and Work of the Seventh Earl of Shaftesbury, Vol. III, 164.

When in the Gospels we hear Jesus talk of "the grass of the field, which to-day is, and to-morrow is cast into the oven," we think of the home in Nazareth where the boys went out to gather hay and stubble for the fire. When we hear him speak of the "leaven, which a woman took, and hid in three measures of meal, till it was all leavened," we see Jesus in Nazareth by Mary's side watching the mysterious bubbling of fermenting dough. When Jesus speaks of a hungry boy asking bread and given bread, not stone, we picture the hungry family as they came to a larder which Joseph and Mary labored to keep ample for their needs. When Jesus speaks of patched garments, or of sparrows that in the market-place are sold two for a penny, we see the practical difficulties which often faced the home from which Jesus came. When he talks of eagles circling about carrion, of birds returning to their nests and foxes to their holes, of hens gathering chickens under their wings, of lost sheep, of a red sunset prophesying a fair morning, of the wind blowing as it lists, how vivid the figure of the Master becomes! So from manger to Cross we naturally endeavor to picture the Master in a concrete historic situation, and the result in many minds was well expressed by a Jewish student: "I do not think he is the Messiah, but I do love him."

Nevertheless, let us look more closely at this historic figure and inquire what he has done for men. If we ask who Jesus *is*, we may be unsure, we may share our generation's doubts and uncertainties. Change the inquiry, therefore; what has Jesus done? what changes has he wrought? what contributions has

he made to life? Such matters belong to history.
They can be stated. And, as we state them, the re-
curring theme of our argument will be: Jesus must
have been the kind of person who could do what he
has done.

For one thing, *Jesus has given the world its most
significant idea of God.* He supremely—some think
he for the first time in history—took ethical monotheism in thorough earnest. He saw the world gathered up into one spiritual sovereignty; his God was
the God of the whole earth and of all men; and the
moral meaning of that insight he took with utter se-
riousness. Fatherhood in God, as Jesus taught it,
was no soft and sentimental quality as much Christian
preaching has represented it. The fundamental attribute of Jesus' God was universal moral will. No
modern scientist, I think, ever sensed the reign of law
in the physical world more grandly and austerely
than Jesus in the moral world sensed the sovereign will
of God. A moral grandeur is exhibited in Jesus' obe-
dience to the divine will, from the first struggle in the
desert until it led him through Gethsemane to the
Cross, which to many of us makes his relationship
with God the most impressive spiritual phenomenon
in history.

This God of sovereign will Jesus interpreted in terms
of utter goodness. All Jesus' love for men was the
expression of God's will. If under the stars at night
we think of the vast, incalculable universe and argue
behind it a purposeful, intelligent power, we believe
in God, but we have not thereby reached the characteristic and distinctive quality of Jesus' Father. If we

philosophize until with intellectual satisfaction we
produce an argument assuring us there is a God, we
may believe in him, but we have not thereby reached
the distinguishing characteristics of Jesus' Father.
When, however, we love men, are merciful to the un-
grateful and undeserving, forgive our enemies, re-
claim the lost, and help the fallen, when, in a word,
we respect personality wherever we find it as the supreme treasure, then in the eternal love behind our
love, the divine will behind our service, we find Jesus'
God.   This idea of God, often hinted at and vaguely
adumbrated, the Master took like so much rough ore,
purified it, minted it, put his image and superscription
on it, and made it current coin.   Such thoughts of God,
which had been fugitive and occasional, he clarified,
made them triumphant affirmations, vivified them in
a gloriously illustrative life, and published them so
that what was before sporadic and dubious has become a persistent and conquering Gospel.   The word
God is only a picture-frame; all its value depends
on the quality of portrait which the frame encloses.
Into that old frame Jesus put a new picture so beautiful because of his own life, so inspiring and win-
some because of his sacrificial death, that men never
had so thought of God before and never since have
been so moved, melted, and transformed by any other
thought of him.   That is an amazing thing to have
done.   In this world where so many have groped after
God, guessed about God, philosophized concerning
God, the Master has lived a life of such self-authenti-
cating spiritual grandeur that increasing millions of
men when they wish to think about God can think

nothing so true, so satisfactory, so adequate, as that
the God they worship is like Christ. Even Paul, who
had been brought up in the Old Testament's noblest
ideas of God, gained a new name for him when he had
met the Master: "The God and Father of the Lord
Jesus."

For another thing, *Jesus has immeasurably heightened
man's estimate of his own worth and possibilities.* Professor George William Knox, who for twenty years
had tried the Gospel out as a missionary in the Orient
before he taught it as a philosophy at home, used to
say that Jesus' faith in the spiritual nature, infinite
value, permanent continuance, and boundless possibilities of human personality was his supreme contribution to man's thought. To believe in men as Jesus
did was in itself a great and adventurous faith; to
believe in men as Jesus did, in spite of all that men
did to him, was magnificent. It was not so much by
his teaching, however, as by his life that Jesus wrought
this heightening of faith in humankind. In himself
he carried our human nature to such heights, so unveiled in his own character what manhood was meant
to be, and by his life of divine sonship so challenged
men to claim their spiritual birthright as children of
God, that he has created new standards of estimation
about mankind's worth and possibilities. Wherever
his real message has gone folk have begun to say such
things as this: that they, too, are children of God; and
if children, then heirs; heirs of God, and joint-heirs
with Christ; that now are they children of God, and it
is not yet made manifest what they will be; they know
that, if he shall be manifested, they will be like him;

that they will attain unto the unity of the faith, and of the knowledge of the Son of God, unto a fullgrown man, unto the measure of the stature of the fulness of Christ.[1] Men never have talked like that about themselves except where Jesus' influence has come.

Yet another thing the historic Jesus has done: *he has made men believe in the possibility of moral reclamation and renewal.* He was the great specialist in the conservation of the waste products of humanity—its prodigals and outcasts. He came at men from one angle, saw them in one light—what might they not become before he was through with them? Habitually he looked at people in terms of their possibilities. He valued men not at all for what they possessed, not primarily for what they had done, not even for what they were, but most of all for what they yet might become. Many people, noting this attitude of Jesus, ascribe it to kindness, but that misses the mark. It was not primarily kindness, but insight. When Robert Browning in the square of San Lorenzo in Florence picked up a yellow pamphlet for a lira, and saw in its sordid tale the possibility of The Ring and the Book, he was exercising not kindness but insight into values actually there. So always it is the greatest minds that see the greatest possibilities in the most unlikely places. The Master exercised this insight supremely on men, and the worth which he saw hidden in immature, perverted, wronged human nature he was sure God saw too, so that for those who would fulfil the conditions were waiting forgiveness, reconciliation, and moral power to become sons of God.

[1] Cf. Romans 8:17; I John 3:2; Ephesians 4:13.

Divine forgiveness had long been taught, but Jesus made the concept thoroughly moral; he cleansed it of ceremonial elements; he made God's pardon dependent on man's right relationship with man; and in faith he supplied the power which could work the transformation. This message Jesus did not originate, but he clarified it and proclaimed it with a singleness of interest, a unity of purpose, a beauty of spirit, which make him its unique expositor. So the possibility of Roentgen Rays always had existed, latent in the radiant energy of which the universe is full, yet they will always bear Roentgen's name. He fulfilled the conditions of their production, disclosed them in their full meaning, brought them out of the darkness into light, and made them available for use. In some such way the message of moral reclamation and renewal is uniquely Christ's. He revealed its depth and range, personalized it, practised it, put the seal of his Cross upon it, and sent it out into the world. That is an amazing thing to have done. This is a hard world in which to believe at all that forgiveness and transformation of life are possible. Law and punishment are the certainties; forgiveness and renewal are the miracles. Yet Jesus has made men believe in them and, what is more, experience them. They are his specialties.

Another item must be added to the achievements of the historic Jesus: *he has given the world its loftiest ethical ideals*. A modern attack has been made upon the ethics of the Master on the ground that he expected a speedy end of the world, that he thus foreshortened his horizon, and that the kind of living that he called for was adapted, not to the real world of slow progress, but to an utterly artificial view of the world swiftly coming to an end. Jesus presents, they say, an interim ethic fitted to the few intervening months before the kingdom should come in glory from the heavens, but not fitted to the needs and possibilities of our progressive world. Suppose that in answer we grant the charge (although I doubt its truth) that Jesus' ethical ideals were deeply affected by apocalyptic expectations. The real question still remains: what would be the nature of that effect? Jesus on this supposition was mistakenly looking forward to a speedy end of the age and the swift inauguration of the best of all possible worlds with God's will sovereign over all the relationships of life. In what direction, then, would his ethical insight turn? Surely it would turn to those absolute ideals whose realization would be the glory of the coming kingdom.

So, when Edward Bellamy wished to make clear what he conceived to be the ultimate moral values, he wrote Looking Backward. He placed himself, that is, in an imagined ideal state and in terms of what is right in such a social system defined the goals and standards of his endeavor. So, too, Plato's clearest thought of ethical values appears in his Republic where in terms of the best social order he could dream he determined what finally is good and evil. If, then, Jesus did share the apocalyptic expectations, what happened in his case was infinitely more vivid and compelling: he thought the ideal order really was at hand, that men must be ready on the moment for the coming of God's perfect kingdom on the earth.

Under such conditions he would not give men prudential maxims such as worldly wisdom might suggest but he would give them a vision of the ideal life fitted to the kingdom's coming. Perfect purity, perfect sincerity, perfect magnanimity and love, perfect devotion to the will of God—such were the ideals he would lift up. He would exalt the kind of life which would make men worthy of God's utterly righteous kingdom. That was in fact the quality of his teaching. His ethical principles leave us many a puzzling problem in this very unideal world, but they have done us more service than any prudential maxims ever could have done. By them we check our little maxims up. By them we decide whether we are going forward or backward in our personal and social life. They have gone before us and go before us still like the pillar of cloud by day and of fire by night leading the way to the Promised Land.

This first answer, however, based upon a granting of the charges, does not exhaust the matter. Personally, I think that this absolute quality would have been in Jesus' ethics whether or no. The plain fact is that wide areas of the Master's most characteristic teaching have no natural connection with apocalyptic expectations at all. The parable of the Good Samaritan or of the Prodigal Son, the Golden Rule, the teaching about anxiety, about goodwill even to enemies, about finding life by losing it, about loving the Lord our God with all our heart, soul, mind and strength, and our neighbor as ourselves—what has all this to do with Jewish apocalyptic? The Master's most characteristic teaching is essentially timeless; it would be as

much at home in our century as in the first, and forty
centuries from now it will be at home still.

Moreover, the real test of any ethical teaching is
not made when folk discuss the frameworks of thought
in which it first appeared, nor yet when they argue
about its abstract rationality. The real test comes
when men apply it, adventure on the basis of it, mold
their lives and institutions to agree with it, and de-
termine what it does when it is put to work. Whenever that test has been applied to Jesus' ethical teaching, that teaching has redeemed life. Christianity
may well be ashamed of many things in its history, but
of some things it need never be ashamed. Wherever
Christ's spirit has welled up in personal character,
wherever homes have been illumined by his teaching
of self-sacrifice, mutual love, and boundless goodwill,
wherever prison systems have been even a little
affected by his attitude toward despised and outcast
men, wherever his ideals have been applied, in ways
however limited, to industrial and international life,
we need never be ashamed. The Master's ideals are
ahead of us, but they are ahead of us because they are
the loftiest, most challenging conceptions of human
character and relationships that mankind has ever
known. They will not let us rest. They condemn us,
haunt us, rally us, and lure us on. Mankind will not
find itself until it works them out and makes them real
in all of life. This immense achievement the Man
of Nazareth has wrought.

Yet again, *the historic Jesus has given the world
its most appealing and effective exhibition of vicarious
sacrifice.* Vicarious sacrifice is not new in man's life.

Gravitation is no more deeply built into the structure cf the physical universe than is vicarious sacrifice into the essential nature of the moral world. Save when some one who need not do it voluntarily assumes the burden of man's misery and sin, there is no salvation from any want or tragedy that mankind knows. All this deepest realm of human experience, universal as it is, is summed up in the Master's Cross. He has given us so perfect and convincing an illustration of the power of a boundless love expressing itself through utter sacrifice that he has become the unique representative on earth of that universal principle and law.

The cold bare words in which we state this truth do no justice to the fact. The Cross of Christ, like every other abiding element in man's life, has passed through interpretation and reinterpretation as the thought of it has been poured from one generation's mental receptacles into another's. It has been run into thought-forms associated with old animal sacrifices; it has been made "a pious fraud" played by God upon the devil, who was promised Christ if he would give up man and who ultimately lost both;[1] it has been poured into the mold of the feudal system by Anselm[2] and into the mold of later European law by Grotius.[3] Yet, warped and distorted out of its vital significance, as it often has been, by categories that had no relation with its original meaning and were essentially unfitted

[1] St. Gregory of Nyssa: The Great Catechism, Ch. XXVI, in The Nicene and Post-Nicene Fathers, Second Series, Vol. V, 495–496.

[2] Cur Deus Homo.

[3] A Defence of the Catholic Faith concerning the Satisfaction of Christ, against Faustus Socinus.

to represent its deepest truth, the Cross of Christ has been the most subduing, impressive and significant fact in the spiritual history of man. Wherever one meets vicarious sacrifice—in Livingstone voluntarily assuming the burden of Africa's misery, in Father Damien becoming a leper to the lepers when he need not have done it, in Florence Nightingale taking on herself the tragedy of battlefields which she never had caused—it always is the most subduing and impressive fact mankind can face.

But when in the supreme character it is supremely exhibited, it becomes uniquely significant. To multitudes it has meant alike a revelation of the divine nature and a challenge to sacrificial living of their own which they could in no wise escape. It has bowed them in gratitude, chastened them into penitence, wakened them to hope, inspired them to devotion. It has made the one who bore the Cross not alone a religious and ethical teacher, but a personal Savior whom to meet, with whom to fall in love, by whom to be chastened, melted, subdued, forgiven, and empowered, has been the beginning of the noblest living that this world has ever seen.

This leads us to the issue of the matter: *Jesus has supplied an object of loyalty for the noblest devotions of the generations since he came.* Men do believe that this world is not a senseless chaos, that it is not

> "a tale
> Told by an idiot, full of sound and fury,
> Signifying nothing," [1]

that it does have a divine purpose running through it.

[1] Macbeth, Act V, Sc. 5.

But men do not fall in love with and devote themselves to the divine purpose in the abstract. It must
become embodied so that they can see it. It must be
lived so that they can adore it. All through the universe the pervading purpose of God runs like blood
through our bodies, but there must be at least one
place where men can put their fingers on it and feel
its pulse. Just that service Jesus has rendered men.
He has been to them the place where they could feel
the divine heart-beat; he has been the one in whom
the eternal purpose came to the surface where they
could be sure of it. The simplest, deepest, most
searching way of expressing the finest consecrations
of men since Jesus came has been devotion to him.

We need not feel this to be unimportant because it is
not easy to state theologically; it is easy to state
psychologically, and that is just as significant. To
live a life so illustrative of all that men in their best
hours aspire to be that they can find no finer way of
phrasing their noblest devotion than in terms of
personal allegiance to the one who lived it, is an
achievement that would be utterly incredible if we did
not know that it had been done. "The devotion of
the leader to his men and to his cause," wrote Montefiore, the Jew, "Jesus shared it. The devotion of the
led to their leader—Jesus inspired it. He kindled a
flame which was to burn more brightly after his death
than ever before it in his lifetime. 'For the sake of
Jesus.' Of what fine lives and deaths has not this
motive been the spring and the sustainment." [1]

[1] C. G. Montefiore: Some Elements of the Religious Teaching of
Jesus, 133.

IV

We thus have rehearsed some of the achievements of the historic Jesus which leap first to the mind, not because we suppose for a moment that such a statement can be remotely adequate, but because even so brief a summary should make clear that, when we try to recover the historic figure of the Master behind the interpretative categories which the church has used, we do not find a diminished man, a thin and uninspiring character despoiled of its glory, a Jewish rabbi who by chance was exalted by being called Messiah. What we do find is a transcendent personality who has done for the spiritual life of man what no one else ever did. Whatever else may be said of Jesus, he must surely have been the kind of person who could do what he has done. When, therefore, I sum up even the few things we have been saying, the consequence seems impressive to the point of awe. Jesus was the kind of person who could do the things that we have said— give the world its loftiest thought of God, lift to its noblest heights man's estimate of his own worth and possibility, bring to men moral reclamation and renewal, give the world its noblest ethical ideals, its most appealing and effective outpouring of sacrificial saviorhood, its most satisfactory object of personal loyalty and devotion. These things at the very least the Master has done for men and he must have been the kind of person who could do them. And if, facing these facts, one says that Jesus was the divinely appointed agent of God's kingdom in the earth, is that too much to say? Is it not the most obvious and simple thing that we could say? I confess frankly that when I say it I do not think that I have said enough. Yet to say that is to call him the Messiah. That is the essential meaning of the New Testament when it interpreted his personality in Messianic terms. For Messiahship was simply the Hebrew category of function and purpose; it was a way of saying that God had specially anointed one to mediate his sovereignty over all mankind.

Nothing more clearly could illustrate the non-speculative character of Hebrew thinking than this fact that its highest category of personal greatness concerned a practical function. Divine substance and nature, ontological equality with God, were not involved in Messiahship at all. No ideas were there which could lead to philosophies of triunity in God or of two natures blended in one person. All that speculative theology came from the Gospel's contact with Hellenistic thought. Messiahship was characteristically and altogether Jewish. There were no philosophic discussions in the Jewish writings about Messiah's nature; his meaning consisted in what he was to do. Sometimes thought of as a Davidic sovereign, sometimes as the pre-existent Son of man, he was one who had been specially chosen to establish God's victorious kingdom in the earth. Of course, there are details associated with these Jewish pictures of the Messiah which our modern minds have no use for and cannot vitally believe. But when one thinks of the crucial matter, the conviction that in Jesus we have one divinely anointed to make real God's sovereignty over men, is not that precisely what we do believe?

Messiahship is only superficially an outgrown category; essentially it is one of the most congenial ways of thinking that modern minds could use. I do not see why one should wish to be a Christian preacher if he does not easily and whole-heartedly approach the Master so. Immeasurably indebted for his unique, costly, and irreplaceable work, tracing all my choicest faiths, hopes, ideals and experience with God to him and to his Cross, convinced that he was divinely appointed to be the world's Savior and that he plays the indispensable part in establishing God's kingdom in the earth—so I, for one, return from trying to see him as he actually lived and died in Palestine. Therefore I call him Christ indeed and when I find an ancient Jewish Christian kneeling before him as Messiah I kneel also, not because I think my fellow-worshiper's category is adequate, but because I share his estimate of the Master, his gratitude, and his devotion.

V

This centrality of Christ in our life and preaching has one crucially important reaction upon our use of the Bible. Men have always gone to any sacred scriptures they possessed primarily that they might find out how to live. That the Bible is "the infallible rule of faith and practise" is one of the most familiar statements which the church has ever framed, but in the historical development of our religion in the Old Testament the second item of that statement came first. The primary use of Scripture was to guide conduct, not to control belief. What ought we to do?

—that was the question with which men first approached their bibles and on account of which they first wanted bibles at all. The roots of this desire to find out what the gods want done go far back into primitive religion. Here, for example, is a Babylonian psalm whose cry expresses one of the most ancient and tragic questionings of man:

"What, however, seems good to one, to a god may be displeasing.
What is spurned by oneself may find favor with a god.
Who is there that can grasp the will of the gods in heaven?
The plan of a god is full of mystery,—who can understand it?
How can mortals learn the ways of a god?
He who is still alive at evening is dead the next morning.
In an instant he is cast into grief, of a sudden he is crushed." [1]

Thus, in dim antiquity men groped after ways of acting, magical, ceremonial, or moral, that would please the gods. Nor did this elemental need grow less when the gods became God and his demands on men were more and more interpreted in terms of righteousness. Still it was the primary interest of religious men to know the will of God that they might do it. When, therefore, among the Hebrews we see the canon of sacred Scripture growing, when Josiah swore the people to a solemn league and covenant— the first example of a formal Hebrew Bible that we know—or when Ezra pledged the nation's loyalty to the keeping of the Levitical law, the Bible which thus was coming into being was primarily a book of divine requirements. It told the people what they ought to

[1] Quoted by Morris Jastrow, Jr., in Aspects of Religious Belief and Practice in Babylonia and Assyria, 333.

do. Moreover, when the prophetic writings were added to the law, this evident purpose of the growing Book to help men to understand in order that they might perform the will of God, became even more explicit. At last the ingenious technicality of scribes, endeavoring to apply to each detail of human life the minute guidance of the Scripture, made legalistic interpretation of the Book a settled and essential use of it.

One might have expected the Christians to break with this legalistic employment of Scripture, as they did break with many of its old results. While, however, Jesus himself and Paul after him were anti-legalists, while they stressed the spirit of men's actions, their motives, objectives, and ideals, and dealt freely with the precise commandment of the written law, the need of an authoritative guide to action was too deep to be easily outgrown. Men who are in earnest about doing the will of God must know what that will is, and they want a book to tell them in definitive terms. When, therefore, the New Testament was added to the Old and the whole Book was bound up into unity by a theory of inerrant inspiration, Christians used the whole Book as the Jews had used part of it; it was a divine oracle to tell men how to live.

This has been one of the major uses of Scripture in Christian history. Ecclesiastical bodies, from the Roman Church citing a text for its justification, to Protestant communions claiming the support of Scripture for their diverse polities and practises, have employed the Bible as though it were a book of canon law to define the procedure and organization of Christian churches forever. Even precise instructions like

Paul's concerning women's uncovered heads or women's speaking in the churches have been used and are used still as binding laws,[1] and religious bodies still exist which denounce innovations such as Bible schools and missionary societies because they are not mentioned in the Bible. Requirements about the sabbath, first emerging among nomads in the desert or among captive Jews in Babylon, are preached and their legal enforcement is attempted in modern cities as though the written word were infallibly to govern mankind's conduct on each seventh day for all time to come. Whole communities have been founded upon the Bible as a legal constitution and, since in the New Testament there is little definite material for the organization of a state, these theocracies have largely been built upon Old Testament laws. Cromwell in England, Calvin in Geneva, the Puritans in New England were endeavoring what Cotton Mather described as "a Theocracy as near as might be to that which was the glory of Israel, 'the peculiar people.'" [2] Even detailed economic processes like the taking of interest on invested capital were forbidden on legalistic grounds.[3] Long ago, in an agricultural community, taking money on a loan would have been trading on the need of a friend, and such meanness stood in Scripture condemned and hated. As a result, every great assembly of the church from Elvira in 306 to

[1] Cf. W. N. Clarke: Sixty Years with the Bible, 149–155.

[2] Irving Berdine Richman: Rhode Island; Its Making and Its Meaning, 8.

[3] For the following point see Andrew D. White: A History of the Warfare of Science with Theology in Christendom, Vol. II. Ch. XIX.

Vienna in 1311 solemnly condemned taking interest;
burial in consecrated ground was denied to any one
who did it; economic expansion was throttled and
interest rates rose to incredible heights because the
church would not recognize changed conditions;
Luther said that taking interest of five or six percent
was robbery; the Jews became money-lenders with
·Isaac of York and Shylock typical, because, being
damned already, they were employed to do what no
Christian could do without incurring eternal penalty,
—until at last relief was found in a rabbinical technicality never thought of until necessity required it, that
a low rate of interest was justifiable but that a high
rate was usury.

At times this endeavor to make the letter of the
Bible a binding law has produced the deepest shames
and tragedies that Christendom has known. "Thou
shalt not suffer a witch to live," [1] used alike as a defense of witchcraft's reality and a call to persecution;
the slave laws of the Hebrews, used in defense of
slavery; "Compel them to come in," [2] used as a commandment requiring religious persecution—such are
a few samples of the cruel consequences of legalism.

Thus to use the Scripture's detailed laws, so often
formulated under circumstances long since gone, and
sometimes enshrining ethical ideas so outgrown that
to obey the law would be to commit a crime, is worse
than folly. Yet the ancient need which the legalistic
use of Scripture tried to meet is with us still. Men
want to know the will of God that they may do it.
They want the Bible clearly to tell them how to live.

[1] Exodus 22:18.   [2] Luke 14:23.

What, then, shall the preacher do who uses the Book and yet cannot use it legalistically as his fathers did?

The spirit and character of Jesus are the answer. He has revealed the quality and principle of true living. Said Matthew Arnold, "Attempt to reach righteousness *by any way except that of Jesus*, and you will find out your mistake!" [1] If some one protests that Jesus does not give us rules and regulations by which in every situation we may know what he would have us do, that he furnishes us no dictionary of conduct giving us a maxim for each contingency, let us be thankful that this is true. Had he written a new Levitical code adapted to his age, the changed circumstances of our modern times long since would have outlawed most of it. Instead, he has given us in timeless terms expressed in universally applicable life a form of conduct, a quality of spirit, which changing circumstances do not affect. What is right in the rest of the Book in him is consummated; what is dim is made clear; what is partial is fulfilled; what is mistaken is corrected. He is the best we know. He is love, and love is the fulfilment of the law.

Preach him, therefore, not as those who timidly suspect that outgrown categories have lost them their cause, but as those who know that all the categories ever used about him have been but partial appreciations of his divine reality.

> "Our little systems have their day;
>   They have their day and cease to be;
>   They are but broken lights of thee,
>   And thou, O Lord, art more than they."

[1] Literature and Dogma, 334.

BIBLIOGRAPHY

The Historicity of Jesus, Shirley Jackson Case. University of
Chicago Press.

Ecce Homo, John Robert Seeley. Roberts Bros.

The Jesus of History, T. R. Glover. Association Press.

Jesus, George Holley Gilbert. Macmillan.

Jesus, W. Bousset, trans. by Janet P. Trevelyan. Putnam.

The Syrian Christ, Abraham Mitrie Rihbany. Houghton Mifflin.

The Character of Jesus, Charles Edward Jefferson. Crowell.

Jesus Christ and the Christian Character, Francis Greenwood
Peabody. Macmillan.

Jesus Christ and the Social Question, Francis Greenwood Peabody. Macmillan.

Outlines of the Life of Christ, W. Sanday. Scribner's.

The Life and Teaching of Jesus Christ, Arthur C. Headlam.
J. Murray.

The Ethical Teaching of Jesus, Ernest F. Scott. Macmillan.

Jesus in the Nineteenth Century and After, Heinrich Weinel
and Alban G. Widgery. T. and T. Clark.

The Life and Teachings of Jesus, Charles Foster Kent. Scribner's.

Jesus Christ, W. P. Paterson, in the one volume edition of A
Dictionary of the Bible, ed. by James Hastings. Scribner's.

Jesus, A. B. Bruce, in the Encyclopædia Biblica, ed. by T. K.
Cheyne and J. Sutherland Black. Macmillan.

LECTURE VIII

JESUS, THE SON OF GOD

I

In our last lecture we laid stress on the indispensable contributions which Jesus has made to the spiritual life of men. We tried to say in our own words what Luther once said with his sure instinct for every question's practical import: "Christ is not called Christ because he has two natures. What does that signify to me? He bears this glorious and consoling name because of the office and the work he has undertaken." [1] Thus describing Jesus in terms of his practical function, we found ourselves not only using a typically modern approach but also understanding better the meaning of Messiahship in the New Testament.

Such functional description is congenial with our modern thinking. When we cannot discover what a force essentially is, as is the case with electricity, but can discover what it does, we do not feel bereft. We are persuaded that anything *is* what it does and that when we can sum up the functions of any force we understand it about as well as there is any use in understanding it at all. There is an easy transition, therefore, when, turning to religion, we waive metaphysical

---

[1] Werke, 2d Erlangen Edition, Vol. XII, 259, quoted by H. R. Mackintosh in The Doctrine of the Person of Jesus Christ, 321.

questions about Christ's essential nature and confine ourselves to his practical saviorhood. We feel at home in that kind of thinking. Perhaps we feel too much at home.

At any rate, in the New Testament there is another category besides Messiahship representing another intellectual interest and tradition. In the New Testament Jesus is the Logos, the eternal Word of God. The background of that conception must be sought in Greek thought, which, setting the realm of pure spirit over against the realm of matter, tended to make God remotely and unapproachably distant from man. The transcendence of God, when highly emphasized, inevitably makes his vital contact with his world and his spiritual creatures difficult to conceive. That problem the Logos solved in the ancient world amid whose prevalent forms of thinking the Gospel made its way. The Logos was the forthgoing of God over the abyss between divinity and man. Sometimes thought of as a principle, sometimes semi-personified as a mediator, the Logos involved the central assertion that God can come into the world which he has made and into man, his child. This was the category which the New Testament used, not only in the Fourth Gospel, but in a disguised form in the Epistle to the Hebrews, and in the great Christological passages of Paul. Jesus was not only practically the Messiah; he was essentially the forthgoing of God himself into his world.

This philosophical approach to the understanding of Jesus is less congenial with our modern minds than is the more practical category of Messiahship. The modern mind often feels positive and indignant aver-

sion against such theological construing of the Master.
Nor is the reason difficult to understand. For so long
a time the theological Christ, with his divine attributes, has been exalted in the church—great creeds
recited about him, great anthems sung to him, great
rituals performed before him—and now after nearly
two thousand years civilization has been shaken by
the most destructive cataclysm in history. The late
war violated everything Jesus ever taught and, pour-
ing the whole world into almost irremediable confusion, has provoked widespread impatience with purely
theological speculations about Christ. The Jesus who
challenges thoughtful men to-day is crying, "Why
call ye me, Lord, Lord, and do not the things which
I say? " [1] Many people, therefore, growing impatient
with the church's worship of the theological Christ,
have been saying:

> Give us Jesus the teacher of righteousness,
> brotherhood, and peace, the proclaimer of prin-
> ciples on which alone civilization can endure.
> For nearly twenty centuries you have been prais-
> ing your theological Christ and yet child labor
> takes our little ones and grinds them like grist
> in our mills, while the real Christ said, " It is not
> the will of your Father who is in heaven, that one
> of these little ones should perish." [2] For nearly
> twenty centuries you have been explaining your
> theological Christ, yet racial hatreds still well up
> bitterly in men, while the real Christ said, " One
> is your teacher, and all ye are brethren." [3] For

[1] Luke 6:46.   [2] Matthew 18:14.   [3] Matthew 23:8.

nearly twenty centuries you have been forming
creeds about your theological Christ yet industrial despotism still grinds its victims with a hard
heel, while the real Christ said, " Whatsoever ye
would that men should do unto you, even so do ye
also unto them." [1] For nearly twenty centuries
you have been controversially debating your theological Christ, but war still curses men, dragging
in its evil train all the abominations that man is
heir to, while the real Christ said, " Blessed are
the peacemakers: for they shall be called sons of
God." [2] Have done with your theological Christ
and give us back Jesus the ethical teacher.

I do not see how any one who knows the Master and
cares for him can fail to sympathize with this movement of thought and to welcome all its positive and
constructive elements. The last thing that the Master could endure would be to be the object of great
creeds, great anthems, great rituals, in a world which
did not do what he said.

Nevertheless, when you have gotten back Jesus
the ethical teacher, when you have exalted his principles of life and have claimed their rightful application to all mankind's relationships, is that all? These
principles for which he stood are lofty in themselves
and difficult of application. They are alien from some
of man's deepest instincts, antagonistic to many of
man's ingrained traditions. Purity in the individual,
altruism in industry, peace in international relationships, brotherhood across racial lines—the very state-

[1] Matthew 7:12.   [2] Matthew 5:9.

ment of such things to multitudes of folk seems sheer contradiction in terms. How can any one intelligently face the revolutionary ideals of Jesus, and imagine what changes their application would imply in human nature's habitual reactions and in man's long-settled institutions without raising inevitable questions: can they ever be made to work? is this the kind of world in which such principles were meant to work? what kind of world is this anyway? in its innermost nature and purpose is it a universe where Christlike principles are natively at home or is it a universe where they are visionary afterthoughts, intruders which have no kinship with reality?

So far as I can see, there are two major positions of which all others are but corollaries, and between which the allegiance of men tends to divide. On the one side, some think of this universe as fundamentally physical. Just as everything in English literature is the arrangement and rearrangement of twenty-six letters, so to these folk all existence consists in the permutations and combinations of eighty-odd constituent elements known to chemistry. Limericks and great poems, cheap romances and the Epistles of Paul, advertisements in the newspapers and the Emancipation Proclamation, are diverse combinations of the alphabet; so this universe, from top to bottom, is to some only the rearrangement of original chemical elements. In this thoroughly materialistic world, with all spiritual life only an accidental episode, they see Jesus, an ethical teacher, an idealist, dreamer, visionary, announcing moral ideals and hopes of regenerated life for humankind that have no contact with creative reality. His ideals are beautiful, they say, but do not fit the nature of the world. Said Nietzsche, "I regard Christianity as the most fatal and seductive lie that has ever existed." [1] Of course he thought that. He knew that in a world with brute force for its creative fact and final arbiter the ideals of Jesus are mistaken, founded on falsehood, that they involve abnormal living, and that in the end, against the deadweight of an antagonistic cosmos, cannot be made to work. He knew that another kind of life than that which Jesus taught is the natural implication of such a world as he believed in.

This issue has been forced on us with startling clearness by the neo-Darwinians. Darwin outlined a picture of the primitive estate of the animal world in terms of the struggle for existence and the survival of the fittest. It was the picture of a hard and bitter fight. Darwin himself, engaged in solving a biological problem, solved it brilliantly and was not responsible for some conclusions that less cautious followers have drawn. But it is a commentary on our low ideals of living that a whole race of neo-Darwinian sociologists has arisen to greet that original animal struggle for existence as the standard to which they can appeal in justifying man's inhumanity to man. Nor in practise have men been less ready than they have been in theory to avail themselves of this defense. Men in industry, desiring to crush their rivals and profiteer upon the public, have done it ruthlessly and have defended it as the struggle for existence and the survival of the fittest. Imperialists in government, looking

[1] Friedrich Nietzsche: The Will to Power, Vol. I, 163, Sec. 200.

with avaricious eyes upon the lands of weaker folk, unscrupulously have seized them, defending their acts as natural: they corresponded with the way the universe is run. Militarists, loving war and glorying in it, have waged it with insatiable blood-lust and have based their conduct's rationality upon the kind of world they live in. The struggle for existence and the survival of the fittest make their actions natural.

This is the Darwinism which Christianity must fight—not the biological truth of evolution, with its endless suggestiveness and value to our thinking, but a philosophic materialism which conceives the world's elemental nature as brutal and bloodthirsty, with war for its basic standard and norm. Nor can this pagan idea of creation's nature be fought by ethical ideals alone, however beautiful. The more beautiful they are the less believable they are in such a world. The doctrine of no-God can be exorcised only by the doctrine of God. We might indeed fight the false science of the neo-Darwinians by true science, pointing out that the mammoths have gone but the bees are here, that the armor-plated ichthyosaurus is as dead as the moon though the ants are not, that even among the animals cooperation has carried species through when brute force has failed. We might insist that even if "Nature, red in tooth and claw with ravine" were an adequate picture of animal life, which it is not, we still are men, not brutes, and will not appeal to an animal struggle as our standard. Slavery was natural and we did away with it; piracy was natural and it has gone; religious wars were natural and we think we have seen the last of them; and to-day race hatred, the liquor traffic, commercialized vice, international armaments, autocratic industries are natural, but for all that we propose to overpass them.

What we Christians, however, are driving at in this necessary protest against neo-Darwinian sociology is something deeper than sociology. We are insisting on another idea of creation's nature altogether from that which materialism presents. We are fighting for a view of the world with spiritual elements at the heart of it and spiritual possibilities ahead of it. Only in such a world can the ethics of Jesus remain credible norms of life.

For this is the other possibility to which men turn when they cannot think that creation is merely physical. They dare to think that spiritual life in man is the revelation of creative reality. They come, by whatever special phrasings, to the fundamental idea for which the Logos stood: that what appears in man as light, life, and love, to use John's favorite terms, comes from God and is God coming into our humanity. Then and then only Christ's ideals cease being visionary; then they become the unveiling of the bases of the real world.

II

A theological interest, therefore, which goes behind the ideals of Jesus to consider whether or not we can see God revealed in him, is not so far-fetched as many superficial minds are thinking. We preachers would better feel this deeply. We who stand for Christian principles of life face a hard fight. We are going out into a difficult, and it may be desperate, generation.

Western civilization may go to pieces under us. It will certainly not be easy to make the way of life which Jesus represents seem possible for men and nations. Waves of skepticism and disillusionment already have overwhelmed the faith of many, and more folk than one likes to think are crying, "Who will show us any good?" In such a generation we cannot make the ideals of Jesus triumphant just because they are beautiful. The Campanile of St. Mark's did not collapse from lack of beauty but from lack of foundations. The ideals of Jesus will as certainly collapse, so far as our generation is concerned, if men, believing that the world is a mere sport of atoms, lose faith in its spiritual bases. Men must know, not only what it would be ideal to do in this world, but whether this world at bottom is meant to have ideals even suggested in it, much more wrought out.

Recently I spent an evening with a young university graduate who had made a brilliant record in his course and has made a brilliant record ever since. He was all at sea about God. He was inherently reverent. He called himself "unescapably religious," and he did not want to be otherwise. He very rarely went to church. He did regularly pray, but he was at sea about God. He told me of his friends, leading men in their college classes, with whom he kept in touch— that they were largely alienated from the church, that they had a kind of private religion which sometimes helped them, that only recently they had talked together all night long about God and immortality, but that in the end they still were all at sea. Now, the upshot of this familiar attitude is ethical. Men wonder what right they have to expect much of human nature and the world. Are not selfishness, brutality, lust, bloodthirstiness, industrial exploitation, war, natural in a world where all moral living is only an accidental episode in an æonic physical process? Must we not take such things for granted and put up with them as the inevitable product of an animal inheritance which it is folly to hope to outgrow? You might as well expect to find a climate without its appropriate results in fauna and flora as to find prevalent materialism without that sort of ethical reaction.

They say that under the snow and ice of Spitzbergen are the remains of tropic forests. Once, where arctic cold now reigns, luxuriant flora grew. If one asks the explanation for this desolation of a once fruitful territory, the answer is plain: the climate changed. Slowly, imperceptibly at first, the climate which had made forests possible began to alter. Perhaps generations passed without obvious effect, but the effect was there. What once grew naturally at last could not grow at all. So religious faith in the spiritual nature of creation, its divine origin, meaning, and destiny, creates a climate. That is perhaps the most important thing religion does. And in that climate it is natural for Christ's ideals of life to grow. But Spitzbergen's forests no more surely surrendered to the ice than those ideals will vanish from a world where materialistic naturalism takes the place of religious faith.

III

Said in other terms, to be sure, but rising from this basic interest in the nature of creation, the idea of the Logos took its place in early Christian thinking. Dr. Henry Sloane Coffin made a wise remark when he said that the deity of Jesus "is not primarily a statement concerning Jesus . . . but a statement concerning the invisible God." [1] How shall men think of God and where shall they find him? how shall God enter into men and redeem them?—these are the profoundest questions of religious life and thought. And men were framing answers to these deepest questions when they said that in Christ the Logos was unveiled, that through him God had crossed the chasm that divides divinity from man, and, taking flesh, had dwelt among us, full of grace and truth. God was in Christ reconciling the world unto himself; in his face we see the light of the knowledge of the glory of God; he is the effulgence of God's glory and the very image of his substance; in the beginning was the Word, and the Word was with God, and the Word was God—this message is an essential part of the New Testament. He who does not proclaim it is not preaching the New Testament; he has parted company not only with the church's theology but with the experience of God in Christ which belongs at the very center of original Christianity. For, in whatever philosophic terms you may phrase it, the norm of Christian experience in the New Testament was to find in Christ, not simply the ideal life, but the in-

[1] In a Day of Social Rebuilding, 58.

carnate God of the world where that ideal life must be wrought out.

Nevertheless one must sympathize with the perplexity of the man upon the street when he sees this question of Christ's divinity debated as a theological controversy and perhaps tossed into the newspapers. One wonders what he thinks when he hears churchmen call one another Arians, Monophysites, Monotheletes, Apollinarians, and other unpronounceable kinds of heretic because they differ in construing the person of our Lord. So much confusion is there in this realm that some people believe in the divinity of Jesus who are not quite sure what that signifies, and many others want to believe in it and try to but find it so beset with knotty questions that they have no freedom and joy in their belief at all. That the divinity of Jesus is not at heart a dry-as-dust theological speculation at all but a warm and vital assertion of religious experience is a fact that multitudes of folk never suspect.

Let us clarify our minds at once by stating plainly that whatever questions there may be about Christ's divinity, there is none about his humanity. Jesus was true man and his divinity must always be asserted and interpreted in such ways as will not cast doubt on that unmistakable fact.

Surely, this is clear in the Gospels. The Master's body was normal like our own. It grew, was weary, hungry, thirsty; it suffered and it died like ours. The Master's emotional life was normally human, too. Sometimes he was astonished, as at the people's lack of faith, or the centurion's excess of it; compassion

moved him when he looked on multitudes unshep-
herded, or, swinging round the brow of Olivet, saw
Jerusalem crowned with the Temple's golden dome;
indignation sometimes swept his spirit like a storm
as when he saw ceremonial law rated higher than
human need, or found his Father's house made a den
of thieves, or faced the cruelty and meanness of
hypocrisy; at times he rejoiced and at times he was
grievously depressed, crying, "My soul is exceeding
sorrowful even unto death," or "My God, my God,
why hast thou forsaken me?"

The Master's mental life, as well, followed the
course of a normal human youth: "Jesus advanced in
wisdom and stature, and in favor with God and men."
He learned the best traditions of his people in his
family, was trained as all children are by habits of
reverence even more than by abstract teaching, and,
later, in the synagogue school he sat on the floor with
the boys of Nazareth and recited in concert the lessons
which the rabbi dictated. The information which his
mind used was gathered, as ours is, by observation
and experience, and was retained by memory, and his
parables illustrate the penetration of his insight and
the tenacity of his recollection. He grew up as we do,
sharing the characteristic forms of thought of his age
and country, and, using thus the ways in which everybody thought to express the truth which he uniquely
saw, he was understood in his own day and so was
preserved for ours.

Beautifully human, too, was his spiritual life. That
is evident in his prayers. Sometimes he prayed in
triumph, as with shining face on the Transfiguration

Mount, and sometimes he prayed in grief, as in Gethsemane when it was written, "And being in an agony
he prayed more earnestly." Occasionally he prayed
all night or went out early in the morning to the hills
alone or at evening withdrew in solitude to seek his
Father's help. At the very center of his spiritual life
was his filial dependence on God. "The Father is
greater than I"; "The words that I say unto you I
speak not from myself: but the Father abiding in me
doeth his works"; "I can of myself do nothing"; "He
that believeth on me, believeth not on me, but on
him that sent me"—such Johannine sayings interpret
the habitual attitude of Jesus' life.[1]   When men
praised him inordinately he resented it: "Why callest
thou me good? none is good save one, even God." [2]
All his life was lived, his work done, his worries borne,
his temptations faced, in this spirit of humble, filial
dependence on God.

With this assertion of Jesus' real humanity in the
Gospels most of us are familiar. But many are not
familiar with the further fact that the church through-
out its early history fought some of its most serious
theological battles to maintain his real humanity
against those who doubted it. The central struggle
of the early church was not to get people to believe
in the divine origin of Jesus. Rather, after the church
achieved power and Jesus was exalted as Lord, current philosophy made it comparatively easy to believe that he came from the supernal realm, that he
was the influx of the Divine into the world. It was
much more difficult then to believe that at the same

[1] John 14:28; 14:10; 5:30; 12:44.   [2] Mark 10:18.

time he possessed a genuinely human life. The difference between the early centuries and our own in this regard is sharp and clear. They started with the certainty that Jesus came from the divine realm and then wondered how he could be truly man; we start from the certainty that he was genuinely man and then wonder in what sense he can be God. Schmiedel is one of the most radical of critics, and Sanday was one of the most cautious and conservative of men, yet Sanday quoted Schmiedel on this point with full approval: "It is not for an instant doubtful that Jesus must be considered as man in the full sense of the term, and that anything divine may be sought in him only under the condition that his humanity is not put in question." [1] This is the almost inevitable attitude for any modern mind when it approaches the personality of Jesus. But the approach through the early centuries of classic theology was precisely the opposite. Jesus was certainly the incarnation of God, but his real humanity often seemed dubious.

It is the more remarkable, therefore, that the early church so steadfastly maintained her insistence on the reality of the Master's human nature and so fiercely attacked and excommunicated those who doubted it. The Gnostics asserted our Lord's deity, but they thought he was not really man, and the church fought the Gnostics tooth and nail for years and drove them out. The Docetists, some of whom were Gnostics and some not, did not doubt Jesus' deity; they asserted it so extremely that they destroyed his manhood, until in their theology he only seemed to be born,

[1] William Sanday: Christologies Ancient and Modern, 209.

seemed to possess flesh, to suffer, and to die. And the church fought the Docetists and drove them out. The climax of the church's effort to maintain its hold upon the real humanity of Jesus despite the pressure of current philosophy came with Apollinaris. Even a theological student might be pardoned for supposing that since this arch-heretic broke with orthodoxy over the question of Jesus' person he must have denied Christ's deity. On the contrary, he asserted it completely and absolutely. He hated the Arians as much as Athanasius could have desired. What he denied was that Jesus had a human will and soul, and the church condemned him utterly and threw him out. When one understands the tremendous pressure of contemporary thought urging the church so to conceive Christ's divine nature that he would not be man at all, one cannot too much wonder and admire as he watches these battles, long drawn out and valiantly fought, in which the real humanity of Jesus steadfastly was maintained.

There are some Protestants in our day, who pride themselves on being orthodox, who need to take this very much to heart. They take a phrase such as "Jesus is God," not to be found either in the Scriptures or the creeds, and set it up as a standard of regularity in doctrine. But to suppose that the phrase "Jesus is God" is an adequate expression of the Christian faith even in its creedal forms is to display abysmal ignorance of what the church has stood for. That statement alone is not orthodoxy; it is heresy. It leaves out of account the unmistakable fact that Jesus was also man.

Jesus was man, and he must be God in what sense he can be God being assuredly man.

IV

This approach to the Master's divinity by way of his obvious and undoubted humanity, so far from being strange, is precisely the approach which the first disciples made. We would better make it ourselves if we wish to understand the reality and power of their experience when they found God in Christ. For the divinity of Jesus was not primarily a doctrine; primarily it was an experience. The disciples felt in him something not of this world. They were sure about his manhood, but it was manhood suffused and irradiated. It subdued them, awed them, fascinated, and mastered them. The glory of their lives came to be that they had known him, loved him, believed in him. They did not start by believing in opinions about him, doctrines concerning him; they started by believing in him. The objective of their faith was not a theory; it was his personality, his life.

They found it impossible, however, thus to believe in him without believing in something more. When the Fourth Gospel reported Jesus as saying, "He that believeth on me, believeth not on me, but on him that sent me," [1] a vital and prevalent experience of the early Christians with their Master was summed up. His life always had a reference beyond itself; it always seemed revelatory of a reality behind him as well as in him.

[1] John 12:44.

There are two sorts of greatness among men. One was illustrated in Napoleon. In many gifts of personal power and genius he deserves to be called great, but his life had no reference beyond itself; he did not stand for nor reveal abiding truths; he was a huge, isolated monolith thrust up out of humanity representing little that mankind finds it possible to love. Think of Copernicus, however, and you think not so much of Copernicus as of the permanent truth which he discovered to the world. Think of Faraday and your thought cannot dwell on Faraday alone; it inevitably goes on to dwell upon the universal force which he unveiled. The significance of such men lies in something which they revealed, into which we can enter now and by which our lives can be enlarged. Such, in the higher realm of spiritual life, was the effect of Jesus on his first disciples. Their thought started with him as an individual but it never could stop there; it went through him and beyond him to the spiritual realities for which he stood, the relationship with God which he illustrated, the divine world to which he was the way and the door. There was nothing artificial about this. It was so truly the natural, spontaneous effect of Jesus' personality on his followers that I do not see how any one can know him in the Gospels even yet and not reduplicate their experience.

This spiritual quality in Jesus that so differentiates him from the rest of us and makes him the supreme revealer of spiritual life faces us with a dilemma. We can do one of two things with it: we can conceive it to be an accident or a revelation. So a man may handle pieces of metal until for the first time he finds magnetized iron. Something new is there. A strange and powerful element has come into his ken. What is it? It may be an accident; it may signify nothing at all beyond its own mysterious uniqueness. But, on the other hand, it may be a revelation—the discovery of a universal force everywhere available and belonging to the substance of creation.

So the first Christians faced the Master, and alike their own immediate impression of his personality and their later reflections on it convinced them that his unique and glorious life was not an accident. Do we think that it was? That differential quality in Jesus is the most impressive spiritual fact that this earth has seen. It is the best we know. It is the fairest production that the race has to show for its millenniums of travail. It has made more difference to the spiritual life of men than anything besides. To call it an accident seems to me the most irrational thing that could be said about it. It is a revelation of creative reality.

Those first Christians, therefore, went out into the Roman Empire with an ardent and convinced assertion, not simply that they had found the ideal life, but that they had found the God from whom it came. When they tried to put their conviction into intelligible and conveyable form they used such categories as they had at hand—in particular, the idea of the Logos was convenient and congenial—but behind all such contemporary formulations of their message was their basic experience. God had welled up among them. God could come, had come, into human life, and they had seen "the light of the knowledge of the glory of God in the face of Jesus Christ." At their best they went out to strive for the ideals of Jesus, not thinking that those ideals were interloping after-thoughts in an unfriendly universe, but crying triumphantly, "In the beginning was the Word, and the Word was with God, and the Word was God."

V

This Gospel of God revealed in Christ, released from literal bondage to old categories and set free to do its work in modern terms of thought and speech, ought to be the central affirmation of our preaching. So far from being a labored, speculative matter, to one who has a spiritual interpretation of life it ought to be a spontaneous and glad expression of his faith. We are wrong when we make belief in the divinity of Jesus a technical, philosophical affair. The men of the New Testament were not primarily philosophers, metaphysicians, theologians. They were primarily men of profound religious life endeavoring to get their vital experiences conveyed to others in such terms as were at hand. I believe that they would have agreed with George Eliot's Adam Bede: "I look at it as if the doctrine was like finding names for your feelings." The doctrine of the divinity of Jesus was thus the expression in current terms of the central experience of the Christian life—finding God in Christ. The divinity of Jesus is not something first of all to be treated as a formula; it is something first of all to be vitally discovered, experienced, and lived upon.

In many minds this experimental approach to the divinity of the Master is impeded and embarrassed by the complicated theological developments which have taken place between the New Testament and our own day. The Apostles' Creed, the Nicene Creed, the Athanasian Creed, are taken as intellectual norms of true belief, and, failing to understand their terms or to believe them when understood, men suppose that they have surrendered the substantial truth which lies behind them. This is the nemesis of all creedalism: the creeds are promulgated to protect faith, and then, their forms of thinking being at last overpassed, insistence on them becomes the ruination of faith.

Nevertheless, it is a pity that even in churches which are not bound to these ecclesiastical creeds of the patristic age, we cannot have a better understanding of what they really meant to say. Personally brought up in an ecclesiastical tradition which has not used these venerable expressions, I have never subscribed to them nor repeated them. But, standing thus outside the tradition to which these creeds belong, when I hear some fresh and flippant modern mind condescending to them, treating the fathers who wrote them as quibblers and fools, I am strongly tempted to bear a hand in their defense.

The Nicene Creed, for example, the noblest of them all, faced a serious problem and handled it in a large way. Still the church was dealing with the old Greek thought which tore God and man apart and left them disparate and unrelated. That chasm between deity and man the idea of the Logos once had bridged. But still the chasm was there and in many Christian minds had its disastrous effect upon the interpretation of Jesus. So far off was God from man that it was easier to think that Jesus was some superior angel, some demigod from heaven, than to suppose that in him men could find the very being and quality of God himself; or, on the other side, if he were the influx of God himself, then he could not have been real man, but only a fantom in appearance like a man. So the unstable thought of the church wavered back and forth. Now this horn of the dilemma, now that, was favored, as the Greek inheritance separating God from man made it desperately difficult to believe in the essential affinity of God with man. And to save her very life the church fought all compromise on this crucial question, and in the Nicene Creed made a resounding declaration that "very God of very God" had come into human life. Of course, they made this declaration in terms of current philosophy. What else could they do? It never would occur to me to use the Nicene Creed as the natural expression of my faith, but the crux of the matter at which the Nicene Creed was driving is my faith. If the church ever loses it the church will have denatured the Gospel. For Christianity is the religion of incarnation and its central affirmation is that God can come into human life.

This truth may readily be translated into present-day terms because we moderns find it easier to conceive than the Nicene fathers did. When they asserted that God in Christ came into human life they were struggling against a philosophy that tore God and man apart. Arius said that God was so utterly transcendent and aloof that he was inscrutable to his own Son. When, therefore, Athanasius against Arius struggled for the Nicene theology, with "very God of very God" incarnate in Christ, he was endeavoring to bridge a chasm that to many seemed unbridgeable. With us, however, the most prevalent and characteristic way of thinking we have had since the middle of the nineteenth century involves the immanence of God and his immediate presence in our lives and in his world. Our poets and prophets for years have been singing and preaching to us that, wherever else God is, he is here. After the sterile frigidity of eighteenth-century deism which put God in exile far from the interests and affairs of men, there came in the nineteenth century a renaissance of life and thought whose most typical intellectual expression is the doctrine of the immanence of God. This upwelling of reliance on and joy in an indwelling, spiritual presence, this rebirth of confidence in the rights of immediate experience to be considered a revelation of eternal reality, was so wide-spread, so deep-seated, so truly a Zeitgeist that no realm of thought and life in the nineteenth century escaped it. The Romantic revival in literature is one expression; the typical theology of Schleiermacher, making the inner emotion of dependence on God the essence of religion, is another; monism in philosophy, in all its forms, as against the preceding deism, springs from the same source; and in evangelical Christianity the fresh insistence on the Holy Spirit as the agent of regeneration reveals the same drift. Divine immanence, as Dr. McGiffert says, has often been called the char-

acteristic religious doctrine of the nineteenth century.[1]

The poets sing it. Says Mrs. Browning:

> "Earth's crammed with heaven,
> And every common bush afire with God:
> But only he who sees, takes off his shoes." [2]

Prophets proclaim it. Says Carlyle:

> "Or what is Nature? Ha! why do I not name
> thee God? Art not thou the 'Living Garment of
> God?' O Heavens, is it, in very deed, He, then,
> that ever speaks through thee; that lives and
> loves in thee, that lives and loves in me?" [3]

Even scientists assert it. Says Sir Oliver Lodge:

> "We are no aliens in a stranger universe gov-
> erned by an outside God; we are parts of a de-
> veloping whole, all enfolded in an embracing and
> interpenetrating love, of which we too, each to
> other, sometimes experience the joy too deep for
> words." [4]

Long since, preachers have resorted to it. Says John
Herman Randall:

> "The relation of this Infinite Power, or God, to
> the universe, is the same as the relation of man's

[1] Arthur Cushman McGiffert: The Rise of Modern Religious
Ideas, 189.

[2] Aurora Leigh, Book VII, p. 275 of Author's Edition, 1857.

[3] Thomas Carlyle: Sartor Resartus, Book II, Ch. IX, p. 150 of
Centenary Edition.

[4] Suggestions Towards the Re-Interpretation of Christian Doctrine,
in The Hibbert Journal, Vol. II, 475 (July, 1904).

soul to his body. The universe as we see it is God's body; then God is the soul of the universe, just as you are the soul of your body. Can you lay your finger on yourself? Is your hand, you? Is your foot, you? Is your brain, you? Where are *you?* Can anyone localize *you* in your body? You pervade your body through and through . . . You are immanent in your body. There is not one atom of your body where *you* are not—but still, *you* are not your body." [1]

Hymnologists are giving it wings in song:

> "Thou Life within my life, than self more near!
> Thou veiled Presence, infinitely clear!
> From all illusive shows of sense I flee
> To find my center and my rest in Thee." [2]

And the theologians themselves no longer can escape it. Says Professor H. R. Mackintosh:

> "One true mode of describing Christ, accordingly, is to speak of His person as representing the *absolute immanence* of God." [3]

Wherever you look at the underlying presuppositions of men's thinking about God to-day you find, not the old dualism against which the ancient church had so long and fierce a conflict, but a gladly recognized affinity between God and man. In our theology no longer are the divine and human like oil and water that cannot mix; rather, all the best in us is God in

[1] The Real God, 26–27, sermon, The Universal Mind.
[2] Eliza Scudder.
[3] The Doctrine of the Person of Jesus Christ, 434.

us. This makes faith in the divine Christ infinitely easier than it was under the old régime. One takes up the Westminster Confession and reads a passage like this about Christ: "Two whole, perfect, and distinct, natures, the Godhead and the manhood, were inseparably joined together in one person, without conversion, composition, or confusion." [1] But that metaphysical puzzle, which Dante put in picturesque form when he portrayed Christ as a griffin [2] —a single creature, composed of an eagle and a lion— is utterly unreal to our thinking, not because what the Westminster Confession was driving at is not true, but because the background of abysmal distance between the divine and the human which the Confession had perforce to bridge, is no longer in our minds. The presupposition of all our thinking is the conviction, not that there is a vast distance between God and man, but that God and man belong together and in each other are fulfilled.

This modern mode of thinking accords with the Christian experience of the New Testament. Where is God in the New Testament? "In him we live, and move, and have our being"; [3] "God is love; and he that abideth in love abideth in God, and God abideth in him"; [4] "Know ye not that ye are a temple of God, and that the Spirit of God dwelleth in you?" [5] "Precious and exceeding great promises; that through these ye may become partakers of the divine nature;" [6]

---

[1] Ch. VIII, Sec. II.

[2] E. g., Purgatory, Canto XXIX, vv. 108–115.

[3] Acts 17:28.   [4] I John 4:16.

[5] I Corinthians 3:16.   [6] II Peter 1:4.

"Behold, I stand at the door and knock: if any man hear my voice and open the door, I will come in to him, and will sup with him, and he with me." [1]   In the New Testament Christianity is a religion of incarnation and its central affirmation is that God has come and can come into human life. When, therefore, the Christians of the New Testament rose up with joy to say that they had found God in Christ, their statement was no tangled, speculative, philosophical matter; it was the glad, spontaneous expression of their religious experience. If we should regain their vital discovery of God in Christ, should interpret it, as we have a right to do, in terms of our thought of divine immanence—the modern counterpart of the Logos doctrine without the antecedent difficulties which the Logos doctrine had to meet—we could make the divinity of Christ once more, not a dry formula, but a living and experienceable reality. Let us refuse to see Christianity reduced to terms lower than that! God is a living God, not far off, but here; he can come into human life and in the face of Christ we have seen the effulgence of his glory.

We need not quibble, either, about a supposed difference that is not really there between his deity and his divinity. That distinction rests back on the old endeavor to think of God in terms of metaphysical Substance, Pure Being, conceived apart from spiritual quality, and then to define Christ's relations with him in the same terms—an endeavor useless for religion and properly outlawed from good philosophy. In everything that matters to our spiritual life, very God

[1] Revelation 3:20.

came to us in Christ. To be sure, nobody should ever
go to Jesus, to his manger and his Cross, to find the
omnipotence which swings Orion and the Pleiades.
Omnipotence in that sense is not revealed there. Nobody in his senses ever went to Jesus for the latest
news in physics or astronomy. Omniscience in that
sense is not revealed there. "He that hath seen me
hath seen the Father"—such was the Master's statement of the truth. That side of God—character,
purpose, redeeming love—we do find incarnate in
Christ.

VI

Such an approach to the divinity of Jesus makes
him as he is in the New Testament, not only unique
but imitable, keeps him not only our Lord but our
brother. Too often the deity of Jesus has been so
presented as to separate him utterly from man until
his injunction, "Follow me," has lost all meaning.
Devotees of his ethical ideals who could not share the
church's faith in his divinity have said: if he was the
incarnation of God, that puts him at a distance from
us impossible to cross, but think of him as a good man
and we can aspire to be like him. I never heard an
argument that seemed so to stand the truth upon its
head. Jesus was, indeed, an extraordinarily good
man. As Sidney Lanier sings,

> "What *if* or *yet*, what mole, what flaw, what lapse,
> What least defect or shadow of defect,
> What rumor, tattled by an enemy,
> Of inference loose, what lack of grace
> Even in torture's grasp, or sleep's, or death's,—

Oh, what amiss may I forgive in Thee,
Jesus, good Paragon, thou Crystal Christ?" [1]

Jesus was a marvelously good man. His goodness was about the only thing he had with which to make his impress on the world—no wealth, no prestige, no worldly learning, nothing but his goodness—and every year that goodness looms so much the higher that there are millions of us who are sure that its chief influence lies, not behind, but ahead. Indeed, he was so marvelously good that one wonders how, being a good man *like that*, we can cheerfully and hopefully set out to imitate him? A sick man in a hospital, surrounded by other sick men, hearing an athlete, perfect in physique, calling others to imitate him, would not be stimulated; he would be discouraged. So may we well be if Jesus, calling us to follow him, be only a good man.

If, however, that is not all the truth, if, not simply a good man, it was God in him who created his quality, and if the same God is seeking entrance to our lives, trying to live out in us, according to our degree and capacity, the same spirit, then we may hope. Let us say it abruptly: *it is not so much the humanity of Jesus that makes him imitable as it is his divinity*. If he be only a good man, he is an isolated phenomenon, like Shakspere or Napoleon in other realms. How can we, pulling on our own bootstraps, set out to lift ourselves by imitation to the likeness of such? But if Jesus is divine and if divinity hedges us all about like the vital forces which in winter wait underneath the frozen ground until the spring comes, that is a

[1] The Crystal, in The Poems of Sidney Lanier, 32.

gospel! Then the incarnation in Christ is the prophecy and hope of God's indwelling in every one of us.

Such is the Gospel of the New Testament about Jesus and his relationship with our lives. He is not an isolated phenomenon—he is "the first born among many brethren;" [1] "Now are we children of God, and it is not yet made manifest what we shall be. We know that, if he shall be manifested, we shall be like him"; [2] "till we all attain unto the unity of the faith, and of the knowledge of the Son of God, unto a full-grown man, unto the measure of the stature of the fulness of Christ." [3] Even in a lofty Johannine passage where Jesus says that he is in the Father and the Father in him, he also prays "that they may all be one; even as thou, Father, art in me, and I in thee, that they also may be in us." [4]

This is the reason why the New Testament is so full of hope about redeemed humanity. Not alone because Jesus was human, but because Jesus was divine, the revelation of the living God who seeks to be incarnate in every one of us, does the whole Book vibrate with expectancy. If one says that we cannot hope to be fully equal to him here, that is painfully obvious. As Emerson said, "A drop of water has the properties of the sea, but cannot exhibit a storm." [5] So we reveal God without the deeps and tides and currents which Jesus knew, without the relations with the world's life which his influence has sustained. He is unique.

> "No mortal can with him compare,
>   Among the sons of men."

[1] Romans 8:29.   [2] I John 3:2.   [3] Ephesians 4:13.
[4] John 17:21.   [5] Representative Men, 100 (Swedenborg).

Yet the God who was in Jesus is the same God who is in us. You cannot have one God and two kinds of divinity. While like drops of water we are very small beside his sea, yet it was one of the supreme days in man's spiritual history when the New Testament started men singing that they were "children of God: and if children, then heirs; heirs of God, and joint-heirs with Christ."

Of all foolish things, I can think of nothing more foolish than, looking back over our race's history and discerning amid its tragedy and struggle this out-standing figure spiritually supreme, to minimize him, to tone down our thought of him, to reduce him so that we can all be like him. Rather let us exalt him! If God be not in him, God is not anywhere. The best hope of mankind is that the living God is in him and through him may flow down through all the secret runnels of the race.

———

Here, then, ends our study where any study of the Bible ought to bring us, standing in reverence before our Lord. For the message of the Book is summed up in Christ. The Book as a whole is best described as the record of the historic preparation for Christ, the earthly ministry of Christ, and the first impacts of Christ's personality and teaching on the lives of those who welcomed him. Nor have the modern uses of the Bible dimmed this fact. They rather have illumined it. From them have come, not simply intellectual liberation from an old literalism, but incalculable spiritual enrichment as well through a quickened and clarified knowledge of Christ.

Let me bear a personal testimony as my closing word. From naive acceptance of the Bible as of equal credibility in all its parts because mechanically inerrant, I passed years ago to the shocking conviction that such traditional bibliolatry is false in fact and perilous in result. I saw with growing clearness that the Bible must be allowed to say in terms of the generations when its books were written what its words in their historic sense actually meant, and I saw that often this historic sense was not modern sense at all and never could be. There, like others, I have stood bewildered at the new and unaccustomed aspect of the Book. But that valley of confusion soon was passed. I saw that the new methods of study were giving far more than they were taking away. They have restored to us the historic Christ. They have led us to the abiding, reproducible experiences of the soul revealed through him. They have given us his imperishable Gospel freed from its entanglements, the Shekinah distinguished from the shrine, to be preached with a liberty, a reasonableness, an immediate application to our own age such as no generation of preachers in the church's history ever had the privilege of knowing before. Have no fear of the new truth! Let us fear only our own lack of wisdom, insight, courage, and spiritual power in using it for the redemption of the souls and societies of men.

BIBLIOGRAPHY

Christologies Ancient and Modern, William Sanday. Oxford University Press, American Branch.

The Early Christian Conception of Christ, Otto Pfleiderer. Putnam.

The Doctrine of the Person of Jesus Christ, H. R. Mackintosh. Scribner's.

Modern Theology and the Preaching of the Gospel, Ch. V, The Deity of Christ in the Light of Modern Thought, William Adams Brown. Scribner's.

INDEX OF BIBLE REFERENCES

GENERAL INDEX

Abbott, Edwin A., 144.

Abraham, 9, 73, 75.

Acts, 145–146.

Akiba, Rabbi, 71.

Allegory, New Testament found in Old by. 9; things not liked disposed of by. 28; prevalent in time of first great exegetes, 37; Ch. III, The Ancient Solution, 65–96.

Amos, 21, 149.

Angelology, angelic visitations, 43; angels stir water of wells, 53; Tertullian on, 112–113; apostrophized in Te Deums, 220; Ch. IV, section on angelology, 123–129; result if angelology had been controlling element in Scripture, 173.

Angels, evil, fallen, see Demonology.

Animistic view of the world, 133–134.

Anselm's interpretation of the Cross, 230.

Anthropomorphism, 28, 66, 74.

Antipodes, attitude of Lactantius and Plutarch toward, 47–48.

Apocalyptic, causing trouble to many, 5; not modern category, 45, 169; replaced in John's Gospel by eternal life, 101; illustration of abiding experiences in changing categories, Ch. IV, Sec. II, 104–110; Jesus relationship to, 106–108, 214, 226–229. See Second Coming of Christ.

Apostles' Creed, see Creed.

Appreciation versus criticism, Ch. VI, Sec. II, 174–182.

Archeology, 7, 37, 41, 219.

Ark, holy, 16, 42.

Ark, Noah's, 82, 89.

Arnold, Mathew, quoted, 106, 212, 240.

Arnold, T., 81.

Ascension, 99, 109, 149.

Asshurbanipal, library of, 41.

Assyria, 15, 38, 105.

Astrology, 49–50.

Astronomy, 34–35, Ch. II, Sec. III, 45–54, 58, 211, 269.

Athanasian Creed, see Creed.

Athanasius, 10, 257, 264.

Atonement, 229–231. See Cross.

Aytoun, R. A., 31.

Azazel, wilderness demon, 118.

Babylonian, creation tablets, 52–53; psalm, 236.

Bacon, Benjamin W., 96.

Badé, William F., 64.

Balfour, Sir Arthur, quoted, 90.

Barton, George A., 64, 130.

Baruch, Jeremiah's biographer, 148–149.

Basil of Cæsarea, quoted, 48.

Beelzebub, 137. See Devil.

Bellamy, Edward, object in writing Looking Backward, 227.

Bethlehem, star of, Chrysostom's effort to dissociate from astrology, 49–50.

Bewer, Julius, 7, 31.

Bible, the preacher's problem, 1–2; necessity of dealing with it, 3–6; first effect of modern study on it, 6–8; a new approach to it, 8 seq.; development of thought in it, 12 seq.; four ways to know it, 19 seq.; results of new approach to it,

281

Deity of Jesus, see Divinity of Jesus.

Democracy, 44, 45.

Demonology, Biblical category, 5; familiar ailments ascribed to, 35; demonic visitations familiar in man's early religious life, 43; in Semitic thought view, 44–45; in modern thought, 45; interpretation of "foreign people" in allegorization of a Jewish law, 73; no longer used in ordinary life, 89; Ch. IV, Section III, on Demonology, 111–122; disbelief in visitation of, 129; animistic idea of miracles, 133; healing of demoniac, 147; demoniac boy, 148; rejection of demonology, 169; result if demonology had been controlling element in Scripture, 173. See Devil.

Determinism, 160.

Deuteronomy, ethics of, 14.

Devil, Calvin attributes allegory to the, 83; development of idea, 118 seq.; chief of demonic host, 119; Tertullian's reference, 112; in early drama, 115; rebellion of, 120; works miracles, 137; Protestants attribute church miracles to him, 152; in Paradise Lost, 173; atonement explained as fraud on him, 230. See Demonology.

Divinity of Jesus, 187 seq., 252–253; 258–272.

Dobschütz, Ernst von, 130.

Docetists, 256–257.

Doctrine, of Trinity found in Old Testament, 9; identity of doctrine supposed to be in Bible, 10, 30, 90; of devils, 116, 119; doctrine and life, 184–191, 208–209; need of doctrine, 189–191, 209; doctrine of no-God, 248; doctrine about Christ, 258 seq.

Documents, of Bible, chronologically arranged, 6 seq; miracle-stories in successive documents, 143–150.

Dragon, in Semitic mythology, 52.

Dreams, 116, 124, 125.

Driver, S. R., 21, 38, 64.

Dumbness, ascribed to demons, 35, 120.

Duty, development of idea, 8, 13 seq. See Ethics; Righteousness.

Ecclesiastes, 26; quoted, 25.

Economics, 44, 45, 58, 131, 198–199, 203, 205, 238–239.

Eden, 53, 74, 77–78, 80, 89.

Edwards, Jonathan, 86.

Egypt, 15, 150, 163, 166; inscriptions of, 38–39.

Elijah, 99, 149, 163–164.

Eliot, George, Adam Bede quoted, 261.

Elisha, 34–35, 149, 155, 163–164.

Emerson, Ralph W., 271.

Enoch, 99, Book of, 39.

Ephesus, 218.

Epilepsy, ascribed to demons, 35, 116, 120.

Eschatology, see Apocalyptic; Resurrection; Second Coming of Christ; Immortality.

Esther, Book of, 26, 86.

Ethics, development in Bible, 13 seq.; contrast between Old Testament and New Testament, 26–27; ethics rated by Jesus above ceremony, 92; Jesus' ethical challenge, Ch. VI, Sec. IV, 191–206; ethics of Jesus defended, 226–231. Jesus, ethical teacher, 244–245; inadequacy of ethics, 245–251. See Duty; Righteousness.

Eucken, Rudolf, 206.

Eusebius, quoted, 48.

Evolution, 44, 51, 61, 185, 215.

Exegesis, versus spiritual insight, 11, 79; Golden Rule of, 37; ancient versus modern equipment for, 37 seq.; allegorical exegesis, Ch. III, 65–96; principle of Reforma-

Holy Spirit, 264.
Homer, 56, 65–67, 69.
Horne, S., quoted, 20.
Hosea, 21–22, 149, 171.
Hugo, Victor, 117.
Hume, David, 153.
Hunnius, 85.
Husic, I., 118.
Huss, John, 82.
Huxley, John, quoted, 163.

Immanence of God, 161, 188, 264–266, 268.
Immortality, development of idea, 22–23; in early Hebrew religion, 25–26; associated with physical resurrection, 45, 98; modern ideas Platonic, 54; interpreted in changing categories, Ch. IV, Sec. I, 98–104; modern interest in, 250.
Imperialism, 44, 203, 247–248.
Incarnation, 217, 252–253, 256, 263, 264, 268, 269, 271.
India, allegory in, 68; ideas of God, 170 seq.
Individual, treated as part of corporate group, 17–18.
Industry, 203, 229, 245, 247, 249, 251.
Inerrancy of Scripture, 30, 163, 237, 273.
Inquisition, 153.
Insanity, ascribed to demons, 35, 115–116, 120, 137.
Inspiration, 30, 68.
Interest, taking interest condemned on textual basis, 238–239.
Interim ethic, 226 seq.
Internationalism, 15, 203, 204–205, 245, 249. See War.
Intervention, miracle regarded as, 139–141, 162.
Isaiah, 15, 19, 23, 149, 180.
Ishmael, Rabbi, 71.

Jacob, 75.
Jastrow, Morris, Jr., 64, 236.

Jefferson, Charles E., 241.
Jehovah, see God.
Jeremiah, 18, 21, 40, 138, 148–149, 213.
Jerusalem, 81, 146, 181, 199, 254.
Jesus, see Christ.
Job, Book of, 23, 56.
John, Gospel of, see Fourth Gospel.
Jonah, 163; Book of, 15.
Jones, Maurice, 31.
Jones, Rufus M., 206.
Josephus, 39.
Jude, 125.
Judgment day, see Day of Judgment.
Justin Martyr, 98, 119.

Karlstadt, 93.
Kautsch, E., 31.
Kent, Charles Foster, 31, 32, 241.
Kháyyám, Omar, Ecclesiastes likened to Rubáiayát of, 26.
King, Henry Churchill, 206.
Kingdom of God, 100, Ch. IV, Sec. II, 104–110, 129. See Apocalyptic.
Kingsley, Charles, quotation from letter of Huxley to, 163.
Knox, George William, 224.
Kohler, Kaufmann, 118, 124, 130.
Koran, 69–70.
Kurios, 212–213.

Lactantius, quoted, 47–48.
Lanier, Sidney, quoted, 173, 269.
Law, see Common Law.
Law, Biblical, allegory of laws, 76; Jesus' appeal from oral to written law, 91; Jesus' appeal from ceremonial to moral law, 92; Jesus' recognition of outgrown elements, 92–93; Luther on Old Testament laws, 93; rabbinical summary of, 199; legalistic use of, Ch. VII, Sec. V, 235–240.
Law, natural, miracle and law Ch. V, 131–167.